S0-DQY-510

TURBO
PASCAL® 5.5
PROGRAMMING

Dedication

To my wife Paula and son Adam,
for making my life twice blessed

Acknowledgments

I would like to thank Borland International for the use of its extraordinarily well-designed and implemented programming environment. I would also like to thank Eric Bloom for his guidance and support.

TURBO PASCAL® 5.5 PROGRAMMING

Jeremy G. Soybel

 WINDCREST®

Windcrest books are published by Windcrest Books, an imprint of TAB BOOKS. The name "Windcrest" is a registered trademark of TAB BOOKS.

Published by **Windcrest Books**
FIRST EDITION/FIRST PRINTING

© 1990 by **Windcrest Books**. Reproduction or publication of the content in any manner, without express permission of the publisher, is prohibited. The publisher takes no responsibility for the use of any of the materials or methods described in this book, or for the products thereof. Printed in the United States of America.

Library of Congress Cataloging-in-Publication Data

Soybel, Jeremy G.
    Turbo Pascal 5.5 programming / by Jeremy G. Soybel.
       p.   cm.
    ISBN 0-8306-3527-0
    1. Pascal (Computer program language) 2. Turbo Pascal (Computer
program) I. Title. II. Title: Turbo Pascal five-point-five
programming.
QA76.73.P2S68   1990
005.26'2— dc20   89-77206
                                          CIP

TAB BOOKS offers software for sale. For information and a catalog, please contact TAB Software Department, Blue Ridge Summit, PA 17294-0850.

Questions regarding the content of this book should be addressed to:

Windcrest Books
An Imprint of TAB BOOKS
Blue Ridge Summit, PA 17294-0850

Director of Acquisitions: Ron Powers
Book Editor: David M. Harter
Production: Katherine Brown

Contents

6   *DOS Shell and the Command Line Recall "Shell" Program*   **157**

7   *The "SlideShow" Graphics Display Program*   **187**

Introduction

Welcome to the amazing world of Turbo Pascal 5.5, and the advanced capabilities of the most popular Pascal compiler available for the PC today. Since its release in the early 1980s, this compiler has provided considerable power and ease of use to beginning as well as expert programmers. Like many distributors of computer software, Borland International, the manufacturer of Turbo Pascal, is constantly trying to improve its product. Unlike the competition, Borland is succeeding.

If I sound like an advertisement for Borland's products, please forgive my zeal. The point I want to make is that Turbo Pascal has consistently provided better functionality, and more of it at a more attractive price, than EVERY other Pascal compiler available.

OVERVIEW

This book has two purposes. First, after reading through this book you will have a working knowledge of many of the most popular features of Turbo Pascal. You will be introduced to advanced concepts that enable you to build complex and useful applications. Second, this book provides source code for four Turbo Pascal applications. These applications are designed to demonstrate intermediate and expert concepts. However, you may also use them as the basis for your own personal applications.

This text is divided into nine chapters. Each chapter serves a specific purpose, and you are encouraged to read them in the order in which they are presented. In many chapters you will find references to the "Turbo Pascal 5.5 User's Guide," "Reference Manual" and the "Object-Oriented Programming Guide." These references are included to provide you with the capability to supplement this text with the manuals provided by Borland. The intention of this book is to teach advanced programming by building upon, not replacing, concepts introduced in the literature distributed with Turbo Pascal 5.5.

CHAPTER 1 contains a review of the basic concepts of structured programming. This includes a history of the Pascal language, as well as the Turbo Pascal Application Development Environment. The advances in PC compiler technology that have been pioneered by Borland and copied by the rest of the industry are described by version number.

CHAPTER 2 is a review of the Turbo Pascal language, including a description and use of the program elements. Elements such as data types, data structures, control structures, pointers, procedures, and functions are discussed.

CHAPTER 3 contains a complete description of the use of the Turbo Pascal version 5.5 interactive application development environment. A description of the menu system including the integrated debugging utility is discussed.

CHAPTER 4 is an introduction to basic and advanced programming concepts using the Turbo Pascal `intr()` and `port()` functions. Specific examples include access to the Basic Input/Output System (BIOS) Video Services as well as direct control of hardware such as the PC's speaker system.

CHAPTER 5 discusses Turbo Pascal's capability to create Memory-Resident or Terminate-but-Stay-Resident (TSR) applications. This chapter includes the source code for a complete TSR that enables you to create a keyboard "click." This application makes use of the sound-generating capabilities of the PC discussed in Chapter 4. A TSR can be used to enhance DOS by adding new functionality to the BIOS system.

CHAPTER 6 discusses Turbo Pascal's capability to create DOS enhancements without modifying the BIOS system. The `exec()` function and its capabilities are discussed in detail. This chapter contains the source code for a DOS command-line recall and line editing system. This application enables users to ignore the single line recall F1 and F3 keys and use the arrow keys to recall 20 or more previously-executed DOS commands. In addition, command-line editing is available to make modifications to current or previous commands and then execute them.

CHAPTER 7 discusses the use of graphics within the Turbo Pascal environment. This chapter includes the source code for a graphics generator capable of creating images from simple text files. Unlike bit map files that can occupy tens-of-thousands or even hundreds-of-thousands of bytes of memory, these text files contain simple ASCII-based graphics, or vector, commands. The application can be used to create presentations or slide shows using a minimum of disk space. And the Turbo Pascal graphics drivers enable you to create a simple and efficient program that can drive virtually any graphics adapter available for the personal computer.

CHAPTER 8 discusses the new and powerful programming concept of Object Oriented Programming (OOP). This chapter contains two versions of one program demonstrating some basic and advanced concepts of OOP. The basic application demonstrates how objects can interact with their environment. The advanced application demonstrates object-to-environment and object-to-object interactions.

CHAPTER 9 contains a review and discussion of the programming concepts discussed in the previous chapters. Emphasis is placed on the need to clearly organize the requirements of an application. Special emphasis is placed on the need to create applications with a user perspective.

1

Pascal and Turbo Pascal

The Pascal language was introduced in 1971 by Professor Niklaus Wirth of the Technical University of Zurich, Switzerland. Pascal is named after the seventeenth century philosopher and mathematician Blaise Pascal. Professor Wirth designed the Pascal language as a teaching aide for beginning programming students. There are a variety of implementations of Pascal available on virtually every computer. The most popular personal computer implementation of this language is Borland International's Turbo Pascal.

Turbo Pascal Versions 1 to 3

The basic capabilities of the Turbo Pascal Application Development Environment have always far surpassed the competition. The basic functionality of Turbo Pascal included an interactive development environment. Users could edit, compile, debug and link a Turbo Pascal program within the same environment. Turbo Pascal provided an interactive source code text editor based on the popular WordStar word processing package. Compilation and linkage of completed programs could be completed within a single step. Syntactical errors could be caught and located during compilation, and the text editor automatically activated and positioned to the location of the offending code.

As releases 2.0 and 3.0 of Turbo Pascal became available, additional functionality was provided. These additional capabilities included DOS access to directories as locations and lists of files. Other procedures and functions were added to increase the basic functionality of Turbo Pascal. All of these additions as well as the price made Turbo Pascal VERY popular. Even so the Turbo Pascal environment was still looked upon by software development professionals as a "toy" compiler. Many cited the fact that Turbo Pascal lacked the ability to create extremely complex data structures. Later versions of the compiler answered these challenges and surpassed the so-called "professional" development environments.

Turbo Pascal Version 4.0

Subsequent versions of Turbo Pascal have included advanced features normally available only through the DOS operating system. Turbo Pascal 4.0 provided the procedures and functions that allow you to read directories, examine file attributes, access specific areas of memory or even specific pieces of hardware. With the introduction of Turbo Pascal version 4.0, the graphics procedures were made available through a "graphics environment." Graphics procedures were modified to eliminate the need to provide ALL attributes of a graphical object in the call to the procedure. Specific procedures to set Color, Fill Pattern, Line Style and Line Thickness were created to simplify calls to graphics procedure calls. This helped to minimize code and provided for much more efficient graphics routines.

Graphics parameters could now be established anytime within a program. Not only could the current color and pattern of the environment be set, but they could also be read. Environmental parameters included not only visible attributes, but also capabilities such as the maximum number of colors available for a driver and its supported graphics modes. The advantage of a graphics environment was, and is, the ability to determine what parameters have been set prior to the current operation. The introduction of the environment provided additional graphics support for fonts such as the Default, Triplex, SansSerif, Small and Gothic. In addition, new device drivers for the EGA, VGA, Hercules, IBM 3270, and ATT 400 graphics drivers were made available.

The advances made available to users of Turbo Pascal version 4.0 were not limited to graphics alone. File attributes such as locking, visibility and others were accessible through enhanced file access functionality. The use of the Include compiler directive was enhanced to allow for 8 levels of file inclusion access, as well as enhanced error detection during compilation. In addition, the need for include-ing source code files and the 64K code limit was circumvented by the introduction of the "unit" concept.

When the source code of a Turbo Pascal program and its related include files are processed to become a program, they must be completely recompiled each time a modification is made. Turbo Pascal 4.0 allowed for the creation of linkable "units" of compiled code. These units contain the compiled code of procedures and functions that have been thoroughly tested and debugged. During compilation, the unit is simply linked to the desired program. If a modification is made to the program, you only need to recompile the program and NOT the unit. The introduction of this concept allowed for faster turnaround time during the development of complex programs.

Finally, version 4.0 of Turbo Pascal moved far beyond the standard Pascal introduced by Niklaus Wirth. New data types included extended real and integer types with ranges far surpassing those of typical Pascal. Turbo Pascal version 4.0 provided easy-to-use functions that gave users the ability to add functionality to the operating system itself. With this capability, programmers could easily create Terminate-and-Stay-Resident (TSR) applications. Many of the most useful programs such as pop-up notepads, calendars, calculators, and clocks can be called up from within any program because they are TSR. Because of these additions, Turbo Pascal now possessed the distinction of being both an "application" and "systems" development environment.

Turbo Pascal Version 5.0

After the major accomplishments of Turbo Pascal 4.0, it seemed unlikely that version 5.0 could make as much impact on the personal computing programming industry. However, once again Borland provided additional functionality that gave Turbo Pascal users a great advantage. Borland added an integrated, source-level debugging utility to the Turbo Pascal environment. The debugger allowed programmers to look "inside" their applications as they executed. Instead of spending time adding write statements to an application to see what's happening, version 5.0 allowed programmers to track values as they were modified.

The Turbo Pascal 5.0 integrated debugger added a new dimension to the environment by giving programmers much more control and versatility over their programs. Individual variables and expressions could be evaluated in "real-time" to allow programmers to see how data is processed.

Turbo Pascal version 5.0 also added new procedures for creating overlay files. Variable size overlay buffers could be created dynamically by a calling application. In addition, third-party vendors could now create drivers and fonts for their own graphics hardware. These drivers and fonts could then be loaded into the Turbo Pascal environment. A new driver for the IBM PS/II 8514 graphics adapter was added to provide graphics in $1024 \times 768 \times 256$-Color resolution. Finally, the documentation for Turbo Pascal was upgraded to include ALL functionality of the environment. This gave users additional information about existing functionality that they did not have before.

Turbo Pascal Version 5.5

The most recent installment to the Turbo Pascal environment is another example of Borland's continuing pursuit of the most advanced compiler for the personal computer. Version 5.5 adds additional overlay support to the Turbo Pascal Application Development Environment. There are enhancements to the development environment's menu system. Last and certainly not least is Turbo Pascal's implementation of Object Oriented Programming (OOP) extensions.

Unlike typical procedural programming languages, Turbo Pascal's OOP extensions provide the programmer with the capability to generate programs using objects as the basic unit of action and data. An *object* is the result of a fusion of data and the procedures or methods that affect that data. Turbo Pascal's implementation of OOP enables programmers to create simple or complex objects. The OOP applications in this text demonstrate how objects can interact with their environment as well as interact with other objects. OOPs are discussed in Chapter 8.

WHAT ARE ADVANCED TOPICS

An advanced topic for Turbo Pascal could be defined as any topic not introduced and explained in an introductory text. This definition is a little too broad for this text. If you have looked through any of the books on the shelves of your local book store, you know that the range of topics considered to be introductory is as varied as the names of the authors.

Although there is a great deal of variation, there are also common threads. Many of the more advanced applications provide for enhanced functionality of the computer or other applications. In order to provide this functionality, an advanced application must have the capability to interrupt another program, provide a service, and then allow the original application to continue executing as though nothing had happened.

These capabilities are normally reserved for the operating system of the computer. They can also be provided by Terminate-but-Stay-Resident (TSR) programs such as SideKick, distributed by Borland International. Many TSR programs provide simple functions such as displaying the date or time. Some provide a calendar, notepad, and calculator. More complex TSRs enable the user to access or modify files while working in a totally different application. However, as with most programming languages, Turbo Pascal allows for alternative methods capable of producing similar results.

Many of the more advanced applications on the market also include the capability to produce graphics. With the release of version 4.0, Turbo Pascal provided the richest set of graphics procedures and functions for any Pascal compiler. In addition, these capabilities were made available for almost every graphics adapter available. Some of the most notable examples of graphics programming are the ''DEMO'' programs sent out by software and hardware manufacturers to demonstrate their product. Graphics demonstration programs enable companies to create visual and audio presentations with a minimum of effort and money and distribute them by mail. Look through any personal computer magazine and you will see several offers to send demonstration diskettes for a minimum price, or even free of charge.

WHY ADVANCED TOPICS

There are many introductory texts for Turbo Pascal that teach the fundamentals of programming, and give examples of programming concepts. There are far fewer advanced texts that provide instruction for more involved concepts and programming examples. One of the major difficulties with these texts is that they take the concepts they present out of the context in which they are used. These texts normally present a single concept at a time, demonstrated within one or two procedures.

This text presents complete applications capable of performing complex tasks, or providing much needed functionality. Each program is an example of a specific programming concept such as TSR, Graphics or OOP. In addition, each application provides a service and can be expanded to provide even greater functionality. The specific capabilities of each application are fully documented for each application chapter.

WHAT IS PROGRAMMING

First of all I'll define what constitutes programming. Programming: The development of instructions, individually or in groups which, when executed, cause a task to be performed. You will notice there is no description of either how the instructions were developed or executed. Programming is defined in this way to emphasize the fact that many of the common tasks people perform each day are based on programs. If you consider yourself an experienced programmer, you were one long before you touched your first keyboard. If you are an inexperienced programmer, just starting with advanced topics, this book will explain things you already know, intuitively. Every time you get out of bed in the morning, get dressed and head off to school or work, you are executing a set of instructions developed for the purpose of starting your day. Programming is nothing more than recognizing that a task exists, and deciding how best to perform it.

HOW THIS BOOK IS DIFFERENT

As you have probably noticed, there are a variety of books available today attempting to teach computer programming. These books generally describe the art of computer programming and the various steps required to create a working program. Some of them go further and elaborate on the art of Structured Programming and the clear, concise programs this method enables the programmer to create. These books are written with two basic limitations: They are too general about the programming languages they are intended to teach, and they are not general enough about the art of programming and problem solving. The intention of this book is to give the user a precise education in four of the more advanced capabilities of Turbo Pascal. This book is not designed to be a general Pascal text. Although many aspects of Turbo Pascal follow the Niklaus Wirth standard, there are variations.

STRUCTURED PROGRAMMING

In the early days of computing, computer hardware was the major contributor to the data processing budget. At that time, with the cost of hardware so high and the cost of programming labor relatively low, it made good business sense to write application programs that used sophisticated and complex algorithms to save memory. This programming emphasis saved on hardware acquisition expenditures at the cost of extensive labor hours and the development of complex software. In many cases, this software was so complex that it could not be modified, even by the original author.

As the price of hardware began to decline, and the cost per programming hour began to increase, the price of developing and maintaining software became a more significant part of the data processing budget. As a result, a technique was developed to improve programmer productivity. This technique became known as *structured programming*.

When structured programming was implemented, improvements became noticeable in many areas. First, because of the self-documenting nature of structured programming, programs became easier to read and thereby easier to enhance or modify. Second, because the program's structure was generally the same from program to program, less time was spent in the program design phase. Also, because of a common formalized structure, many programs could be created just by copying and modifying previously written programs. This was especially noticeable with regard to programs that generated reports. Third, due to the modular nature of structured programs, they were easier to test and debug. Lastly, as a result of the previously discussed benefits, the developed software was more reliable, and had a longer production life.

Structured Programming is a method of programming. In previous paragraphs, I defined programming but not how it is done. Programming is not merely a matter of sitting down at a keyboard and entering the code. The programmer must determine many aspects of the program before a single line of code is written. How will the program be used? Will the program require user input? Will it need to generate output in a particular manner? Will it need to store data? Will it need to retrieve stored data? The well-organized programmer will think carefully about all aspects of his program before considering what the program code will actually look like.

As an experienced programmer, you recognize all of these questions either intuitively or as a matter of experience. The most important reason to review this thought process is to make sure that you are asking yourself the proper questions. Remember, planning and preparation are the best defense against bugs finding their way into your applications.

Problem Definition

The first step in writing any program is to have a problem. If you don't have a problem then you don't need a solution. Some people call this "program conceptualization." All programs begin with an idea. Someone says "Could we make the computer do . . . ," or "How can we do this job better . . . ." The idea might not start with the programmer. Many applications have come from people who were just looking to make a job easier, or to accomplish a task more efficiently. In either case, an idea comes into existence. Regardless of its source, the programmer must take this idea and construct a program.

The programmer takes the idea and starts to break it down into its smallest individual components. From a problem-solving perspective, the idea is a problem. In some cases, an idea is only a single problem with a very clear solution. In other cases, the problem is actually composed of a number of component problems, each with an individual solution. In the latter instance the problem is called a "mess." The object of a problem definition is to determine the extent of the problem or the complexity of the idea, and then break it down into manageable pieces, each more easily solved.

This phase of program development might also require that you establish a line of communication with the individual who has requested, or who requires, the program to be written. If the originator of the idea is you, then don't worry. However, if the originator is someone else, then you must begin the problem-definition phase by determining exactly what the idea originator really wants. The definition might be determined from a single conversation or memo, or it might require several exchanges between the originator and the programmer. Throughout the process each side must maintain an open mind. The programmer must be sympathetic to the requirements of the originator. Similarly, the originator must be made to realize the limitations of the system on which the program will run, and the programmer who will write it. When all of the requirements of the problem have been discussed and accepted by both sides, the programmer can proceed to the next step.

Solution Definition

The second phase of programming is to take the individual problems one at a time, and decide how best to solve them. An individual problem can range from deciding how data might be entered into a program, or how best to perform a calculation. The solution definition should be a short description of how the individual problem was solved.

The solution to a problem should be concise and to the point. It does not need to be a fully elaborated code segment. The solution description only needs to be as complex as you require it to be. Remember, you are the programmer, and these are your personal notes. Later in the process you must create fully detailed solution descriptions which should be understandable by anyone who reads them. For the initial phases of program development, however, you need only be as detailed as you and the originator of the idea require. Even though you and the originator have developed a complete problem definition, it is still important to maintain contact. Remember that the original program requirements might have changed. You might not always be required to change your solution description to accommodate the change in the problem, but maintaining contact will prevent any unwanted surprises.

Program Design

You have developed a complete problem definition, identifying all aspects of the problem to be solved. You have diligently studied the individual tasks required to solve the problem, and have developed separate solutions for each one. The next phase of the development of the program is to assemble the problems and their solutions into a logical structure representing the first crude version of the program. The assembly process requires a more formalized or structured approach than the problem definition or solution description phases.

Technical Design

Technical design is the process of defining a program's structure and detailed logic. To effectively describe this logic, the program being discussed should be divided into bite-size sections called *modules*. Modules are distinct program segments, each of which performs a specific function. The program structure is the way these modules interrelate. Detailed logic outlines the steps and algorithms that must perform within each module to complete its logical function. These modules are the individual solution descriptions you should have previously developed.

Pseudocode

Pseudocode is a tool used to design and later document the processes within a module. This is done by using regular English words, within a Pascal-like format. The difference between this process and the structured English previously mentioned is that this includes all programming steps needed to execute the module and not just selected pieces of logic. In fact, the format of the pseudocode used on the design of a given application is dictated by the language in which the application will be programmed.

However, because pseudocode is so close to the actual program coding, most programmers dislike it. The general feeling among most programmers is that the text being written is almost the actual program—why not, therefore, just write the actual code?

Most programming professionals will tell you about the benefits of pseudocode, and how it can actually save time during the development of code. On the other hand, there are a number of programmers who feel that pseudocode is unnecessary, time consuming, and is NOT required if you properly document your code. In my opinion, both views are valid. As long as there is some form of reasonable documentation—either internal to the source code, or in a pseudocode document—you have performed your task. However, if you program by the "seat of your pants" and start out from point A, not even thinking about where point B is located, then you will do yourself and the users and maintainers of your software a great disservice.

Writing the Source Code

There are two basic ways in which programs are actually written and entered into the computer. The first method is to write the program out by hand on either plain lined paper, or on some type of special coding form, and keying in the entire program. Second, as programmers become more experienced, they tend to try to type the program directly into the computer without first writing on paper. The success of this second method is solely based on the talent of the programmer and the complexity of the application being developed. In either case, proper design specifications greatly assist in the process.

Preliminary Testing

During the programming and compilation process, there are two basic types of programming bugs that can, and usually do, occur. They are syntactical errors and logical errors. Syntax errors are easy to find because the program listing that is created during the compilation process tells the programmer exactly where the error occurred, and provides some explanation of the problem. These errors are caused by statements that are not in the correct Pascal format. For example, the statement "whiile (x < 1) do" will cause an error because "whiile" is not a valid statement, and therefore cannot be understood by the compiler.

Once the program being written is free of syntactical problems, logical errors must be identified and corrected. Logical errors are mistakes in the way the program processes the data. These errors are much more difficult to find and might periodically turn up months or even years later depending on the complexity of the program and the thoroughness of the testing process. To identify these errors, the programmer should develop a small set of test data. This data should contain information that is representative of that used in the application as well as information with "out of range" values and invalid formats. The valid data will assist in the testing of the program's processing logic, and the invalid information will test the program's error checking capabilities.

Program Implementation and Maintenance

The implementation of a program or system is the final step in the software development process. This step is comprised of final testing, implementation and program maintenance.

The Final Testing and Implementation Process   Once the program is completed and seemingly ready for production, it should go through one or more rounds of testing. When possible, these tests should NOT be performed by the program's author. The person who wrote the program tests it to see if it works. Others test a program to find the errors. It is this difference in mental attitude that helps to provide a more thorough and complete test. Also, the programmer has presumably tested the program prior to implementation, and might therefore take a second round of testing less seriously than a newcomer to the process.

A very common practice in testing new programs is to develop a testing team. This team usually consists of the program's author, a fellow programmer, and a user of the program once it is implemented. The program's author is present only to provide technical background about the program's development. The testing is performed by the second programmer and the user.

This team approach seems to work well because the second programmer can evaluate the program's technical aspects without being hindered by a pride of authorship, and the user has the application knowledge to analyze the program's functional merit. Also, the user has a strong vested interest in that they will have to rely on the ability and correctness of this program for the foreseeable future.

There are many techniques that can be used to test programs. Three of the most common are parallel testing, prior testing and simulation testing. *Parallel testing* is the process of running two systems simultaneously. Using this technique requires continuing the old methods, and also taking on the task of doing it the new way. This additional responsibility might mean running another report over the weekend, or it might mean manually inputting data into two systems. Once complete, the outputs of the two systems are compared. If the results are the same, or at least reconcilable, then the new system continues and the old mode of operation is discontinued. If the test results are unsatisfactory, it's back to work, to discuss the problems and make the appropriate changes.

Parallel testing sounds good in theory, but in actuality it can be impractical, or even impossible, to perform due to a lack of the resources needed to do twice the work, or the inability to capture the data in two places at once. Therefore, two alternate approaches were developed that can be performed by just the testing team. The first of these techniques is called *prior testing*. This process uses the same principles as parallel testing except that it uses data from past months. For example, if a new payroll system is being installed in November, establish the test files as of a few months before, say March. Then, enter April's actual data and compare the test reports to the actual April numbers. Continue this process through October, and if all looks good, go with only the new system in November.

The third testing process, *simulation testing*, is similar to the second, except that the test data is strictly simulated. This alternative will not produce as thorough a test. However, if the test data is selected carefully, it should suffice. To implement a system using this test method, the files being used by the new programs should be copied from the old system and converted to the new format. On an appropriate day, the old method is discontinued and the new method is activated.

Program Maintenance   Regardless of the method used to implement the new program or system, there is usually a need for maintenance programming. Maintenance programming becomes necessary for many reasons. Errors might be found in the code that must be corrected. Company policies or procedures might change. Growing firms might outgrow current systems or enhancements might be made to meet new business challenges. Whatever the reason, this task can be made easier if the software is well-documented, written in a clear concise structured format, and carefully modified so as not to violate structured principles or outdate the documentation.

The Compilation Process

Once the source code is written and typed into the computer, it must be translated from a human-readable format into a computer-readable form. To compile a program, the programmer must execute the Turbo Pascal compiler and specify the name of the program to be transformed. This process leaves the input source code unchanged, and creates the compiled code in either memory or in a disk file. In order to run the program, the user need only compile to memory by selecting from the menu to "compile" and then "run." If the program runs correctly, the user may then save the compiled code to a disk file and run independently of the Turbo Pascal programming environment. Unlike many other languages, the Turbo Pascal compilation process is performed in a single stage. Other compilers require the user to compile the source code to an object code, and then link the object modules to form an executable program. The name of the executable program file ends with a ".EXE" extension. Turbo Pascal compilation also offers a variety of compilation directives embedded in the source code of your program, allowing for even more versatile functions. These directives are discussed more fully in chapter 7 of the Turbo Pascal User's Guide, and Appendix A of the Reference Guide.

DISCUSSION

Turbo Pascal offers a complete programming environment for the development of simple and complex applications. Pascal has been used for years in schools to teach the basic, and many of the advanced, concepts of computer programming. With the coming of age of the personal computer, home enthusiasts and professional programmers alike have turned towards Turbo Pascal for its ease of use, its speed of compilation, and its ability to produce fast, efficient code.

This book allows you to take advantage of the advanced capabilities of the Turbo Pascal development environment. The text and examples in the later chapters of this book will provide you with the instructions and skills necessary to create your own advanced applications. After reading this book and examining the example programs, I believe you will understand why I am so enthusiastic about Turbo Pascal.

2

A Technical Review
of Turbo Pascal

This chapter reviews the basic elements of the Pascal language, and Turbo Pascal specifically. As an intermediate or an advanced programmer, you may decide to skip over this chapter, but you might find a review of the basics of the language helpful. Although you might have some experience with Turbo Pascal, you might find additional information in this review. You could be reminded of elements of the language that you have not used in some time, and which you might find useful now.

DATA TYPES

In order for a procedure, function or program to operate, it must have data upon which to perform. Turbo Pascal's data types are varied and greatly enhanced over the data types available in a standard implementation of Pascal. As an intermediate or advanced programmer, you have learned the use of variables and constants. This section reviews the Turbo Pascal data types, their capabilities, and their ranges.

Variables are portions of memory set aside to hold specific pieces of data. Standard Pascal defines Boolean, Char, Integers, and Reals. Each of these variable types is used to hold a specific piece of information. In addition, there are subtypes for these variable types which have specific uses and ranges of value. Each of the variable types, and their subtypes, is described in the following section.

Variables are defined within the Var section of a program, procedure or function. There are restrictions on what you can call a variable, and the length of a variable name cannot exceed 127 characters. Variable names can only begin with alpha characters. No numbers or punctuation will be accepted as leading characters for a variable's name. Punctuation characters other than the underscore character "_" cannot be used in any portion of a variable name. Figure 2-1 contains some acceptable and unacceptable names for Turbo Pascal variables.

Valid Names	Invalid Names
count	1_name
total_pay	name-1
name_1	total$pay
last_name	last name
help_flag	123
f110_type	100_type
_my_var	

Fig. 2-1. List of valid and invalid variable names.

Variables are declared in the "Var" section of an application or its procedures. A sample variable declaration is shown in FIG. 2-2.

```
Var
   Bool_Variable : Boolean;
   Char_Variable : Char;
   Int_Variable  : Integer;
   Real_Variable : Real:
```

Fig. 2-2. Variable declarations in the VAR section.

Variable names CANNOT be the same as Pascal keywords such as BEGIN, END, VAR, TYPE, or PROCEDURE.

Boolean

The Boolean variable type is used to hold values of TRUE or FALSE. These variables allow the user to establish conditions, and are used for selective evaluation of portions of program code. Through the use of Boolean expressions, extremely specific conditions may be established. An example of a Boolean variable and its use is shown in FIG. 2-3.

```
condition := (number_variable = 4);
```

Fig. 2-3. A Boolean variable.

The example in FIG. 2-3 demonstrates the assignment of a Boolean expression into a Boolean variable. As you might recall, variables are declared in the "var" section of a program or procedure. Figure 2-3 also demonstrates the Boolean equality operator " = " which is used to determine if the value to the left of the operator and the value to the right of the operator are equal. In addition, the assignment operator ": = " is used. Do not confuse the assignment and equality operators. Remember, one is used to assign a value into a variable, the other determines if one value is equal to another, respectively. Boolean expressions are usually placed between parentheses "( )" to distinguish between multiple expressions. In FIG. 2-3 the expression within the parentheses can evaluate to TRUE or FALSE. The Boolean result of the evaluation of the expression is assigned to the CONDITION variable. When declaring a variable, you need not declare all variables of a specific type on one line (see FIG. 2-4).

Fig. 2-4. Multiple Boolean variable declarations.

```
Var
  Bool1, Bool2, Bool3 : Boolean;
  Bool4 : Boolean;
```

The ability to declare several variables as being of the same type is not limited to Boolean variables. However, two variables cannot have the same name, even if they are of different types. Finally, a variable which is defined to be Boolean cannot be redefined to hold integer, character, or any other values.

Char

The Char or character variable type is a simple variable used to hold the ASCII character set. Char variables occupy a single byte of memory as do Boolean variables. However, Boolean variables can only hold two different values TRUE and FALSE.

A Char variable can assume the value of any of the printable characters "A" to "Z," "a" to "z," "0" to "9," as well as punctuation and special language characters. The Char variable can hold up to 256 different values. Not all of the ASCII characters are printable characters, but a Char variable can still hold them.

Integer

Unlike the Boolean and Char variable types, the Integer type represents a class of variable types. The Boolean and Char types each have only one range and a specific set of values that they can hold. There are six ranges and subtypes which an Integer variable can be assigned. The common thread among these subtypes is the ability to hold only whole counting variables. Integers are counting numbers, and as such have a special function in Turbo Pascal control structures that will be reviewed later in this chapter (see FIG. 2-5).

Fig. 2-5. Valid and invalid integer types.

Valid	Invalid
4	4.2
123	1.23
65535	655.35
128	−12.8

Byte   The Byte type is a simple counting integer type. It has a range of 0 to 255. If a value less than 0 or greater than 255 is assigned to a byte variable, the result will be unexpected. For instance, if you assign the value 300 to a Byte variable and then output the contents of that variable, the value 44 will be displayed. The reason for this apparent error is Turbo Pascal's effort to try and make the number fit into the variable type. Because a Byte variable can only hold a maximum value of 255, any values exceeding it automatically wrap around the variable such that 256 is 0, 257 is 1, and 300 is 44. Like the Char and Boolean types, A Byte variable needs only a single byte of memory to hold its value.

Comp   The Comp data type is used to hold extremely large integer values ranging from $-2E+63$ to $+2E+63$. The Comp variable type is listed in the Turbo Pascal User's Guide as a Real. However, a Comp variable can only hold integer values. A variable defined as Comp is invaluable for holding extremely large integer numbers for use in prime number cyphers, or other encryption or decryption work. Because of the extremely large range of integer values it can assume, a Comp variable requires 8 bytes of memory to store it. This is fine if you have the memory to spare. However, variables that occupy relatively large portions of memory usually take longer to process.

Integer   There is not only an integer data type class, but an Integer subtype as well. An Integer variable can hold values for -32768 to 32767. Like the Byte and Comp integer subtypes, Integer variables can be used for counting and calculations involving moderately sized numbers. However, if the result of an operation exceeds the operating range for an Integer variable, and that value is assigned into such a variable, then you will see results similar to the Byte variable. Unlike the Byte subtype, an Integer variable can assume negative values. This allows for more versatility in numeric operations where negative numbers might result. The Integer variable requires more memory to store a number utilizing 2 bytes where the Byte variable required only 1.

LongInt   The Longint integer subtype is an extended Integer type variable. It can hold values from $-2,147,483,648$ to $2,147,483,647$. The advantages of such a variable over the standard Integer variable are obvious. The disadvantage of this subtype is memory. The Longint type requires 4 bytes of memory to hold a value.

ShortInt   The Shortint subtype is very similar to the Byte subtype. The Shortint requires only a single byte of memory. It can hold 256 different values. However the Shortint subtype holds values from -128 to 127. Although the Byte and ShortInt integer subtype can each assume up to 256 different values, they each have their own value ranges. I believe you will find these two subtypes extremely useful.

Word   The Word subtype is similar in scope to the Integer subtype. Like Integer, the Word subtype can accommodate 65536 values. Unlike an Integer which can assume negative numbers, a Word ranges from 0 to 65535. Like an Integer, a Word variable requires only 2 types of memory to accommodate this range. This subtype enables programmers to count twice as many positive numbers as an Integer, without using additional memory.

Larger amounts of memory are usually required for greater precision, or in this case, greater counting range. Because most personal computers today come with a minimum of 512K or 640K of memory, any restrictions on the use of more memory for variables should be avoidable. A programmer must often take into account the capabilities of the platform on which his application runs. Turbo Pascal version 5.5 provides an extremely rich set of Integer subtypes that can serve a variety of purposes.

Real

Unlike integer variables that cannot assume values other than whole numbers, Real variables have the ability to take on a wide variety of numbers with whole and real portions as well as exponents, that can be either positive or negative. In addition, real numbers can take on integer values such as 4 or 65535.

However, an integer variable cannot hold a real value. If an attempt is made to assign a real value to an integer variable, the code will likely be caught by Turbo Pascal during the compilation of your program. If it is not, then a run-time error will likely result. Figure 2-6 lists some valid real numbers.

Valid
4.2
1.23
655.35
−12.8
1.444E10
−2E−2

Fig. 2-6. Valid real values.

Real variables are used for complex calculations where the result is not a whole number. Real numbers are used to hold trigonometric results, or the results of arithmetic operations of real and integer numbers. Any operation between a real and an integer value will likely result in a real number. Many of Turbo Pascal's mathematical functions are designed to take and return real values. Real variables are used to hold real world values.

Like the Integer data type, the real data type is actually a class of variable types. Each real subtype has a specific range of values. Unlike integers, real subtypes also have a precision attribute which may be used to determine which type of real variable you should use in your applications.

Double   The Double precision subtype is used for complex arithmetic where the precision of the result of an operation must be high. Remember, precision is not accuracy. Precision is the degree of exactness with which a quantity is defined. Accuracy is the ability of an operation to yield the correct answer. The Double subtype allows for a precision of up to 16 significant figures. A Double variable can range from $5.0E-324$ to $1.7E308$. Like the integer variables which provide larger number ranges, a Double variable requires a relatively large amount of memory (8 bytes) to store a value. However, as I stated before, when precision of a result of an arithmetic operation is important, use of a larger amount of memory for variable storage is easily justified.

Extended   The Extended subtype provides even greater precision and range than the Double subtype. Extended variables allow for ranges of real values from $1.9E-4951$ to $1.1E4932$. That is an incredible range, and it also requires more memory for storage of values. The Extended subtype requires 10 bytes of memory for storage and in return provides 19 to 20 digits of precision. Like the Double precision variable subtype, Extended variables are used to hold the results of numeric operations where the precision of the result is extremely important.

Real   Like the integer variable class, the real class also has a namesake subtype. The Real subtype provides for variables with a precision of 11 to 12 digits. For this precision, each Real variable occupies 6 bytes of memory. With the original Turbo Pascal and for versions prior to 4.0, the Real variable subtype was the only type available for real numbers. For general purpose use, the Real subtype provides moderate precision, and uses a relatively small amount of memory.

Single   The Single precision subtype is similar in range to the Real variable subtype. Unlike the Real, Single variables have a precision of only 7 to 8 digits. They range from $1.5E-45$ to $3.4E38$. For this precision and range, each Single precision variable uses only 4 bytes of memory. There are certain advantages to using Single precision variables, most important of which is the relatively small amount of memory required for storage. Because fewer bytes of memory are actually used to store a value, Turbo Pascal can process these variables faster. This difference in speed of evaluation of Single as opposed to Real or Double precision variables is negligible for a small number of real number operations. With numeric operations numbering in the thousands or higher, a substantial difference in speed of evaluation is observed. Single precision variables are used for low-precision arithmetic results where speed of execution is important and limited precision is not.

String

The string variable is a superset of the Char variable described earlier. Character strings can be up to 255 characters in length. A String type is defined in the "type" section of a procedure or application. The String variable is declared in the "var" section of a procedure or application. Some sample string definitions and declarations are shown in FIG. 2-7.

Fig. 2-7. String variable definitions and declarations.

```
Type
    str25  = string[25];
    str50  = string[50];
    str100 = string[100];
Var
    string1 : str25;
    string2 : str50;
    string3 : str100;
    string4 : string;
```

The type section of FIG. 2-7 shows the definition of various length string types. The STR25 type can be used to create a character variable string 25 characters long. The STR50 type can be used to create a character string variable 50 characters long. And the STR100 type can be used to create a character string variable 100 characters long. As you can see in the type definition section, the number between the square brackets "[ ]" defines the length of the character string type. The String variable can then be declared in the Var section. You might have noticed the last declaration for the STRING4 variable is simply "string." The string type without brackets is defined by Turbo Pascal as string[255] or the maximum length a String variable can assume.

Variables are portions of memory that contain specific pieces of information. This information can be numeric, character, Boolean or, as you will see later in this chapter, a combination of the three. Turbo Pascal offers a rich selection of variable types and subtypes. Specific variables have specific ranges, precisions, or specific values they can assume. The nature of your applications determines the necessity for character, Boolean, integer, or real data and the ranges and precisions required to enable your application to execute properly.

OPERATORS

Like all programming languages, Turbo Pascal has the ability to perform mathematical tasks by combining numeric variables and arithmetic operators into mathematical expressions. The numeric variables are defined using the various numeric data types previously discussed. The arithmetical operators are the symbols like " + " and " - " that tell the compiler which mathematical process to perform.

There are four standard and two integer arithmetical operators. They are: " + ", " - ", " * ", "div" and "mod" standing for addition, subtraction, multiplication, integer division and integer remainder respectively. Table

**Table 2-1. Standard
Expressions Mathematical Examples**

	Before			After		
Expression	a	b	c	a	b	c
a := b + c	1	2	3	5	2	3
a := b − c	1	2	3	−1	2	3
a := b * c	1	2	3	6	2	3
a := b / c	1	5	2	2.5	5	2
a := b div c	1	24	10	2	24	10
a := b mod c	1	24	10	4	24	10

2-1 lists some examples of the operators and the outcome of their equations.

The "div" operator calculates the integer portion of the result of the division operation. The "mod" operator calculates the remainder after an integer division. For example, given the equation "a := 5 div 2;", "a" would be given a value of 2. Similarly, in the "a := 5 mod 2;" "a" would be given the value of 1.

When combining these operators into a single formula, care should be taken to assure that the mathematical processes are performed in the expected order. Turbo Pascal evaluates mathematical equations in a way that is consistent with mathematical principles of precedence. This precedence first processes expressions within parentheses left to right, then multiplication and division left to right, then addition from left to right. For example, the equation "a := 1 + 2 * 3;" will give "a" a value of 7. First the 2 and 3 are multiplied giving a value of 6, then 1 is added to 6 making a total of 7. Therefore, "a := 1 + 2 * 3;" and "a := 1 + (2 * 3);" are equivalent expressions. If however, you wish to add the 1 and 2 first and then multiply the sum by three, the equation should be written "a := (1 + 2) * 3;". The general rule regarding when to use these parentheses is to ALWAYS use them, thus forcing the proper order of operation and as a by-product, improve the formula's readability. Table 2-2 lists example formulas and displays their expected results.

Expression	Result
a := (1 + 2) * 3;	9
a := 1 + 2 * 3;	7
a := 1 + (2 * 3) ;	7
a := 2 * (1 + 1) / 2;	2
a := 1 + (2 + 6) / 4;	3

Table 2-2. Example Mathematical Formulas

RELATIONAL EXPRESSIONS AND OPERATORS

Relational operators allow the programmer to establish whether an inequality exists between two pieces of data. Comparisons can be performed between two numbers, two characters or even two strings of characters. These comparisons, when combined into a program, become expressions which evaluate to TRUE or FALSE. If the comparison evaluates to TRUE, the value TRUE can be placed into a variable designed for a Boolean value.

The operators in TABLE 2-3 are used to determine the relationship between two pieces of data. The expression "(2 < 3)" is a relational expression which compares the numbers 2 and 3. If the number 2 is less than the number 3, the expression "(2 < 3)" evaluates to TRUE. If the number 2 were greater than the number 3, the expression would evaluate to FALSE. Because the result of a relation operation is a value of TRUE or FALSE, these expressions are referred to as "Boolean expressions." You will recall that Boolean variables can contain only values of TRUE and FALSE. Booleans are used to control the execution of programs. Because the result of a relational operation is such a value, it may be used in the same way. An example of a relational operation in program control is shown in FIG. 2-8.

Table 2-3. The Basic Turbo Pascal Relational Operators

Operator	Meaning
=	Equals To
<	Less Than
>	Greater Than
< =	Less Than or Equal To
> =	Greater Than or Equal To
< >	Not Equal To
in	Contained In Set

In FIG. 2-8 a comparison occurs between the results of two arithmetic operations. The first operation yields the value of the counter divided by 3. The second operation yields the integer part of the value of the counter divided by 3. The control statement asks whether the results of the two operations are "equal" with the "if ((counter/3) = TRUNC (counter/3)) then" statement. If the results of the two arithmetic operations are "equal" the statements contained within the "if..then" statement are executed. Obviously, the comparison will evaluate to "True" when the counter is an integer multiple of the number 3.

```
Program :        Program demonstrate_relational_control;
                 Var
                    counter : integer;
                 Begin
                    writeln('Numbers between 1 and 20 divisible by 3:');
                    writeln(' ');
                    for counter := 1 to 20 do
                      begin
                         if ((counter/3) = TRUNC(counter/3)) then
                           begin
                              writeln(counter,' is divisible by 3.');
                           end
                      end;
                 end.

Program Output : Numbers between 1 and 20 divisible by 3:
                      3 is divisible by 3.
                      6 is divisible by 3.
                      9 is divisible by 3.
                      12 is divisible by 3.
                      15 is divisible by 3.
                      18 is divisible by 3.
```

Fig. 2-8. Relational operations programming example.

THE "IN" RELATIONAL OPERATOR

In addition to the six basic relational operators =, <, >, <=, >=, and <>, there is an additional operator which provides for some extremely useful comparisons. This operator is called the in operator. The in operator evaluates a piece of data for its inclusion in the specified data set. If the data is a member of the specified set, the in comparison returns a value of TRUE. If the data is not in the set, then a value of FALSE is returned. A data set is a set of data grouped together. The data can be used separately, but the programmer has defined a set to contain certain elements. Typical sets of data are shown in TABLE 2-4.

Table 2-4. Some User Definable Sets

User Defined Set Name	Contents
days_of_week	Sun, Mon, Tues, Wed, Thurs, Fri, Sat
Months_of_year	Jan, Feb, Mar, Apr, May, Jun, Jul, Aug, Sep, Oct, Nov, Dec
some_letters	A, H, J, K
some_numbers	3, 6, 9, 12
yes_no_answers	YES, Yes, yes, Y, y, NO, No, no, N, n

Sets can contain characters, numbers, words, phrases or any valid data recognized by Turbo Pascal. One of the most widely used applications of sets is to evaluate responses to "yes/no" questions. A thoughtful programmer will make provisions for a wide range of responses to questions in a program. One of the questions that has such a wide range of responses is a question which requires an answer of "yes" or "no." This simple question can receive responses of "Yes," "Yes," "yes," "Y" or "y" when the response is meant to be affirmative. All of these responses are valid, but to program for all five responses is a waste of source code. Instead of performing five comparisons, a program with a set of responses can be evaluated with one in comparison. The use of in for a response to a "yes/no" question is shown in FIG. 2-9.

```
Program :    Program Yes_or_No_Response;
             Type
               string255 = string[255];
               yes_no_set = set of ('YES','Yes','yes','Y','y');
             Var
               responses : yes_no_set;
               answer : string255;
             Begin
               write('Do you wish to continue : ');
               readln(answer);
               if (answer in responses) then
                 begin
                   writeln('The answer is affirmative.');
                 end
               else
                 begin
                   writeln('The answer is negative.');
                 end;
             end;
```

Fig. 2-9. An example of the "in" relational operator.

LOGICAL EXPRESSIONS AND OPERATORS

Relational operators form the basis for all logical control of Pascal programs. Pascal provides a method for evaluating more than one comparison within a single line of code. Using logical operators such as and, or, not and xor the programmer can combine several comparisons into one statement or logical expression. A typical logical expression might generate an output of names of individuals who are between twenty and forty years of age. There are actually two comparisons that must be performed as part of this comparison. First, the age of the individual must be greater or equal to 20. Second, the age of an individual must be less than or equal to 40. Some comparisons of individuals and their ages are shown in TABLE 2-5.

Table 2-5. Individual Ages and Comparisons to 20 and 40

Name	Age	Age Greater Than or Equal to 20	Age Less Than or Equal to 40
Joe	14	False	True
Ann	22	True	True
Mike	41	True	False
Donna	39	True	True
Gary	52	True	False

The results of TABLE 2-5 show that all of the data in the list satisfies one or the other of the two conditions. Some people's ages are less than or equal to 40, while others are greater than or equal to 20. Because there are two conditions that must be TRUE for a correct output, it is necessary to combine the two comparisons to form a logical expression.

When both comparisons must be TRUE for the expression to be TRUE then the comparisons must be combined with an and operator. One condition is "age > = 20)." The second condition is "(age < = 40)." In TABLE 2-5, the first condition is TRUE for Ann, Mike, Donna, and Gary. The second condition is TRUE for Joe, Ann and Donna. Both the first and second conditions are TRUE for Ann and Donna. The results of the individual and combined comparisons are shown in TABLE 2-6.

Table 2-6. Individual Ages and Comparisons to 20, 40, 20 AND 40

Name	Age	or Equal to 20	or Equal to 40	AND (Age < = 40)
Joe	14	False	True	False
Ann	22	True	True	True
Mike	41	True	False	False
Donna	39	True	True	True
Gary	52	True	False	False

Using the and operator enables the programmer to establish extremely complex criterion for a final evaluation of TRUE. In addition to the "and" operator, there are three other operators known as or, not, and xor.

The or operator like and allows the programmer to link two or more individual comparisons together to generate a logical expression. The or does not require both conditions to be TRUE to evaluate the entire condition as TRUE. When the or operator is combined with the age example in TABLE 2-5, the results are different than with the use of "and." The results of the age example with the or operator is shown in TABLE 2-7.

Table 2-7. Individual Ages and Comparisons to 20, 40, 20 OR 40

Name	Age	Age Greater Than or Equal to 20	Age Less Than or Equal to 40	(Age > = 20) OR (Age < = 40)
Joe	14	False	True	True
Ann	22	True	True	True
Mike	41	True	False	True
Donna	39	True	True	True
Gary	52	True	False	True

The use of or allows the programmer to establish comparisons and logical expressions that might require only one or two conditions to evaluate to TRUE for the entire expression to evaluate to TRUE and a specific portion of the code to execute.

The not operator does not link two or more comparisons to form an expression. Instead it is used to negate the value of a comparison. If a condition evaluates to TRUE then the expression "NOT(True)" evaluates to FALSE. Similarly, the expression "NOT(False)" evaluates to TRUE.

The xor operator also allows the programmer to link two or more comparisons together into an expression. The xor operator, however, requires the first condition to be TRUE and the second condition to be FALSE. Like the and operator, xor requires each comparison to evaluate to a specific value before the expression can evaluate to TRUE. The results of each logical operator on two conditions is shown in TABLE 2-8.

Table 2-8. The Logical Operators

Evaluated Condition One	Comparisons Condition Two	Logical Operator	Evaluated Combined Expression
True	True	AND	True
True	False	AND	False
False	True	AND	False
False	False	AND	False
True	True	OR	True
True	False	OR	True
False	True	OR	True
False	False	OR	False
	True	NOT	False
	False	NOT	True
True	True	XOR	False
True	False	XOR	True
False	True	XOR	False
False	False	XOR	False

Judicious use of these operators makes a program both efficient and easy to use. However, care should be taken to ensure that the logic of these expressions is not improperly evaluated. Although all individual comparisons must be evaluated before a logical expression can be evaluated, there is a precedence of evaluation from left to right along the statement line. All logical operators have the same precedence, so the logical expression "A

OR B AND C" would not necessarily evaluate to the same value as "C AND B OR A."

If A is TRUE, B is TRUE and C is FALSE then the first expression evaluates to FALSE, however the second evaluates to TRUE. In both cases, the first logical operator is evaluated first. "A OR B" is TRUE, and TRUE "AND C" is False. "C AND B" is FALSE, and FALSE "OR A" is TRUE. As in arithmetical expressions, where precedence may be circumvented by the use of parentheses, evaluation precedence may also be superceded by the use of parentheses. The use of parentheses around the desired expression is the best way to ensure evaluation order. If parentheses are placed into the original equations "A OR (B AND C)" and "(C AND B) OR A" the evaluation order is made consistent between the two expressions. Using the values for A, B and C, both of these expressions now evaluate to TRUE.

THE "BYTE" OPERATORS

The logical operators and, or, not and xor perform vital operations to create logical expressions. In addition, they enable the programmer to perform fast and useful operations of "byte" variables.

Previously, Byte variables were defined as a subrange of the Integer data type. A byte variable can assume a value between 0 and 255. This number range is extremely significant because it is the maximum range a byte variable can assume, and because it is the value of 2^8. A byte consists of eight "bits" which are strung together to form a small section of memory. Each bit can have a value of either 1 or 0. As you will notice, this is extremely similar to a Boolean variable, which can assume values of only TRUE and FALSE. This is significant because of the capabilities of the "and," "or," "not" and "xor" operators.

Each bit in a byte has a specific integer value associated with it, based on that bit's value of either 1 or 0. When all of the associated bit values are added together, they amount to an integer value between 0 to 255 associated with the entire byte. A schematic of a typical byte is shown in TABLE 2-9.

Bit Number	Associated Byte Value if value in bit is "1"		
7	128	decimal	$80	hexadecimal
6	64	decimal	$40	hexadecimal
5	32	decimal	$20	hexadecimal
4	16	decimal	$10	hexadecimal
3	8	decimal	$08	hexadecimal
2	4	decimal	$04	hexadecimal
1	2	decimal	$02	hexadecimal
0	1	decimal	$01	hexadecimal

Table 2-9. The Values Associated with each "Bit" of a "Byte"

If bit 1 has a value of 1, and all other bits have values of 0, the value of the byte is 1. If bits 1 and 2 have values of 1, and all other bits have values of 0, the value of the byte is 3. In general, the value of a byte is the sum of the associated values of the bits with values of 1. The display of a bit's position and value is called a *bitmap*. Some values between 0 and 255 and their associated bit maps are shown in FIG. 2-10.

Decimal Value	Bit Map Values Position								Sum of Associated Values
	7	6	5	4	3	2	1	0	
47	0	0	1	0	1	1	1	1	0 + 0 + 32 + 0 + 8 + 4 + 2 + 1
140	1	0	0	0	1	1	0	0	128 + 0 + 0 + 0 + 8 + 4 + 0 + 0
201	1	1	0	0	0	1	0	1	128 + 64 + 0 + 0 + 0 + 4 + 0 + 1
3	0	0	0	0	0	0	1	1	0 + 0 + 0 + 0 + 0 + 0 + 2 + 1
255	1	1	1	1	1	1	1	1	128 + 64 + 32 + 16 + 8 + 4 + 2 + 1

Fig. 2-10. Example bitmaps and associated byte values.

Because each bit in a byte so closely resembles a Boolean variable in itself, one might assume the logical operators to have some effect on the bits of a byte variable—such an assumption is entirely correct. The logical operators and, or and xor can be used to perform *bitwise* addition of byte variables. Bitwise simply refers to the effect of the operator on each bit of the byte. Because it is necessary to combine two comparisons with a logical operator in a logical expression, it is also necessary to combine two bytes—hence these operations are called "addition."

The addition of bytes using the logical operators can provide some helpful information about a particular number. Some basic bitwise addition expressions, their bitmaps, and their results are shown in FIG. 2-11.

Each of the bitwise addition operators and, or and xor provides the ability to combine two numbers into a third. The not operator performs a simple subtraction of the byte value from 255.

In addition to the bitwise addition operators, there are two more bitwise operators called shl and shr. The shl operator stands for "shift left." What this means is that the pattern of 1's and 0's is shifted in the bitmap by a specified number of bits. For the "shift left" operator this means a shift towards the seventh bit location. For the "shift right" operator this means a shift towards the zeroth bit location. The results of these shift operators are shown in FIG. 2-12.

There are additional operators that exist in Turbo Pascal. There are operators on sets. There are operators which transform portions of integers into bytes that can then be manipulated using the bitwise operators. The review of these operators is left to the reader.

Decimal Value	7	6	5	4	3	2	1	0	Sum of Associated Values
Bit Map Values				**Position**					
150	1	0	0	1	0	1	1	0	128 + 0 + 0 + 16 + 0 + 4 + 2 + 0
43	0	0	1	0	1	0	1	1	0 + 0 + 32 + 0 + 8 + 0 + 2 + 1

(150 AND 43) = 2

	7	6	5	4	3	2	1	0	
	0	0	0	0	0	0	1	0	0 + 0 + 0 + 0 + 0 + 0 + 2 + 0

(150 OR 43) = 191

	7	6	5	4	3	2	1	0	
	1	0	1	1	1	1	1	1	128 + 0 + 32 + 16 + 8 + 4 + 2 + 1

NOT (43) = 222 (* This is the same as 255 − 43 *)

	7	6	5	4	3	2	1	0	
	1	1	0	1	0	1	0	0	128 + 64 + 0 + 16 + 0 + 4 + 0 + 0

NOT (150) = 105 (* This is the same as 255 − 150 *)

	7	6	5	4	3	2	1	0	
	0	1	1	0	1	0	0	1	0 + 64 + 32 + 0 + 8 + 0 + 0 + 1

(150 XOR 43) = 148

	7	6	5	4	3	2	1	0	
	1	0	0	1	0	1	0	0	128 + 0 + 0 + 16 + 0 + 4 + 0 + 0

Fig. 2-11. Typical "bitwise" operations and results.

Decimal Value	7	6	5	4	3	2	1	0	Sum of Associated Values
Bit Map Values				**Position**					
255	1	1	1	1	1	1	1	1	128 + 64 + 32 + 16 + 8 + 4 + 2 + 1

(255 shl 3) = 248

	7	6	5	4	3	2	1	0	
	1	1	1	1	1	0	0	0	128 + 64 + 32 + 16 + 8 + 0 + 0 + 0

(255 shr 3) = 31

	7	6	5	4	3	2	1	0	
	0	0	0	1	1	1	1	1	0 + 0 + 0 + 16 + 8 + 4 + 2 + 1

Fig. 2-12. The "bitwise" shift operators.

INPUT AND OUTPUT

The most basic input procedure in Turbo Pascal is the read procedure. This procedure allows the programmer to import information into a program from an input device. The most common input device is the keyboard. From the keyboard, numbers, characters, or strings of characters may be entered. The information that is entered might be used for arithmetic operations. Entered information might correspond to a menu for which an integer number is required to select one of the items. Information may be textual, as might be entered into a text editor. The read procedure may be used to allow all of this information to be entered into a program. An example of a typical program using the read procedure is shown in FIG. 2-13.

The program in FIG. 2-13 demonstrates the use of the read function for data entry from the keyboard. The program asks for two numbers to be entered by the user. The values are entered and their sum is returned. The user must type the response and then press the ENTER or RETURN key to cause the response to be accepted.

One of the most important aspects of the program in FIG. 2-13 is the demonstration of how to preface a call for information with a question. The statement that usually occurs before a read procedure is the write procedure. The write procedure is exactly identical to a writeln procedure except that it does not cause the cursor to move to the next lower line on the screen after it is executed. The lack of a newline after a "write" allows the cursor to stay on the same line as the text. This enables the answer to a question to be entered on the same line as the question. An example of a typical data input statement combination is shown in FIG. 2-14.

```
Program Demonstrate_Read;
Var
   num_a, num_b, sum : real;
begin
   writeln('This program asks for two numbers');
   writeln('and returns their sum.');
   write('Enter the first number and press RETURN : ');
   read(num_a);
   write('Enter the second number and press RETURN : ');
   read(num_b);
   writeln(' ');
   writeln(' ');
   sum := num_a + num_b;
   writeln('The sum of ',num_a,' and ',num_b,' is ',sum);
end.


Program output: This program ask for two numbers
                and returns their sum.
                Enter the first number and press RETURN : 5.1
                Enter the second number and press RETURN : 3.6


                The sum of 5.1 and 3.6 is 8.7
```

Fig. 2-13. An example of the use of the "read" procedure.

```
        Partial Program Listing:
                  .
                  .
                  .
                  write('This is the question portion : ');
                  read(input_variable);
                  .
                  .
                  .

        Partial Program Output:
                  .
                  .
                  This is the question portion : _
                  .
                  .
```

Fig. 2-14. A typical series of statements for data entry.

When the read procedure is prefaced with a write procedure as in FIG. 2-14, the cursor stays on the same line as the question. This allows the person who must enter the data to better relate the position at which to enter data, with the question that asks for it. The read procedure itself does not provide a means for displaying a question. Instead, when used with the write procedure, the question and the prompt for an answer may be grouped together.

The standard syntax for the "read" procedure allows for the input of data from the keyboard, a file, or some other input device. The read procedure allows the programmer to design input statements for one or many pieces of data within one statement. The use of the write procedure to preface the read statement with a question, however, usually results in only a single piece of data being entered per read statement. However, when input is from a file, or a specially designed entry screen, more than one piece of data entered per read statement is more the rule rather than the exception. The standard Pascal syntax for the use of the "read" procedure is shown in FIG. 2-15.

Name: READ
Function: Allow Input into Specified Variable or Variables from specified input channel.
Syntax: READ ([channel,] var1 [,var2, . . . , varn]);
Rules: 1) All items within brackets ([ ]) are optional.
2) Variables may be of any valid Pascal or user defined datatype.
3) The "channel" variable is a correctly defined file identifier which has been assigned to an existing file or device.
4) If no "channel" variable is specified, input is assumed to be from the standard input device: the keyboard.

Fig. 2-15. The standard syntax for the "read" procedure.

The syntax of the read procedure allows for some particularly useful input techniques. Most input is made from either the keyboard or a file. Turbo Pascal defines several constant names that can be used synonymously with the specific input devices. These names are listed in TABLE 2-10 along with their devices.

For most purposes the INPUT, CON and TRM channels are identical for both input and output functions. For input from a channel that points to the standard input device, pressing ENTER is required. Beyond the simple input methods that require the use of the RETURN or ENTER key, Turbo Pascal provides a method for reading data from the keyboard one character at a time. An example of a typical single character input program is shown in FIG. 2-16.

Figure 2-16 contains a specific example of a program capable of capturing keys as they are pressed on the keyboard. While the key pressed is neither upper- nor lowercase "q" the program loops through a series of statements.

Table 2-10. Turbo Pascal Pre-Defined Input Channels

Channel Name—Indicated Input Device

INPUT Standard Input. This channel is assigned to the primary input device of the computer, usually the keyboard.

CON Console. This channel is assigned to the console device of the computer.

TRM Terminal. This channel is assigned to the terminal device of the computer.

AUX Auxiliary Communications Device. This channel is assigned to the primary "SERIAL" communications device. This channel may be used for either input or output.

USR User Defined Device. Consult your DOS manual for defining "devices" in the CONFIG.SYS file.

```
Program Get_Single_Key_Stroke_For_Version_4
Var
   char_a : char;
begin
   char_a := 'a';

   (* Loop Until either the 'Q' or 'q' key is pressed *)
   while NOT((char_a = 'q') AND (char_a = 'Q')) do
     begin
        writeln('Enter the letter 'Q' to stop the loop');

        (* Do nothing until a key is pressed *)
        (* When a key is pressed, READKEY sends it to the CHAR_A *)
        char_a := READKEY;

        (* Compare character to known characters to *)
        (* determine what kind of character it is   *)
        if ((char_a >= chr(0)) AND (char_a <= chr(32))) then
          begin
             writeln('The entered character is not printable!');
          end;
        if ((char_a >= chr(33)) AND (char_a <= chr(47))) OR
           ((char_a >= chr(58)) AND (char_a <= chr(64))) OR
           ((char_a >= chr(91)) AND (char_a <= chr(96))) OR
           ((char_a >= chr(123)) AND (char_a <= chr(127))) then
          begin
             writeln('The entered character is punctuation!');
          end;
        if ((char_a >= chr(48)) AND (char_a <= chr(57))) then
          begin
             writeln('The entered character is a number!');
          end;
        if ((char_a >= chr(65)) AND (char_a <= chr(90))) then
          begin
             writeln('The entered character is a capital letter!');
          end;
        if ((char_a >= chr(97)) AND (char_a <= chr(122))) then
          begin
             writeln('The entered character is a lower case letter!');
          end;
     end;
end.
```

Fig. 2-16. Examples of programs to read and interpret single keys as they are pressed on the keyboard.

The uses of the program in FIG. 2-16 range from interpretation of menu selections to interpretation of pressed keys as movements of game pieces for a computer game. The programmer could design a simple painting program that could use either regular or cursor keys on the keyboard to direct a "paint brush" across the display screen.

The read procedure provides for input of data from the keyboard as well as from files. Along with the "read" procedure the readln procedure allows access to data files. These procedures are identical in action when used to gather data from the keyboard. However, the read and readln procedures exhibit significantly different behavior when gathering data from files.

Line Editing

The Turbo Pascal read procedure also incorporates extra features which simulate crude line editing. The read and readln procedures have special interpretations for certain control characters. The function of the backspace character should be well known to any computer user. However, this character deletes the displayed character to the left of the cursor and repositions the cursor one character to the left. The ESC key causes the current input line to be deleted. The character that results from pressing CTRL and the letter A keys simultaneously (^A) performs the same action as ESC. The ^S character performs the same function as backspace. The ^D character recalls one character from the previous input line. The ^F character recalls the previous input line in its entirety. The ^Z terminates the current input line, and passes an EOF "End Of File" marker to the read or readln procedure.

Data Output

In previous examples the actions of the writeln procedure and some of its capabilities for standard as well as formatted data output have been demonstrated. The write statement described in FIGS. 2-17, 2-18, and 2-19 does not cause a new line to be produced when it is executed. However, the writeln procedure causes the cursor to move to the next line and the left side of the screen once the specified text has been output. This allows for the combination of write and read statements to produce questions and gather responses on a single line of the display screen.

The write and writeln procedures allow for output to standard output devices such as the terminal, a printer, or a file. Table 2-11 lists the standard output channel names, and the devices to which they point.

The CON and TRM devices can be used for either input or output. In addition, the AUX and USR devices may also be used for either input or output, depending on the equipment to which they are directed.

Name: WRITE

Function: Allow Output from Specified Variable or Variables to a specified output channel.

Syntax: WRITE ([channel,] var1 [,var2, . . . , varN]);

Rules:
1) All items within brackets ([ ]) are optional.
2) Variables may be of any valid Pascal or user-defined datatype.
3) The "channel" variable is a correctly defined file identifier which has been assigned to an existing file or device.
4) If no "channel" variable is specified, output is assumed to be for the standard output device: the display screen.

Fig. 2-17. The standard syntax for the "write" procedure.

Source Code	Destination: Output
write("Hello There");	Display: Hello There
write(10*3.1):	Display: 31
write(.000000000001)	Display: 1E-12
write(LST, "This goes to the Printer");	Printer: This goes to the Printer
write(f1, "This goes to a file");	File f1: This goes to a file
write ('3.05 + 1.47 = ',4.52);	Display: 3.05 + 4.07 = 4.52
write('3.05 + 1.47 = ',3.05 + 1.47);	Display: 3.05 + 4.07 = 4.52

Fig. 2-18. Example output from the "write" procedures.

```
Program Display_Character_A;
Var
  var_a;
begin
  var_a := 'A';
  writeln('The first letter of the alphabet is :',var_a:10,'.');
end;


Output :   The first letter of the alphabet is :          A.
```

Fig. 2-19. Formatted output of the letter "A."

The write and writeln procedures provide the programmer with the capability to generate output which may be characters, numbers, strings or combinations of all of them. The syntax for the use of the "write" procedure is shown in FIG. 2-17.

Output from the write procedures can be sent to the display screen, a printer, to a file, or a user specified device. The channel variable corresponds to the destination to which output data will be sent. When no channel is specified, the display screen is used. When the predefined LST channel is used the output data is sent to the primary printer. When a valid file channel is used, output is sent there. Examples of the use of the write procedures are shown in FIG. 2-18.

Table 2-11. Turbo Pascal Pre-Defined Output Channels

Channel Name—Indicated Input Device

OUTPUT	Standard Input. This channel is assigned to the primary output device of the computer, usually the display screen.
CON	Console. This channel is assigned to the console device of the computer.
TRM	Terminal. This channel is assigned to the terminal device of the computer.
LST	Printer Port. This channel is assigned to the primary parallel printer port. This port almost invariably attaches to a printer or a spooling device which is linked to a printer.
AUX	Auxiliary Communications Device. This channel is assigned to the primary "SERIAL" communications device. This channel may be used for either input or output.
USR	User Defined Device. Consult your DOS manual for defining "devices" in the CONFIG.SYS file.

The write can incorporate literal strings of characters or numbers, variables containing characters of numbers, or functions that return characters or numbers.

In addition, the write and writeln procedures enable the programmer to format output. Formatting can be applied to all basic data types in Turbo Pascal. Because the number and complexity of data types that can be developed by users is so great, no provision is made in Turbo Pascal to accommodate them as complete entities. However, because complex data structures can only be composed of basic data types, the format options of the write procedure can be applied, indirectly, to these data types as well.

The formatting of output is the predetermination of the amount of output area that a piece of data might assume. Output area is the amount of space or the number of characters on the output device that are required to display a particular datum. Formatting for character variables allows the programmer to specify the number of characters to be used in the output area. To output the character "A" the programmer might specify the line in FIG. 2-19.

The actual output formatting of the character takes place in the portion of the write procedure where the variable is identified. The variable var_a appears as var_a:10 in the write procedure. This indicates to the procedure that the contents of the character variable should be output in a display area of 10 characters, with the actual variable contents right-justified within the area. In the case of FIG. 2-19 the content of the variable is "A." The output area is 10 characters. The resulting formatted output area for the variable is "<   >A."

All formatted output created with the write procedure format options is right-adjusted within the output area. This applies to formatted output of Boolean, integer, real and string as well as character variables. The Turbo Pascal data types and the syntax of the available output format options within the write procedure are shown in TABLE 2-12.

Table 2-12. Output Formatting Syntax for the "WRITE" Procedures

Data Type	Format Option	Explanation
Boolean	:n	n - The total number of characters in the output area. Boolean variables can produce output of TRUE or FALSE only. Minimum value of "n" should be 5.
Char	:n	n - The total number of characters in the output area.
Integer	:n	n - The total number of digits in the output area.
Real	:n:d	n - The total number of digits in the output area. The decimal point (.) as well as the total number of decimal digits is included in this number.
		d - The number of digits required for the real or decimal portion of the real number.
String	:n	n - The total number of characters in the output area.

The format options for all data types except for real number variables allow the user to modify only the length of the output area. For character and string variables, the theoretical limit for the length of the output area should be the amount of memory available to the display screen. For practical purposes the limit is 80 because most display screens allow only 80 characters per line. These practical limitations apply to Boolean variables as well. The Boolean variables may only contain values of TRUE and FALSE. If the contents of a Boolean variable are output using the write procedure the word "TRUE" or "FALSE" will be written based on the Boolean value. The practical length of the output area may be up to 80 characters. However, only five characters, at most, are required to display either value.

The formatted output of integer values is similar to that of the previously discussed data types. The limitations imposed by the use of integer data should be fairly obvious. The range value for integer values in Turbo Pascal is −32768 to 32767. The maximum amount of output area required to accommodate this number range is five digits. A larger output area may be specified to incorporate spaces to the left of the integer value, if desired.

Unlike Booleans, Characters, Integers and String variables, Real numbers should be formatted with two parameters. The first parameter is used to define the length of the output area. The second parameter defines the number of digits within the output area that will be used to display the "real" or "decimal" portion of the real value. For the number 43.21, the number "21" is the decimal portion. If a format of ":6:3" is applied to the number 43.21 the resulting output will be "43.210." The parameter ":6" defines the total length of the output area as 6 digits or characters. The parameter ":3" allocates 3 digits or characters of the output region for display of the decimal portion of the real value.

A real variable can be formatted with only a single parameter if desired. If only the parameter is specified, it will be assumed to be the length of the output area. In addition to the total number of digits that should be used to format a real number, the length of the output area must also include the number of characters required to display the decimal point, the sign of the number and its exponent, and the character "E" which indicates the use of exponential numeric display format. Unlike other data type format options, Turbo Pascal imposes a limit of 24 characters for the total length of an output field for a real value. And, if a format of zero is specified for either a real or an integer number, no output will result. Finally, the number of digits allocated for the decimal portion of a real number CANNOT exceed the total length of the output area.

Some example data values, applicable formats and the output based on those formats can be seen in TABLE 2-13. The underline character represents a blank space. If the data is smaller than the specified area, any unused output area is filled with blank spaces.

Data	Format	Output
14.01	:10:2	_____14.01
14.01	:12:6	_____14.010000
3.000001	:4:1	_3.0
3.59	:4:1	_3.6
6	:10	_____6
TRUE	:1	T
FALSE	:3	FAL
A	:5	_____A
Hello	:2	_____He
Hello	:10	_____Hello

Table 2-13. Typical Output Data Formats Available with the "WRITE" Procedures

The use of formatted output can often make a program more appealing to the end user. These options within the "write" allow for standardization of output. This in turn makes the output of your programs appear more professional.

One example of the benefit of formatting can be found in the financial world where calculations never incorporate numbers with the real value requiring more than two decimal places. Although integer values do not require formatting, values expressed in dollars and cents do. Integer numbers can always be expressed without the formatting option, because they are stored as whole values within the memory of the computer. Each bit within an integer variable represents a specific integer value. Within a real number only an approximation of the number can be made. The precision of this approximation was discussed earlier in this chapter. If the number "123456.789999" is output using no formatting then it will appear as "123456.789999." This is unacceptable to the business world. When the number is formatted using ":10:2" as a format, the output area contains " 123456.79."

This is a limited example. However, in the course of programming you will notice certain inconsistencies in the ability of real numbers to approximate integer values. Depending on the application, numbers such as 5 have been represented by the real value "4.99999999." This is not an error in Turbo Pascal. Rather, it is a limitation of the internal precision of the computer. If your programming career extends to the "Mini" or "Main Frame" computer world, you will see that this precision problem can also occur with larger machines as well.

Generally the use of formatting will make the output from your programs appear more professional. It will be easier to read because information will always appear at specific locations on the display screen, regardless of the actual values contained within the output variables. Some programmers find the use of formatted output somewhat tedious, and therefore ignore it. This is fine for applications which only the programmer will use. However, for the end user who might not be as knowledgeable about your program as you are, formatting of output should be considered. The formatting of output is not required for all data written by your program. However, it should be used for that data which must always be displayed in a standard fashion.

The Use of Input and Output Procedures

The input and output procedures read, readln, write and writeln form the basis for all of the basic methods of entering data into, and outputting data from, your programs.

Without these procedures, only the programmer knows what is happening within the program. Without the input and output procedures, the program becomes a "black box" from which the user can gather no information. The programmer must design an interface with these procedures that allows the user to understand what the program requires for data. In addition, the programmer must create meaningful output which the user can understand.

Most well-designed programs are "user friendly." This means they are thoughtfully designed with questions and displays that give the user as much information about the running of the program as the manual. These programs rarely frustrate the user and provide help where frustration can occur. The internal mechanisms of a "user friendly," program might actually be extremely poorly written and inefficient. Most users would rather work with these programs than the most efficient and hard-to-use programs.

As a program developer, equal attention must be paid to the needs of the program originator and the program user. The originator must have a program that correctly performs the task for which it was written. The user must have a program that can be executed easily, and with a minimum of frustration. The user might be trained to work with the program, but if the program can provide a pleasant interface for the work that must be performed, the user will be the happier for it. This is not to imply that all programs must make the user happy to run them. On the contrary, too much user friendliness will almost certainly result in a program that runs too slowly, and requires too many responses to perform a task.

The necessity to create a user interface for your program which balances the needs of the originator as well as the user is not meant to create apprehension for you as a new or improving programmer. However, as a programmer you have certain responsibilities to the people who will be using your programs. After you have developed full-fledged problem and solution descriptions for your program, take some additional time to consider the user.

CONTROL STRUCTURES

New programmers generally begin their careers by creating programs that proceed through a sequence of steps, generate and make known a result, and then cease execution. Sequential execution is the linear execution of program steps from statement "A" to statement "Z." There is no conditional execution of statement "H" rather than statement "G" based on the result of function "F." The only "logical flow" to the program is to begin at the first statement and to end at the last statement, executing each statement in between them in the order in which it appears in the code.

Sequential execution allows the programmer to create programs that barely utilize the smallest fraction of the potential of Pascal. Turbo and Standard Pascal provide six basic structures to selectively execute portions of the code. Selective execution allows the programmer to establish conditions for the execution of one program statement over another. An example of a selective execution structure is shown in pseudo and Pascal source code in FIG. 2-20.

```
Pseudo Code    : if (variable equals number 5) then
                   writeln('The variable equals the number 5');

Pascal Source  : if (var_a = 5) then
                   writeln('The variable equals the number 5');
```
Fig. 2-20. A typical selective execution statement.

Figure 2-20 demonstrates the use of the "if..then" statement. When the condition within the parentheses "( )" evaluates to TRUE the statement or statements associated with the "then" portion execute. If the condition evaluates to FALSE the "then" statement or statements do NOT execute.

The six control structures within Pascal are called for..do, while ..do, repeat..until, if..then..else, case, and goto. The for, while, and repeat commands are called *looping* structures. The if..then..else and case statements are called *conditional branches*. And finally the goto statement is called an *unconditional branch*. Conditional branches allow programmers to create structures that execute a statement or statements based on the evaluation of a condition.

The "if..then..else" Structure

The least complex of the conditional branch statements is the if.. then..else statement. This statement allows the programmer to choose a set of statements for execution based on a condition that occurs when the program is running rather than when it is written. An example of the "if..then" portion of this statement was shown in FIG. 2-20. The entire statement is demonstrated in FIG. 2-21.

```
Program Demonstrate_if_then_else;
Var
   var_a : integer;
begin
   write('Enter an integer between 1 and 10 : ');
   read(var_a);

   (* evaluate entered number *)
   if (var_a < 5) then
     writeln('The entered number is less than 5.')
     else
     writeln('The entered number is greater than or equal to 5.');
end;
```
Fig. 2-21. The "if..then..else" statement.

Besides demonstrating simple logical flow control, the if.. then..else structure also demonstrates one of the few inconsistencies in the syntax of Pascal. The writeln statement, executed when the value in var_a is less than 5, is not terminated with a semicolon ";." The writeln statement which is executed if the condition evaluates to FALSE is terminated by a semicolon. The reason for this apparent inconsistency is the structure of the conditional statement. When an else is present the writeln associated with TRUE evaluations is not the last portion of the if..then..else. As an individual statement, and as the command in an if..then statement, writeln can stand on its own, but as part of the conditional branch it does not require a semicolon command terminator. If a semicolon is included when it is not required, a compilation error will occur. Similarly, if a semicolon is required and not present, an error will also occur. The syntax of the if..then..else conditional branching statement is shown in FIG. 2-22.

Name: IF-THEN-ELSE

Function: Allows for conditional execution of statement(s) based on the evaluation of a condition or conditions.

Syntax: If (condition) then
    [begin]
        statement1[;]   (* "True" statement(s) *)
        [statement2;]
    [end[;]]
   [else
     [begin]
        [statementA;]   (* "False" statement(s) *)
     [end;]

Rules:
1) All items within brackets ([ ]) are optional.
2) Conditions may be based on any valid Pascal or user-defined datatype.
3) The "True" statement does not require a semicolon if the next line is an "else."
4) A group of "True" or "False" statements must be placed between a set of "begin .. end" statements.
5) The "end" statement of a group of "True" statements does not require a semicolon if the next line is an "else."
6) If-Then-Else statements may be "nested" within other If-Then-Else statements.

Fig. 2-22. The syntax of the "if..then..else" statement.

More than one command may be associated with either side of an if..then..else statement. When more than one command is present, they are grouped together with the begin..end reserved words. When the begin..end words are present, any statements between them are exe-'cuted together. The use of begin..end in if..then..else statements allows the programmer to specify several actions to execute when a condition evaluates in a particular manner. An example of several statements within the if..then..else conditional branch is shown in FIG. 2-23.

```
if (answer = 'Y') or (answer = 'y') then
  begin
    record := record + 1;
    writeln('Based on the answer of ',answer,' : ');
    writeln('The current record is ',record);
  end
else
  writeln('The record could not be located');
```

Fig. 2-23. Multiple statements in a conditional branch.

Like all Turbo Pascal control structures, the if..then..else construct may be nested within another if..then..else construct. In addition, a condition for the if..then..else structure might actually be a complex set of individual logical evaluations. Figure 2-23 shows a complex condition where a variable called answer is evaluated for its equality to either "Y" or "y." Depending on the circumstances, it might be more advisable to evaluate all possible conditions at one time on one line of code. In other situations, it might be more logical to evaluate each condition separately. The final decision belongs to the programmer. Some more examples of possible if..then..else structures are shown in FIG. 2-24.

```
If (answer = 5) then writeln('The answer is 5');

if (answer < 5) then
  writeln('The answer is less than 5')
else
  writeln('The answer is greater than or equal to 5');

if NOT((answer < 5) OR (answer = 5)) then
  begin
    counter := counter + 1;
    writeln('The answer is greater than 5');
    writeln('Total answers greater than 5 is ',counter);
  end;

if (answer < 5) then
  begin
    less_counter := less_counter + 1;
    writeln('The answer is less than five');
  end
else
  begin
    if (answer > 5) then
      begin
        greater_counter := greater_counter + 1;
        writeln('The answer is greater thn five');
      end
    else
      begin
        equal_counter := equal_counter + 1;
        writeln('The answer is equal to five');
      end;
  end;
writeln('Total less than ',less_counter);
writeln('Total greater than ',greater_counter);
writeln('Total equal to ',equal_counter);
```

Fig. 2-24. Further examples of "if..then..else" usage.

The last example in FIG. 2-24 should be of particular interest because it demonstrates nesting of the if..then..else structure within itself. In the last example, two conditions were evaluated to arrive at one of three different conclusions. If the number is less than 5 then a statement is executed and a counting variable is incremented. If the number is not less than 5 then it is evaluated for being greater than 5. If the number is not less than 5, and not greater than 5, then it must be equal to 5.

At first glance it might appear that, of the two methods in FIG. 2-25, the second method is more efficient. The first method requires twenty lines of code to arrive at the same conclusion as the second method which requires only 17 lines of code. Further study shows this to be false. Method two always evaluates three conditions. Method one at most evaluates two conditions. It does not always evaluate two, because if the first condition is TRUE then the "TRUE" commands are evaluated and the FALSE commands are ignored. Because the second condition in method one is part of the FALSE commands, it is not evaluated every time the program is executed.

```
Method 1:
─────────

if (answer < 5) then
  begin
    less_counter := less_counter + 1;
    writeln('The answer is less than five');
  end
 else
  begin
    if (answer > 5) then
      begin
        greater_counter := greater_counter + 1;
        writeln('The answer is greater thn five');
      end
     else
      begin
        equal_counter := equal_counter + 1;
        writeln('The answer is equal to five');
      end;
  end;
writeln('Total less than ',less_counter);
writeln('Total greater than ',greater_counter);
writeln('Total equal to ',equal_counter);

Method 2:
─────────

If (answer < 5) then
  begin
    less_counter := less_counter + 1;
    writeln('The answer is less than five');
  end;
if (answer > 5) then
  begin
    greater_counter := greater_counter + 1;
    writeln('The answer is greater than five');
  end;
if (answer = 5) then
  begin
    equal_counter := equal_counter + 1;
    writeln('The answer is equal to five');
  end;
writeln('Total less than ',less_counter);
writeln('Total greater than ',greater_counter);
writeln('Total equal to ',equal_counter);
```

Fig. 2-25. Two methods to evaluate the same conditions.

These two methods of evaluating the same set of conditions also demonstrate the difference between a novice and an experienced programmer. The first method is a well thought out, efficient structure that minimizes the number of commands required to perform a task. The second method is sequential execution in disguise. All conditions are evaluated regardless of the result of previous evaluations. When a condition evaluates to TRUE the commands associated with it are executed. Although the second method uses conditional branching, the logic is still somewhat sequential.

The if..then..else structure may be used in both simple and complex situations. Single or multiple commands may be selected for execution based on the control branch established. In addition, the condition used for evaluation can be constructed of either single or multiple conditions. Using the logical operators to link these individual conditions, extremely complex criteria may be established for selective execution of a command or group of commands. The if..then..else structures may be nested within one another to provide even greater flexibility in the condition evaluation structure.

The "case" Structure

The case structure allows the program to execute a specific command or commands for several conditions simultaneously. Unlike the if..then..else structure, case allows the user to identify all possible equalities for a condition to be satisfied. If the condition in the if..then..else structure is "(answer = 5)" then there are two possible outcomes, TRUE or FALSE. The case structure allows the programmer to define several exclusive conditions such as (answer = 1), (answer = 5), or (answer = 9). By the first method in FIG. 2-25 it would be necessary to establish a nested if..then..else structure to properly anticipate the possible values of the variable. Using the case statement, these other possibilities can be incorporated into a single structure. An if..then..else structure and a corresponding case structure are shown in FIG. 2-26.

The variable answer is called the "case variable." The numbers 1 to 9 which appear before the colons (:) are called matching values. When the answer variable is found to be equal to a matching value, the command or commands associated with that value are executed. Single commands may be placed directly after the matching value with a colon (:) as a separator. Groups of commands may be associated with each matching value by placing these commands between a begin..end set, with the begin placed directly after the matching value and colon.

The case structure allows the user to establish unique conditions for each possible value for the variable. The case structure can be used with integer numbers as well as character variables. Real numbers cannot be used because exact matches cannot be made. In addition, the case structure can accommodate set variables. In general, any ordinal data type can be used within a case structure. However, only a single data type can be used within each case statement.

```
'If..then..else'

if (answer < 5) then
  begin
    less_counter := less_counter + 1;
    writeln('The answer Is less than five');
  end
 else
  begin
    if (answer > 5) then
      begin
        greater_counter := greater_counter + 1;
        writeln('The answer is greater thn five');
      end
     else
      begin
        equal_counter := equal_counter + 1;
        writeln('The answer is equal to five');
      end;
  end;
writeln('Total less than ',less_counter);
writeln('Total greater than ',greater_counter);
writeln('Total equal to ',equal_counter);

'case'

case (answer) of
    1,2,3,4 : less_counter := less_counter + 1;
    5 : equal_counter := equal_counter + 1;
    6,7,8,9 : greater_counter := greater_counter + 1;
  end;
writeln('Total less than ',less_counter);
writeln('Total greater than ',greater_counter);
writeln('Total equal to ',equal_counter);
```

Fig. 2-26. Comparison of "if..then..else" to "case."

The case statement is particularly useful for menus, where a specific task has been assigned to a numbered menu item. If that item is chosen, the task associated with it is executed. The item is usually chosen by entering a number or letter associated with the menu item as it is displayed. When the number or letter is entered, it may be compared directly to the information in the case statement. When a match is found, the commands within the particular option chosen are executed. If two options within the case statement use the same number or character, only the option appearing first in the case list will be executed. The Turbo Pascal case statement allows only a single option to be executed during a given call.

The standard Pascal case statement allows the user to define a set of matching values to the case variable. However, if a match does not occur, an error will. This error occurs frequently for poorly planned programs that cannot anticipate all possible values of a case variable. Turbo Pascal is less strict and will not cause an error for an unmatched case variable. In fact, Turbo Pascal will allow the user to define a set of commands for the situation where a match does not occur. The syntax of the Turbo Pascal case statement is shown in FIG. 2-27.

Name: CASE

Function: To provide a conditional branch structure for predefined matching values, based on the contents of a variable of the same type.

Syntax: case (variable) of

```
        match1[,match2] : [begin]
                              statement;
                              [statement2;]
                          [end;]
    [match3 : begin
                 statement1;
                     .
                 statement2;
              end;]
  [else]
    [begin
       statement1;
     end;]
  end;
```

Rules:
1) All items within brackets ([ ]) are optional.
2) Matching values may be defined on any valid Pascal character, integer, defined ordinal variable.
3) Only a single match is performed per case statement.
4) A single command or a group of commands in between "begin .. end" statements may be associated with each matching value.
5) When no match is found, the command or commands associated with the "else" are executed.

Fig. 2-27. The syntax of the "case" statement.

Although case and if..then..else structures can sometimes be used interchangeably, they do not perform the same function. A single if..then..else structure has only two possible results for its evaluation. A single case statement provides an unlimited number of results for its evaluations. The operators that may be used for the if..then..else structure include all of the relational and logical operators and resultant expressions. The case statement utilizes only the "equality" operator to determine if the command associated with a matching value should be executed.

In general, the if..then..else structure provides a much more flexible environment for evaluating the contents of a variable. However, the case structure provides a more direct method of evaluating equalities and executing commands based upon them. In addition, the Turbo Pascal implementation of the case statement provides for added flexibility in processing nonmatches.

The situations in which a conditional branch should be employed should also indicate the structure to use. Generally, those situations where all possible values of a variable can be predetermined should be implemented with the case statement. There should be more than two possible matching values, and these values must be ordinal. An *ordinal* number is simply an integer or a member of a group of data that may be referenced by its integer location or occurrence in the group.

In situations where two possible values result, an if..then..else structure is more appropriate. If the programmer does not wish to create commands for particular values, rather for ranges of values, the if..then..else structure is the conditional branch of choice. In FIG. 2-26, the if..then..else structure has been designed to determine a range such as "if the number is less than 5." To create a case statement for this would require the program to evaluate all numbers from − 32768 to 4 to see if the case variable matched. Clearly the if..then..else structure with the "less than" (<) operator would be more appropriate.

In the final analysis, the programmer determines the conditional branch structure most suited to the program's needs. As you continue to program and gain experience, you will develop your own rules for use of these structures.

The Looping Structures

Looping structures allow the programmer to generate code that may perform the same task again and again. These structures provide an additional level of program control, as well as a method of reducing the amount of code necessary to perform a task. In addition, case and if.. then..else structures may be nested within loops to provide for even more versatility in control branching.

The for..do loop   The for..do structure allows the programmer to establish a control structure to perform a group of commands for a specified number of cycles. These commands may be any valid Turbo Pascal procedure, or function calls as well as calls to control branches, or even other looping structures. The for..do structure requires the programmer to specify the exact number of times the commands within the loop will be executed. A typical for..do loop is shown in FIG. 2-28.

The counter variable is the loop "increment," or count holder, variable. The value 1 represents the low or starting value of the increment. The value 20 represents the high or ending value of the increment. The counter variable begins with value 1 and proceeds to value 20, increasing its value by 1 after the completion of each cycle of the loop. Unlike other languages, the counter variable normally increases or decreases its value by 1 during each cycle of the loop. The value may be changed by an arithmetic operation within the loop, but without such a modification only increments of 1 or − 1 are possible. The syntax of the for..do loop is shown in FIG. 2-29.

```
Program Test_for_do;
Var
   counter : integer;
begin
   for counter := 1 to 20 do
     begin
       writeln('The current number is : ',counter);
     end;
end;
```

```
Output : The current number is : 1
         The current number is : 2
         The current number is : 3
         The current number is : 4
         The current number is : 5
         The current number is : 6
         The current number is : 7
         The current number is : 8
         The current number is : 9
         The current number is : 10
         The current number is : 11
         The current number is : 12
         The current number is : 13
         The current number is : 14
         The current number is : 15
         The current number is : 16
         The current number is : 17
         The current number is : 18
         The current number is : 19
         The current number is : 20
```

Fig. 2-28. A typical "for..do" loop.

Name: FOR .. DO

Function: Execute a group of commands contained within its "begin .. end" while a counter variable increments between a starting and ending value.

Syntax: for counter : = starting_value to ending_value
   [begin]
      statement1;
      statement2;
   end;]

or

for counter : = starting_value downto ending_value
   [begin]
      statement1;
      [statement2;
   end;]

Rules:
1) All items within brackets ([ ]) are optional.
2) Starting and Ending loop values may only be integer or byte variables.
3) When a starting value is greater than an ending value the "for .. do" loop must incorporate the "downto" rather than the "to."
4) Increments by the looping mechanism alone can only be made with values of "1" and "–1."
5) The value of the "counter" variable may be changed from within the loop if desired. This allows for modification of the increment size.

Fig. 2-29. The syntax of the "for..do" loop.

The for..do loop is extremely useful for creating a structured counting loop in which a command or group of commands might be executed a specified number of times. The counter variable may be used and manipulated within the loop. This gives the programmer the ability to prolong execution of the loop simply by keeping the value of the counter different from the ending value. The programmer may also terminate the loop prematurely by setting the counter equal to the ending value.

The while..do loop   Like the for..do loop, the while..do loop allows the programmer to establish a control structure containing a command or group of commands. Each time the loop is called, the command or commands within the loop execute. However, unlike the for..do loop, no increment is used to determine when the while..do should finish executing. Instead, a condition is defined. This condition is evaluated each time the loop executes. If the condition evaluates to TRUE the loop continues to execute. If it evaluates to FALSE, the loop ceases execution. A typical while..do loop is shown in FIG. 2-30.

```
Program Test_While_Do;
Var
   counter : integer;
begin
   counter := 1;

   while (counter <= 15) do
     begin
        writeln('The value of the counter is : ',counter);
        counter := counter + 2;
     end;
   writeln;
   writeln('The final value of the counter is : ',counter);
end.


Output :          The value of the counter is : 1
                  The value of the counter is : 3
                  The value of the counter is : 5
                  The value of the counter is : 7
                  The value of the counter is : 9
                  The value of the counter is : 11
                  The value of the counter is : 13
                  The value of the counter is : 15

                  The final value of the counter is : 17
```

Fig. 2-30. An example of the "while..do" loop.

The condition of the loop is "(counter < = 15)." While this condition evaluates to TRUE the loop continues to execute. If the condition evaluates to FALSE, the loop ceases execution. Unlike the for..do, the loop increments or modifications that affect the condition must take place within the loop. If nothing within the loop affected the value of the counter variable, then the loop would continue to execute forever.

The value of the counter can be modified within the loop using simple arithmetic operations. If the looping condition is based on arithmetic evaluations, any of the arithmetic operators may be used. If several separate evaluations are required, any or all of the logical operators may be utilized.

It is also important to note the final value of the counter variable after completion of the loop. In the for..do loop the final value of the counter is the upper limit of the loop. In the while..do loop, when a counter is employed, the final value of the counter is the value that does not pass the evaluation. In the case of FIG. 2-30 the final value was 17. If it had been a for..do loop, the final value would have been 15. It is important to be aware of the differences in counting variables—especially if the contents of these variables will be used later in the program.

When a while..do loop is poorly planned or incorrectly written, it might fail to terminate properly. If a while..do loop does not terminate at all, it is called an infinite loop. This simply means that the loop has no logical finishing point. If the computer cannot find an end point, it will execute as long as it can. An example of an infinite loop is shown in FIG. 2-31.

The loop continues to output the phrase "In the loop!" The program never terminates, because the loop will not terminate. As a beginning programmer, you likely run into this error more often that you want. As your experience grows, the occurrence of such errors will be less, but always be aware of the possibility.

```
Program Infinite_Loop;
Var
   counter : integer;
begin
   counter := 5;

   writeln('Before the loop!');
   While (counter = 5) do
      begin
         writeln('In the loop!');
      end;
   writeln('After the loop!');
end.
```

Fig. 2-31. An infinite "while..do" loop.

```
Output :        Before the loop!
                In the loop!
                In the loop!
                In the loop!
                In the loop!
                  .
                  .
                  .
```

Because the while..do loop is based on a condition, it need not be based on a numeric evaluation. The loop condition may be based on the result of a function, or the contents of a Boolean variable. The while..do loop is particularly useful for programs that have menu interfaces. A simple menu program is presented in FIG. 2-32.

The program in FIG. 2-32 represents only the least potential of the while..do loop. It also highlights the more attractive features of this control structure. The programmer does not need to know how many times the loop must be executed. The user running the program can determine when to continue and when to terminate the loop. The condition for the loop can be based on the evaluation of characters as well as numbers. In

```
Program Simple_Menu;
Var
   enter_char : char;
begin
   enter_char := ' ';

   while (NOT(enter_char = 'Q') AND NOT(enter_char = 'q')) do
      begin
         clrcls;   (* Turbo Pascal command to clear the display *)
         writeln;
         writeln('                Main Menu');
         writeln('                ————————');
         writeln;
         writeln('      Code           Option');
         writeln('      ——             ——————');
         writeln('       1             Add two numbers');
         writeln('       2             Subtract two numbers');
         writeln('       3             Multiply two numbers');
         writeln('       4             Divide two numbers');
         writeln;
         writeln('       Q             Terminate Program');
         writeln;
         writeln;
         write('   Enter the code number or letter of your choice');
         read(enter_char);

         case (enter_char) of
            '1' : writeln('This is the addition option');
            '2' : writeln('This is the subtraction option');
            '3' : writeln('This is the multiplication option');
            '4' : writeln('This is the division option');
           else
            begin
              if NOT(enter_char = 'Q') AND (enter_char = 'q') then
                begin
                   writeln('Invalid menu entry. Please try again');
                   writeln('Press ENTER to Continue');
                   read(enter_char);
                end;
            end;
         end;
      end;

   clrcls;
   writeln('Menu loop terminated ... ');
end.
```

Fig. 2-32. A simple menu program using the "while..do" loop.

addition, conditions may incorporate evaluations of Booleans, strings of characters, or more complex data structures. like any logical construct, the condition may also incorporate mixed evaluations, such as numbers and characters, in two simultaneous evaluations linked by a logical operator.

Figure 2-32 also highlights some of the more basic, and yet extremely profound, aspects of programming. The condition in the while..do loop will accept either uppercase "Q" or lowercase "q" to cease execution. This particular example allows the user to enter one of two characters to cause the same result. To the user, "Q" and "q" are the same character. By allowing either character you make your program more user friendly and less aggravating. In addition, the else portion of the case structure tells the user when he or she has selected an invalid character. Of course, these are limited examples, but little additions such as these make your program more intelligent and professional. More importantly, they demonstrate a concern for the user.

The repeat..until structure   The repeat..until structure is identical in all respects, except one, to the while..do control structure. The execution of the loop is based on the evaluation of a condition. The condition may be based on a single evaluation or a combination of evaluations connected with logical operators. The definition of the commands within the repeat..until structure must be carefully planned and executed to ensure against the possibility of an infinite loop. The only difference between the while..do and the repeat..until structures is the place in the loop where the condition is evaluated.

The while..do performs the evaluation at the beginning of each loop. If the condition evaluates to TRUE then the loop and the commands contained within it are executed. If the condition evaluates to FALSE the commands within the loop do not execute. If the condition in the while..do loop evaluates to FALSE before the loop starts, the command or commands contained within the loop do not execute even once. The repeat..until performs the evaluation at the end of the loop. The commands contained within the loop execute, and then the condition is evaluated. If the original condition evaluates to FALSE the contents of the loop have executed at least once.

The commands contained within the repeat..until structure are guaranteed to execute at least once—even if the original condition is FALSE. Figure 2-33 contains a comparison of the while..do and repeat..until loops.

```
Program Compare;
Var
   counter : integer;
begin
   counter := 1;
   while (counter <= 4) do
     begin
       writeln('The WHILE counter is <= 4, with value ',counter);
       counter := counter + 1;
     end;

   writeln;

   repeat
     begin
       counter := counter + 1;
       writeln('The REPEAT counter is <= 4, with value ',counter);
     end;
   until (counter <= 4);
end.


Output :    The WHILE counter is <= 4, with value 1
            The WHILE counter is <= 4, with value 2
            The WHILE counter is <= 4, with value 3
            The WHILE counter is <= 4, with value 4

            The REPEAT counter is <= 4, with value 6
```

Fig. 2-33. Comparison of "while..do" and "repeat..until."

The repeat..until and while..do structures, except for the minimum number of executions, are identical. They may be used interchangeably in most circumstances. In some situations one structure might be more appropriate, such as reading files character by character until an end marker is reached.

Choosing the looping structure for a program or procedure is a matter of programming style. However, there are basic guidelines that help make the selection easier. If the loop requires a finite number of iterations that might be expressed as a valid integer value, use the for..do loop. If the loop must be executed an indeterminate number of times, but can still be expressed as an integer value, use the while..do loop—but you can use the for..do loop. If the loop must be executed an indeterminate number of times based on an evaluation of one or more non integer data, use the while..do loop. If the initial conditions of the loop cannot be determined at the time of the writing of the program, but you know the termination condition, use the repeat..until loop. And finally, if it is necessary for the loop to execute at least once during the running of the program, use the repeat..until loop.

Other reasons for utilizing specific looping structures are left to you. As your experience grows, you might find these general rules inadequate for your programming needs. By this time, however, you will have defined your own rules for using the capabilities of Turbo Pascal.

The Unconditional Branch or "goto"

Unlike the if..then..else and case structures, goto does not accept conditions for its usage. When a goto is reached, it causes control of the program to move directly towards a labeled section of the code. This section of the code is then executed as though it were the first command or commands within the program. When a goto is called from a loop, the loop ceases to execute. The loop stops executing, not because the condition has evaluated to FALSE, but because program control has passed out of it. A sample of a goto within a program is shown in FIG. 2-34.

In FIG. 2-34, the last 100 iterations of the for..do loop were by-passed using the goto command. This capability might actually prove to be beneficial in certain instances, but the risks of using several goto commands far outweigh any benefits. When several goto commands are utilized to move program control from section AA to section CC to section BB or section DD of the code, errors are bound to happen. An example of a while..do structure, and similar control logic in a series of goto commands, is shown in FIG. 2-35.

Because the use of goto statements is nonconditional, program logic becomes difficult to follow. If enough goto commands are used, the program becomes incomprehensible to almost everyone. The program might even become a jumble of code to the programmer who wrote it. This type of programming CANNOT be tolerated. If it cannot be understood and

```
Program Demonstrate_Goto;
Label LAST_COUNT;
Var
   counter : integer;
begin
   counter := 1;
   while (counter < 100) do
     begin
       writeln('Counter < 100 with value : ',counter);
       counter := counter + 1;
       if (counter > 4) goto LAST_COUNT;
     end;

   LAST_COUNT : begin
                  counter := counter + 1;
                  writeln;
                  writeln('Final counter value : ',counter);
                end;

   writeln('Program terminated ...');
end.

Output  :   Counter < 100 with value : 1
            Counter < 100 with value : 2
            Counter < 100 with value : 3
            Counter < 100 with value : 4

            Final counter value : 6
            Program terminated ...
```

Fig. 2-34. An example of the "goto" unconditional branch.

The 'WHILE..DO' Method
_____

```
counter := 0;
while (counter < 100) do
  begin
    if (counter < 50) then
      writeln('Less than 50.')
    else
      writeln('Greater than 50');
  end;
```

The 'GOTO' Method
_____

```
counter := 0;
AA : begin
       if (counter < 50) then
         goto CC
       else
         goto BB;
     end;
BB : begin
       counter := counter + 1;
       if (counter > 100) then goto DD;
       goto AA;
     end;
CC : begin
       writeln('Less than 50');
       goto BB;
     end;
DD : begin
       writeln('Program Terminated ...');
     end;
```

Fig. 2-35. Comparison of "while..do" and "goto" control structures.

maintained by a programmer of comparable experience and knowledge as the creator, a program cannot be considered complete. Incomplete programs are not acceptable. If you must use a goto, it is necessary to observe the same caution about the possibility of an infinite loop as with any of the looping structures.

PROCEDURES

Knowledge of the separate capabilities of the Turbo Pascal language is important. Knowledge of how they may be assembled into a working program is invaluable. Data input, storage, evaluation, manipulation and output are all individual parts of programming. These separate, but related, concepts are brought together in the smallest executable portion of a program called a "procedure." A *procedure* can be likened to a thought, or a single task. When a procedure is executed, the task is performed or the thought is completed. A procedure might be as simple as the display of a greeting. A simple procedure is shown in FIG. 2-36.

```
Procedure Greetings;
begin
    writeln('Welcome to Turbo Pascal.');
end;
```
Fig. 2-36. A simple procedure.

A procedure may be as complex as the human mind can conceive. For most programs, however, the procedure should be considered a solution for the smallest indivisible portion of a problem to be solved.

To use a procedure within a program, or even another procedure, it is necessary to first declare it. The declaration enables the programmer to name the procedure. In addition, the declaration allows the programmer to define what arguments the procedure should take. An argument is a value needed within the procedure for calculation or manipulation, that does not originate within the procedure. An argument may be a number, a character, a string of characters, or just about any piece of data. The data is passed to the procedure and manipulations take place. When the procedure finishes, a result is output. A simple procedure to output a number multiplied by two is shown in FIG. 2-37.

```
Procedure Double_Number(input : real);
begin
    writeln('The number ',input,' multiplied by 2 is : ',input*2);
end;
```
Fig. 2-37. A simple procedure declaration with arguments.

The procedure declaration in FIG. 2-37 defines the name of the procedure as double_number. The argument variable is called input and it is defined as a real variable, capable of accepting numbers from – 1E38 to 1E38. The value of the input variable is passed into the procedure by another procedure which calls double_number. As long as the value is of the type specified by the variable definition in the procedure declaration,

```
Program Test_Procedure;
Var
  entry_value : real;

  Procedure Double_Number(input : real);
  begin
    writeln('The number ',input,' multiplied by 2 is : ',input*2);
  end;

Begin (* Main Program *)
  write('Enter a number : ');
  read(entry_value);

  double_number(entry_value);
end.
```

Fig. 2-38. A sample program using the "double_number" procedure.

the procedure will execute. A program that makes use of the double_number procedure is shown in FIG. 2-38.

The program in FIG. 2-38 is typical of a program that uses a procedure or procedures to accomplish its task or tasks. In any program, the definition of a procedure or procedures is placed after the variable declarations for the program and before the Begin statement of the main program.

The read procedure in the main body of the program in FIG. 2-38 enables the user to enter a number into the entry_value variable. This value is then passed to the double_number procedure, where the number, and the number multiplied by 2, are output to the screen. A procedure can take more than one argument, and is not limited to taking arguments of only one type. Samples of multiple argument procedure declarations are shown in FIG. 2-39.

```
Procedure Test(A,B:integer; C:real);
Procedure Test(A:char; B,C:real; D:string255);
Procedure Test(Value1,Value2 : real);
Procedure Test(Greet_Text:string255; Number_of_Greetings:integer);
Procedure Test(Value:real; double:real);
```

Fig. 2-39. Sample procedure definitions.

Different data type declarations are separated by semicolons ";". The last variable defined should not have a semicolon following it. However the procedure declaration line must be terminated by a semicolon. It is important to note that there should be no effective limit on the number of arguments a procedure may take. However, if the number of arguments is greater than 15, the programmer might wish to redesign the procedure. Remember, a well-designed and -written procedure should be the expression of a single thought, or the completion of a single task.

Procedures may be written to perform more than one task. However, to write procedures that perform multiple tasks defeats the intent of structured problem solving. Remember, in structured problem solving and programming, each procedure is designed to solve a single aspect of a larger problem specification. When the procedures are combined, the complete problem might be solved by the resulting program. Procedures performing multiple tasks might require complex control logic. This removes program control from a central controlling loop or conditional branch. When this occurs, program logic might become more complex than necessary to solve a problem. Programs written using the structured method do not preclude the use of multiple task procedures. However, the user must make sure the use of such procedures does not cause the program logic to become incomprehensible.

Functions

In FIG. 2-37 the double_number procedure was defined to take a real number and output that number multiplied by two. What if the programmer wanted to retain the result of the operation in a variable rather than output it to the screen. Turbo Pascal allows the user to return a value from a structure known as a function. A *function* is simply a procedure that returns a value. This value can be returned into a variable, or it can be passed to another procedure such as writeln( ) for output to the screen. Figure 2-40 shows the double_number procedure as a function.

```
Function Double_Number(input : real):real;
begin
  double_number := input*2;
end;
```

Fig. 2-40. The "double_number" function.

This declaration of a function is similar to a procedure. Any values passed to the function must be defined in the function declaration section. In addition, the data type of the result or value returned by the function must be declared. The declaration line Function Double_Number(input : real):real; shows the input variable defined as a real variable. The name of the function Double_Number is also defined as a real variable. The use of this function is demonstrated in FIG. 2-41.

```
Program Test_Function;
Var
  entry_value, double_value : real;

  Function Double_Number(input : real):real;
  begin
    double_number := input*2;
  end;

Begin (* Main Program *)
  write('Enter a number : ');
  read(entry_value);

  double_value := Double_number(entry_value);

  write('The value of ',entry_value,' times 2 is ',double_value);
end.
```

Fig. 2-41. The use of the "Double_Number" function.

The program in FIG. 2-41 defines two variables to hold real numbers. The first variable ent ry_va l ue holds the value of the number entered by a user in response to the input question. The second variable doub l e_va l ue holds the value of twice the entry_value returned by the Double_Number function. In each case a variable is required to hold a value. The program in FIG. 2-41 also demonstrates the manner in which a function is called. A variable is assigned a value or the result of an operation through the use of the assignment ":-" operator. The value returned by a function is assigned to a variable as though it were a simple value. The call to a function is an assignment to the variable of the value returned by the function.

A procedure is evoked by using the name of the procedure in a line of code. If the procedure requires arguments, these are provided with the procedure call. A function is also called by using its name in a line of source code. However, where the call to the procedure can stand as a complete statement, the call to the function must be part of another operation. Because functions return values, they can be used in arithmetic operations, value assignments, even calls to other procedures or functions. Figure 2-42 demonstrates some function calls and locations in which return values may be placed.

```
Program Demonstrate_Function_Calls;
Var
   entry_value, double_value, quadruple_value : real;

   Function Double_Number(input : real):real;
   begin
     double_number := input*2;
   end;

Begin (* Main Program *)
   write('Enter a number : ');
   read(entry_value);

   (* Function value returned to variable *)
   double_value := Double_Number(entry_value);
   writeln('The value of ',entry_value,' times 2 is ',double_value);

   (* Function value returned as argument to another procedure *)
   write('The value of ',entry_value,' times 2 is ');
   writeln(Double_Number(entry_value));

   (* Function value returned to a function then a variable *)
   quadruple_value := Double_Number(Double_Number(entry_value));
   writeln('The value of ',entry_value,' times 4 is ',quadruple_value);
end.
```

Fig. 2-42. Calling functions.

The return value of a function should be treated as any value held in a variable. In the code for a function, the actual function name is used to hold the return value. Unlike a variable name, however, the function can only be assigned a value within itself.

Recursion

One of the more interesting features of functions in any high level language is their ability to call themselves. The act of a function calling itself is called recursion and it lends itself to some particularly useful tasks. The result is a small amount of code capable of performing extremely complex calculations and data manipulations. A simple example of recursion would be the mathematical concept called factorial.

The calculation of a *factorial* is simply the calculation of a product of all numbers between a chosen number and 1. The factorial of the number 5 is "5 * 4 * 3 * 2 * 1" or 120. The factorial results from the number 5 multiplied by (5 − 1) multiplied by (5 − 2), etcetera, until five minus a number equals 1. The product of the multiplication becomes the factorial of the original number. Recursion is used because the function seeks to satisfy a condition where the number entered minus another number is equal to 1. A sample factorial program is shown in FIG. 2-43.

```
Program Calculate_Factorial;
Var
  entry_value, factorial_value : real;

  Function Factorial(input : real):real;
  begin
    if (input = 1) then
      Factorial := 1;
    else
      Factorial := Factorial(input - 1) * input;
  end;

Begin (* Main Program *)
  write('Enter the value for which a factorial is desired : ');
  read(entry_value);

  factorial_value := Factorial(entry_value);
  writeln('The factorial of ',entry_value,' is ',factorial_value);
end;
```

Fig. 2-43. An example of recursive programming.

The program in FIG. 2-43 demonstrates the recursion capabilities of a function. The function seeks to create the sum of all the integer numbers between the contents of the input variable and the number 1. The if..then..else statement is key to the recursive call of the function. When the content of the input variable is greater than 1, the Factorial function is called with the value of the variable minus 1. Each call to the function creates a new copy of the function in memory. The input variable in the second Factorial function is different than the input variable in the fifth Factorial function. When the value of the input variable is 1, the function starts to return values. A map of the values of the variables, and levels of recursion for the factorial program in FIG. 2-43 with an initial value of 5, is shown in FIG. 2-44.

Level	Input Value	Function Call	Return Value
1	5	Factorial(4)	Factorial(4)*5
2	4	Factorial(3)	Factorial(3)*4
3	3	Factorial(2)	Factorial(2)*3
4	2	Factorial(1)	Factorial(1)*2
5	1		1

Fig. 2-44. Recursion: Factorial function calls and results.

When the factorial function is called, the value passed to it is evaluated for equality to 1. If this is not found, the function calls itself with the input value minus 1. This recursive call is made until the value of 1 is found. When the condition evaluates to TRUE some very interesting operations take place. The 5th level factorial function returns the number 1 to the 4th level factorial which called it. The 4th level factorial function returns the value of the return value multiplied by the original input value, or 2. So the 4th level factorial function returns 2*1 or 2 to the 3rd level. The 3rd level function returns 3*2 which is 6. The 2nd level function returns 4*6 or 24 to the 1st level. Finally, the 1st level function returns 5*24 or 120 to the original call to the function.

Functions and procedures have a lot in common not only with each other, but also with the general structure of a Pascal program. A typical program might contain not only a variable declaration section, but also constant, type and label sections as well. Procedures and functions may also have these sections. These sections may be included or excluded from procedures and functions at will. The requirements of the procedure determine which sections are necessary.

When a variable is declared within a program it is referred to as a *global* variable. When a variable is declared within a procedure, the variable is called a *local*. The difference between the two is extremely important to the proper execution of programs, procedures and functions. The basis of the difference is the range of availability of the value contained within that variable. When a global variable is defined, the value assigned to that variable is available anywhere in the program. When a local variable is assigned a value within a procedure, the variable and its contents exist only as long as that procedure executes. A demonstration of the difference between global and local variables is shown in FIG. 2-45.

The value assigned to the global or G_var variable in the First procedure is retained after the execution of the procedure is complete. The value within this variable can be accessed throughout the program and is in the Second procedure where it is output to the screen. The value assigned to the local or L_var variable in the first procedure is not retained. After the procedure ceases execution, the variable and its contents are lost. The Second procedure also defines a local or L_var variable. Even though the variables are named identically, they are totally unrelated. Any variable

```
Program Demonstrate_Variables;
Var
  G_var : real; (* Global variable *)

  Procedure First;
  Var
    L_var : real;
  begin
    writeln('The global variable is assigned the value : 10');
    G_var := 10;
    writeln('The local variable is assigned the value : 5');
    L_var := 5;
  end;

  Procedure Second;
  Var
    L_var : real;
  begin
    writeln('The value of the global variable is ',G_var);
    writeln('The value of the local variable is ',L_var);
  end;

Begin (* Main Program *)
  First;
  writeln(' ');
  Second;
end.


Output : The global variable is assigned the value : 10
         The local variable is assigned the value : 5

         The value of the global variable is 10
         The value of the local variable is 0
```

Fig. 2-45. The difference between global and local variables.

defined in a given procedure is local to that procedure. Any value stored within that local variable would be lost when the procedure ended, unless the value was also assigned to a global variable, or passed to another procedure.

It is extremely important to keep track of local and global variables. In languages such as BASIC this is easy, because every variable is global. In Pascal the rules vary because of the structure of the procedures and functions utilizing these variables.

Just as variables may be defined to the global and local, constants and types may also be defined in this manner. This is especially helpful for declaring arguments to be of a complex data type. Constants such as PI or other mathematically significant data may be made local to a procedure that requires them, or global for all procedures. In this case PI is a predefined Turbo Pascal function so it is global to any program you create in Turbo Pascal. Because a label for a goto statement is declared in the program or procedure header, it may also be declared to be global or local. This capability for a label makes it even more confusing to use. The importance of NOT using, or minimizing the use of, a goto statement cannot be overstressed.

Passing arguments to procedures and functions has already been discussed in detail, however, there are some additional Turbo Pascal procedure declaration capabilities that should be discussed. It was stated previously that functions and procedures differed mainly in the fact that functions returned values. In several of the figures in this chapter, the difference in the method of calling each type of routine was also demonstrated.

Actually, procedures as well as functions are capable of returning values. This can be done by a method of declaring argument variables to be *passed by reference*. When a procedure or function argument is declared in the normal fashion, it is defined to be *passed by value*. Passing by value simply means that the variable in the procedure declaration is different from the variable in the procedure call, but the value is the same. Passing by reference means that the memory location of the variable is passed rather than the value contained within it. Data passed by value and by reference are demonstrated in FIG. 2-46.

```
Program Pass_Value;
Var
   value : real;

   (* Data is passed by value *)
   Procedure A(a_var : real);
   begin
     writeln('The original value is ',a_var);
     a_var := 10;
     writeln('The new value is ',a_var);
   end;

   (* Data is passed by reference *)
   Procedure B(var b_var : real);
   begin
     writeln('The original value is ',b_var);
     b_var := 15;
     writeln('The new value is ',b_var);
   end;

Begin (* Main Program *)
   value := 5;
   A(value);
   writeln('The value after procedure A : ',value);
   B(value);
   writeln('The value after procedure B : ',value);
end.


Output : The original value is 5
         The new value is 10
         The value after procedure A : 5
         The original value is 5
         The new value is 15
         The value after procedure B : 15
```

Fig. 2-46. Passing data by value and by reference.

The "value" variable is a *passing* variable because information passes from it to the called procedure. The a_var and b_var variables are *receiving* variables because information passed to the procedure is received into these variables. When data is passed by value, only the contents of the variable are passed to the procedure. The procedure declaration contains definitions for local variables to accept the passed values. In "Procedure A" the value 5 is passed. The value of the local variable may be output or modified. However, when the procedure ceases execution the value contained within the a_var variable is lost. Even though the values within the value and a_var variables were identical to start, the manipulation of a_var has no effect on the value variable. This occurs even when the passing and receiving variables have identical names.

When the value is passed by reference, the passing and receiving variables are linked. The value of the passing variable is not transferred to "Procedure B." Instead, the memory location of the value variable is passed to b_var. In essence the value and b_var variables are the same. Whatever manipulations are performed on the data in b_var will also be performed on the data in the value variable.

An argument may be declared as a reference variable simply by placing the word var in front of the definition of that variable in the procedure or function definition. Some examples of defining arguments as reference variables are demonstrated in FIG. 2-47.

```
procedure first(var value : real);
procedure second(value_a : real; var value_b : real);
procedure third(var a,c : integer; b,d : real);
procedure fourth(var a : string255; var b : integer; var c : real);
procedure fifth(var a,b : char, var c,d : integer; var e : real);
```

Fig. 2-47. Examples of arguments defined as reference variables.

The "first" procedure defines the "value" argument as a reference variable. The "second" procedure defines only one of two arguments as reference, although all are defined to accept real values. The "third" procedure defines two of four arguments as reference and leaves the other two arguments as "pass by value." The "fourth" procedure defines all arguments as reference variables even though they are all of different types. Finally, the "fifth" procedure defines all arguments as reference variables allowing for more than one data type as well as more than one variable of each type.

The use of reference variables is fairly common and extremely powerful. It can also be dangerous. The ability to pass arguments by reference gives the programmer the capability to circumvent the difference between a global and a local variable. Local variables are supposed to exist only as long as the procedure executes. When the procedure ends, the variables cease to exist as do the values contained within them. When a variable is defined as reference, any manipulations performed upon that variable in a local procedure will be incorporated into the passing variable.

You might never make use of all of the capabilities of the structure of procedures and functions in Turbo Pascal. These capabilities allow the programmer to design and implement procedures of phenomenal functionality and value. The best method to further develop your own understanding of these capabilities is to work with them. You should enter the procedures in the figures of this chapter into Turbo Pascal and run them. Make modifications to see what works and what doesn't. Remember, if the manual fails you, experimentation will likely provide you with a reasonable understanding of a procedure or function.

Forward Procedure and Function Declarations

Turbo Pascal, like Standard Pascal requires that any procedure called by other procedures be defined prior to the command that calls it. Up to this point procedures calling other procedures have been defined after the procedure they call. However, situations will arise requiring two or more procedures or functions to call each other. Pascal provides for this possibility with the forward declaration. The forward declaration allows the programmer to define the header line of a procedure or function before the actual code for procedure or function is available. A typical forward declaration is shown in FIG. 2-48.

```
Program Test_Forward;
Var
 position : integer;

  (* Forward Declaration of Procedure B *)
 Procedure B; FORWARD;

  (* Declaration and Definition of Procedure A *)
 Procedure A;
 begin
   position := 1;
   B;
 end;

  (* Definition of Procedure B *)
 Procedure B;
 begin
   position := 2;
 end;

Begin (* main *)
  A;
  B;
 end.
```

Fig. 2-48. The FORWARD procedure and function modifier.

Procedure A calls procedure B, but procedure B also calls procedure A. Under normal circumstances, this situation would be unacceptable to the "top-down" programming philosophy behind a structured programming language like Turbo Pascal. However, because this philosophy was understood to be too limiting when the Pascal language was created, the forward declaration capability was added.

The forward declaration of the procedure is identical to the normal declaration. All variables must be declared in the procedure header, or the header must be defined as a variable type if the declaration is for a function. After the declaration is complete the text "FORWARD;" is appended to the procedure or function declaration. The definition of the procedure or function routine is identified by the word "Procedure" or "Function" followed by the name of the procedure or function.

SETS AND RECORDS

Beyond the use of simple variables to hold character or numeric data, Turbo Pascal enables the programmer to create complex data structures with even greater functionality. These structures include "sets" and user definable data structures called "records." In addition to enabling the programmer to assign values to memory for later storage, these structures enable the programmer to define basic relationships between the data stored. Data may be stored in any variable, and by virtue of this assignment the data can be referenced not only by the variable to which it is assigned, but by any other variable included in the structure. Database applications make direct use of structured variables for data entry and retrieval.

Sets

Sets enable the programmer to establish relationships between data. A *set* may be the counting numbers from 1 to 10 or the lowercase letters of the alphabet. In either case, the components of the data set are defined in some sequence that might be used by the computer. A typical set declaration is shown in FIG. 2-49.

```
Program Demonstrate_Sets;
Type
   Days = (Sun,Mon,Tue,Wed,Thr,Fri,Sat);
Var
   day : Days;
Begin
   day := Mon;
   writeln('The day is : Mon');
   writeln('The number of the day is : ',integer(day));
   writeln('The previous day is : ',integer(day)-1);
   writeln('The next day is : ',integer(day)+1);
end.

Output :   The day is Mon
           The number of the day is : 1
           The previous day is : 0
           The next day is : 2
```

Fig. 2-49. The definition of a set.

A "set" may be defined in the Type and Const sections of a program, a procedure or a function. As always with Turbo Pascal, the sequencing of the Type and Const sections in the program is optional. The set type is defined in the Type section of the program in the line Day = (Sun,Mon, Tue,Wed,Thr,Fri,Sat);. After this type of set is defined, a variable may be declared as being of that type. After a variable is declared as a set variable it may be assigned one or more of the values associated with the set. In FIG. 2-49, the value Mon would normally be considered a string of characters. In a set, it is regarded by Turbo Pascal as an ordinal or finite value within the declared set. The value Mon is not the string of characters "MON," rather it is the second item in the set of "DAYS." Based on this internal representation Turbo Pascal allows the programmer to perform backwards referencing within the set—a function not provided within Standard Pascal.

The function INTEGER(day) normally returns the integer portion of a real number. When used in conjunction with set variables, this function returns the sequence number of the data as it appears in the defined set. The value "MON" is the second item in the set of "DAYS." The value returned by the INTEGER function is 1. The reason for this seemingly bizarre numbering scheme is explained in the internal structure of Turbo Pascal. Programmers have the option of defining and indexing arrays and complex variables as they see fit. Sets require more stringent declaration rules to enable Turbo Pascal to recognize the constituents of a set and their sequence. Sets may contain up to 256 individual elements, numbered from 0 to 255. Therefore the first element in the set of "DAYS" is "Sun" and its number is 0. Hence the value for "Mon" as the second element in the set of "DAYS" is 1.

Set types may be declared in a variety of ways in both the Type and Const section. In the Const section, a set is defined and assigned to a constant. These constants can be used to hold pieces of data relating to specific responses to queries for input, or simply separate pieces of data that relate to each other. Remember that information declared as a constant cannot be modified during the running of a program.

Set types may also be defined within the Type section for later use during variable declaration. These variables may then be used for input, or output, depending upon the type of data used in the set. Although set variables may be defined to hold entire sets of data, they are usually assigned one piece of data at a time for comparison to the entire set. The program in FIG. 2-50 shows some additional examples of defining and assigning values to sets variables.

The program in FIG. 2-50 demonstrates the most basic use of a set. The contents of a set represent a finite number of responses to a specific question. Several constants were defined as sets that contained possible answers to the question posed by the procedure. Each of the individual data sets of positive and negative response values may be incorporated into an even larger data set. The larger set would contain all positive or all negative responses as in the "positive_answer" and "negative_answer" sets.

Set declarations and definitions in conjunction with the "IN" operator provide the most efficient method of determining set membership. The "IN" operator, demonstrated in FIG. 2-50 provides the basis for a Boolean evaluation of set membership. The format of the evaluation is shown in FIG. 2-51.

The "Element" variable is a variable defined to be of the same type as the basic component of the set. The Set variable is a variable defined as a variable of type "set" and assigned one or more values declared to be a part of the set. If the value in the element variable is a member of the set variable, a value of TRUE is assigned to the Boolean variable. If the value

```
Program Demonstrate_Sets_Part_II;
Type
   answers = set of char;
Const
   yes_answer : answers = ['Y','y'];
   no_answer : answers = ['N','n'];
   True_answer : answers = ['T','t'];
   False_answer : answers = ['F','f'];

   positive_answer : answers = ['Y','y','T','t'];
   negative_answer : answers = ['N','n','F','f'];
Var
   answer : char;
Begin
   write('Do you wish to continue  : ');
   readln(answer);

   writeln('The response was YES : ',(answer IN yes_answer));
   writeln('The response was TRUE : ',(answer IN True_answer));
   writeln('The response was NO : ',(answer IN no_answer));
   writeln('The response was FALSE : ',(answer IN False_answer));
   writeln(' ');
   writeln('The response was Positive : ',(answer IN positive_answer));
   writeln('The repsonse was Negative : ',(answer IN negative_answer));
end.


Program Output :
                 Do you wish to continue : n
                 The response was YES : FALSE
                 The response was TRUE : FALSE
                 The response was NO : TRUE
                 The response was FALSE : FALSE

                 The response was Positive : FALSE
                 The response was Negative : TRUE


                 Do you wish to continue : T
                 The response was YES : FALSE
                 The response was TRUE : TRUE
                 The response was NO : FALSE
                 The response was FALSE : FALSE

                 The response was Positive : TRUE
                 The response was Negative : FALSE
```

Fig. 2-50. The use of SETS and the IN operator.

in the element variable is not a member of the set, a value of FALSE results. The yesanswer function in FIG. 2-52 is an excellent representation of the power of the "IN" operator and the set data type in general.

The yesanswer function demonstrates how sets can be used to determine not only that an input value is either YES, NO, TRUE or FALSE, but in a general aspect whether the response to the question is in the affirmative or negative. This function could be written with if..then..else logical constructs, but the code would be two to three times longer, and less logically precise. The same results would be generated from the if..then..else procedure, but the procedure would not be as efficient nor as intuitively obvious. In addition, the modification of the yesanswer function in FIG. 2-52 would require far less effort because all of the comparison values are assigned in one location in the code. If the if..then..else structure were used, several comparisons in as many locations would require modification.

Fig. 2-51. The "IN" operator.   `Boolean = (Element IN Set);`

```
Function yesanswer : boolean;
Type
  response_type = string[5];
  answer = set of char;
Const
  answers : answer = ['Y','y','N','n','T','t','F','f'];
  True_answer : answer = ['Y','y','T','t'];
Var
  response : response_type;
Begin
  readln(response);

  (* Make sure the response is within the set of  *)
  (* allowable responses based on the ANSWERS set *)
  while NOT(COPY(response,1,1) IN answers)
    begin
      write('Enter a YES or NO : ');
      readln(response);
    end;

  (* Determine if the response is AFFIRMATIVE or NEGATIVE *)
  (* based on set membership to the TRUE_ANSWER value set *)
  if (COPY(response,1,1) IN True_answer) then
    yesanswer := TRUE
  else
    yesanswer := FALSE;
end.
```

Fig. 2-52. The "yesanswer" function.

Besides the "IN" operator, there are a variety of set operators available within the Turbo Pascal environment. These operators include intersection, union, difference, and equality comparison. The results of these operations will be sets only if both components of the operation are sets also.

"∗" - Set Intersection   This operator requires three "set" variables A, B, and C in the formula "A : = B ∗ C;." The variables A, B and C are defined as set variables of the same type. When an element shared by B and C is located, it is assigned to the variable A. The variable A is assigned all values shared by B and C.

"+" - Set Union   This operator requires three "set" variables A, B, and C in the formula "A : = B + C;." The variables A, B and C are defined as set variables of the same type. All elements in B and C are assigned to the variable A. If any element appears in both B and C only a single copy of that element is assigned to A.

"−" - Set Difference   This operator requires three "set" variables A, B, and C in the formula "A : = B − C;". The variables A, B and C are defined as set variables of the same type. When an element found in B is not found in C it is assigned to the variable A. The variable A is assigned all values found in B and not found in C.

There are set comparison operators such as equality "=" and inequality "<>." These operators allow the programmer to quickly determine if all of the elements in one set are contained within another set.

There are two additional comparison operators ">=" and "<=." The greater than ">=" operator can be used in the Boolean expression "(A >= B)" where A and B are set variables. When ALL of the elements contained in B are also present in A, the Boolean expression evaluates to TRUE. The less than "<=" operator can be used in the Boolean expression "(A <= B)" where A and B are also set variables. When ALL of the elements in A are also present in B, the Boolean expression evaluates to TRUE.

The value of sets and set operators cannot be overstressed for higher level applications. Turbo Pascal provides all of the functionality of Standard Pascal and adds the capability of treating a set as an array capable of backward and forward referencing when applicable. Obviously, the most important function of sets emphasized in this chapter is their use in response functions. Many of the responses to queries and menu options are based on a finite number of choices determined at the time an application is compiled. Rather than spending more time and effort than is necessary to create a complicated and verbose structure of if..then..else evaluations, please take the time to consider how a set variable can simplify the logical structure of an evaluation.

Records

As important as the use of "sets" can be to advanced Turbo Pascal applications, "records" provide the programmer with an infinitely greater variety of programming choices. Records enable the programmer to develop and manipulate data structures of unlimited complexity. Unlike basic Pascal data types, *records* are multiple variable structures that may be used to store more than one piece of data of more than one type at one time. Pascal arrays can store more than one piece of data at one time. However, arrays must be declared to hold only a single type of data.

A record variable can be defined to hold integer, real, character, Boolean and string data all at the same time. Records are defined in the Type section of a Turbo Pascal program, procedure or function. Like any variable type, a record structure may contain values local to a procedure or global to the entire program. In addition, any component of a record may be output using the writeln procedure, or used within readln to receive input data. The program in FIG. 2-53 demonstrates the declaration and one of the possible uses of record variables.

Records can only be declared from previously defined data types. Records may be based on basic and complex types including arrays, or even other records. The Phonebook record generated in FIG. 2-53 could be

```
Program Phonebook;
Type
  string25 = string[25];
  string40 = string[40];
  phonebook_type = record
                        lastname, firstname : string25;
                        address : string40;
                        town, city : string40;
                        phonenumber : string25;
                      end;
Var
  phone_entry : phonebook_type;
Begin
  with (phone_entry) do
    begin
      write('Enter the last name for the record : ');
      read(lastname);
      write('Enter the first name for the record : ');
      read(firstname);
    end;

  write('Enter the address for the record : ');
  read(phone_entry.address);
  write('Enter the town for the record : ');
  read(phone_entry.town);
  write('Enter the city for the record : ');
  read(phone_entry.city);

  write('Enter the telephone number for the record : ');
  read(phone_entry.phonenumber);
end.
```

Fig. 2-53. The use of a "record" variable.

used as the basis for a phonebook database if the Type section of the program included an array declaration of type "phonebook_type." Some critics of Pascal claim that it fails to provide the programmer with a complete set of variables types for data storage. Although Turbo Pascal version 3.0 might have suffered from this malady, versions 4.0, 5.0 and 5.5 have as wide a range of basic data types as any implementation of the C programming language. In addition, the capability to declare advanced data structures such as the record in FIG. 2-53 more than compensates for any perceived deficiency in previous versions of Turbo Pascal.

The program in FIG. 2-53 depicts the usage of a record variable. As stated previously, values may not be assigned directly to a record variable. Instead, each component of the structure must be addressed separately, although the information is stored together. Each variable of the record is addressed by using the name of the structure and the name of the target variable component when assigning or retrieving data. In FIG. 2-53 the address portion of the structure is accessed with the assignment phone_entry.address. The structure phone_entry is the name of the record. The variable address is a portion of the record structure. A value is assigned to address by combining it with its parent structure name using a period character. Once this is coded, the construct phone_entry .address can be used as if it were a string variable type.

Another method of using records is the with ( ) do structure. This structure is simply a shorthand method of accessing individual portions of a record structure. Figure 2-53 demonstrates the use of this structure. When the name of the record variable is placed within the parentheses of the with ( ) do structure, any variable names used within its begin..end statements are compared to the record structure. If a match is found then any assignment to, or manipulation of, that variable will result in a manipulation of the value stored in the portion of the record of the same name. The lastname and firstname variables in the phone_entry record may be manipulated directly when they are accessed using the "with ( ) do" structure.

Variant Records   The combination of a record structure with an array variable can lend itself to the creation of even more complex data structures with even greater value. In addition, record structures may be declared with variable internal structures based on input at run time. Such a structure is shown in FIG. 2-54.

```
Type
   country_type = (USA,CANADA);
Const
   country : country_type = [USA,CANADA];
Type
   state_type : string[2];
   province_type : string[20];

   phonebook_type = record
                    lastname, firstname : string25;
                    address : string40;
                    town, city : string40;
                    phonenumber : string25;

                    case  nation : country_type  of
                      USA : (state : state_type);
                      CANADA : (province : province_type;
                               state : state_type);
                    end;
```

Fig. 2-54. A variant record structure.

All of these structures enable the programmer to create data structures of exceptional versatility within the Turbo Pascal programming environment. If the variable component "nation" of the record structure is assigned the value "USA" the record will be assigned an additional variable called "state." If the value of nation is "CANADA" two additional variables state and province will be associated to the record structure.

DYNAMIC MEMORY ALLOCATION

Along with the creation of complex data structures—such as records, arrays, variant records—comes the task of allocating memory to hold all of the data stored within these structures. Normally this memory allocation is performed for you. When you declare a byte variable, a pointer to that variable is defined and a byte of memory is allocated for storing the value.

Similarly, for simple integers two bytes are allocated; simple reals require six bytes; character and Boolean variables require a byte each; and string variables may contain up to 256 bytes. These variables require such a small amount of memory in a typical program that their combined memory utilization is not worth mentioning. If larger structures are required, arrays can usually provide the variable spaces needed to store data. However, when you begin to construct complicated variables that require more than 65,520 bytes total, Turbo Pascal does not allow them. A *static* variable would simply be an array requiring more than 65,520 bytes of contiguous memory for storage. This apparent limitation can be overcome by the use of dynamic variables. Turbo Pascal does not allow for the definition of static variables utilizing more than 65520 bytes, but because dynamic variables do not actually require memory until run time, they are acceptable to the compiler.

Pascal provides the user with the capability to *dynamically allocate* memory—that is, allocate and use memory as it is required. Pointers and records can be combined to create structures that point to each other. Each structure forms a link in a larger collection structure called a *chain*. The programming term for such a linked data structure is a *linked list*. This linked list forms the basis for some of the most advanced applications available on the PC, such as Databases.

In a Database, data of different types are grouped together to form discrete units called *records*. Each record is a collection of data related to a specific portion of the record called the *key*. For the phonebook, the key is the lastname variable. The key also forms the basis for the arrangement or linkage of each of the unique records to form the database. In a linked list, the structures are linked by pointers that point from one record to another. An individual link in a linked list is shown in FIG. 2-55.

Record Structure -

A^	value	B^

Declaration -

```
Type
    link_pointer = ^link_type;
    link_type = record
                    A, B : link_pointer;
                    value : integer;
                end;
Var
    link : link_type;
```

Fig. 2-55. A simple linked list and the code to define it.

The code in FIG. 2-55 can be used to create individual links within a linked list structure. Each record has two pointers used to point to as many as two other links within the list. Remember, the actual pointer memory address value may be assigned from one pointer to another, as well as the values to which they point. Each record also contains a value variable used to hold an integer. There are two basic forms of linked list, the "single" and "double" linked list. The single linked list is simply a record containing one pointer variable. This variable is used to point to the next or previous link in the list. An example of a single linked list is shown in FIG. 2-56.

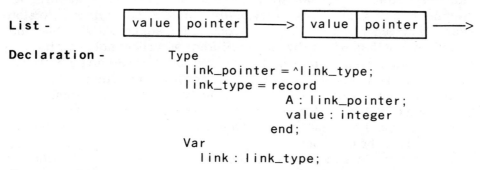

List -

Declaration -
```
Type
    link_pointer = ^link_type;
    link_type = record
                    A : link_pointer;
                    value : integer
                end;
        Var
            link : link_type;
```

Fig. 2-56. A single linked list.

As you can see, the single linked list is simply a string of values pointing to the next value in the list. When a value is required from within the list, a procedure must first trace through the links until the desired data is found.

The double linked list is different from a single because its records are defined with two pointers each. One pointer of the record points to the next link, and the other points to the previous link in the list. This pointer structure allows the program to trace both forwards and backwards through a list, adding flexibility and improving list search efficiency. An example of a double link list and how it may be used is shown in FIG. 2-57.

```
Program Link_List_Counter;
Type
  link_pointer = ^link_type;
  link_type = record
                  front, back : link_pointer;
                  value : integer;
              end;
Var
  start, endd, link : ^link_type;
  counter : integer;

Procedure Start_Link_List;
Begin
  new(link);              (* Create First Link *)
  start := link;          (* Set List START Pointer to Address of New Link
  link^.front := nil;     (* Set Front of List to NIL *)
  link^.back := nil;      (* Set Back of List to NIL *)
  link^.value := 0;       (* Set Link Value to 0 *)
  endd := link;           (* Set List ENDD pointer to Address of New Link *
end;
```

Fig. 2-57. Linked lists and dynamically allocated memory.

"Fig. 2-57
continued."

```
Procedure New_Link;
begin
  new(link);                (* Create New Link for List *)
  link^.front := nil;       (* Point the Front of New Link to NIL *)
  endd^.front := link;      (* Point the Front of Old End to New Link *)
  link^.back := endd;       (* Point the Back of New Link to Old End *)
  link^.value := 0;         (* Set New Link Value Link Value to 0 *)
  endd := link;             (* Set End of List Pointer to New Last Link *
end;

Procedure Printout_Link_Values;
Var
  count : integer;
begin
  link := start;            (* Assign LINK Pointer to Beginning of List *
  count := 0;

  (* While the current link points to another link perform the loop *)
  while (link^.front <> NIL) do
    begin
      count := count + 1;
      writeln('The value in link ',count,' is ',link^.value);
      link := link^.front;
    end;

  (* Printout the value contained in the last link of the chain *)
  count := count + 1;
  writeln('The value in link ',count,' is ',link^.value);
  writeln(' ');
end;

Begin (* Main Procedure *)
  (* Initiate the List *)

  Start_Link_List;
  link^.value := RANDOM(1000);
  Printout_Link_Values;

  (* Extend the List to Five Links, Assign Values and Display *)
  for counter := 1 to 4 do
    begin
      New_Link;
      link^.value := RANDOM(1000);
      Printout_Link_Values;
    end;
end.


Program Output : The value in line 1 is 924

               The value in line 1 is 924
               The value in line 2 is 474

               The value in line 1 is 924
               The value in line 2 is 474
               The value in line 3 is 237

               The value in line 1 is 924
               The value in line 2 is 474
               The value in line 3 is 237
               The value in line 4 is 259

               The value in line 1 is 924
               The value in line 2 is 474
               The value in line 3 is 237
               The value in line 4 is 259
               The value in line 5 is 97
```

The program shown in FIG. 2-57 is the foundation for nearly every linked list program you might ever need to create. Each of the procedures demonstrates one of the basic features of linked lists—including starting a list, adding a link, adding information to a link component variable, and manipulation of the data stored within a link component variable. Each of these operations is essential to proper declaration, assignment and use of a linked list whether it is singly or doubly linked. Although the program in FIG. 2-57 is declared and linked as a double link list, it is manipulated in only one direction. However, the task of modifying this code into a double link list program is made simpler by the fact that the code already accommodates double link records.

Each of the procedures in FIG. 2-57 represents an important part of list maintenance and manipulation within a Turbo Pascal program. Each portion of the code is examined in detail.

Initializing the List

A link list requires three separate pointers to be declared and assigned. The *start pointer* points to the first element or link in the list. The *end pointer* points to the last element or link in the list. The *link pointer* points to the current list element. When a link list is initialized, all three of these pointers point to the same record structure. The initialization of these pointers is shown in FIG. 2-58.

```
Procedure Start_Link_List;
Begin
  new(link);              (* Create First Link *)
  start := link;          (* Set List START Pointer to Address of New Link
  link^.front := nil;     (* Set Front of List to NIL *)
  link^.back := nil;      (* Set Back of List to NIL *)
  link^.value := 0;       (* Set Link Value to 0 *)
  endd := link;           (* Set List ENDD pointer to Address of New Link *
end;
```
Fig. 2-58. Starting a linked list.

Of the three pointers, only the link pointer is assigned a space of memory with the new( ) function. Remember, this function allocates the memory specified in the record structure and assigns the address of that memory location to the link variable. When the start and endd pointers are assigned the address contained in the link pointer, they also point to the newly allocated record. Even though the list has only one element after this procedure is executed, it is the starting point for any list.

When using a single link list, it is unnecessary to know the location of the last element of the list. Regardless of the last element of the list, the list will always be searched from the start element until the last element points to a value of nil. The double link list requires the use of an end pointer, because elements point both backwards and forwards in the list. Depending on the method of searching the list, either the beginning or ending of the list may be used as the first element of a search.

Adding Elements to the List

After the list has been initialized, it will likely be extended by adding links. The addition process is essential to all list manipulations and dynamic memory allocation. In dynamic memory allocation, the program uses only as much memory as required to process data. In the program in FIG. 2-57, links were added to the list when a new variable was required to store data. The list could easily have been declared as an array of five elements. The use of a link list would allow the programmer to develop an application that could allow the user to enter the number of random numbers to generate. Based on that number, the program in FIG. 2-57 could generate as many random numbers as could be held in memory. An array would need to be predefined before the user could use it, necessarily limiting the number of random numbers that could be generated and stored in 56535 bytes of memory.

The procedure New_Link in FIG. 2-59 demonstrates the addition of a link to the link list at the end of the list. The addition could just as easily be in the middle or at the start of the list. Because this list is double linked, the addition procedure must point the last element of the list to the new link, point the new element to the previous last link, and point the endd pointer to the new end of the list.

```
Procedure New_Link;
begin
   new(link);                  (* Create New Link for List *)
   link^.front := nil;         (* Point the Front of New Link to NIL *)
   endd^.front := link;        (* Point the Front of Old End to New Link *)
   link^.back := endd;         (* Point the Back of New Link to Old End *)
   link^.value := 0;           (* Set New Link Value Link Value to 0 *)
   endd := link;               (* Set End of List Pointer to New Last Link *
end;
```
Fig. 2-59. Adding links to a linked list.

The addition of links to a link list is demonstrated in FIG. 2-60. The linking schemes are fairly straightforward, but usually require some contemplation. A simple analogy sometimes helps the thought process. Imagine adding a short piece of rope to the middle of a longer piece of rope. The long rope must first be severed. One end of the short rope is tied to the first piece of the severed rope. The other end of the short rope is tied to the second piece of the severed rope. The first piece of the severed rope is now connected to the middle piece and the middle piece to it. The second piece of the severed rope also points to the middle piece and the middle piece to it as well. The addition can be likened to the addition of a link to a list. The connections are established by placing the address of the "short rope" into the pointers of the "severed long rope." Similarly, the addresses of the severed pieces must be placed into the pointers of the newly added "short rope." Please take some time to consider the linking process.

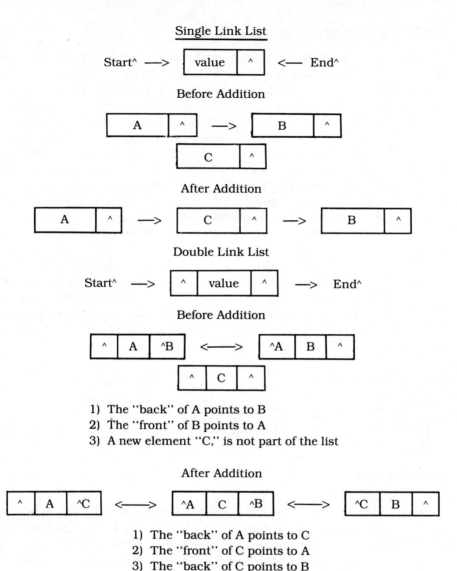

Fig. 2-60. Linking schematic for single and double link lists.

Manipulating Linked Lists

After a link list is created, and data is stored within its structure, the next logical step in a program is to manipulate the data. To retrieve the data, it is necessary to retrieve it from the linked list. As you have seen, single lists can be scanned in one direction, forward, while double linked lists may be scanned both forwards and backwards. The procedure in FIG. 2-61 demonstrates the retrieval of information from a double linked list of

```
Procedure Printout_Link_Values;
Var
   count : integer;
begin
   link := start;    (* Assign LINK Pointer to Beginning of List *)
   count := 0;

   (* While the current link points to another link perform the loop *)
   while (link^.front <> NIL) do
     begin
       count := count + 1;
       writeln('The value in link ',count,' is ',link^.value);
       link := link^.front;
     end;

   (* Printout the value contained in the last link of the chain *)
   count := count + 1;
   writeln('The value in link ',count,' is ',link^.value);
   writeln(' ');
end;
```

Fig. 2-61. Accessing and manipulating link list data.

records holding random numbers. The sequence numbers assigned to each random number output is related to the position of the record in the list rather than the actual data value held in the record.

Information is retrieved from each record in the list and output to the screen. The intermediate link pointer is repositioned in the output loop by setting the link pointer equal to the address value in the front pointer of the current record. If the front pointer in A points to B, and link points to A, then the assignment "link := link^.front;" causes the link pointer to point to B. The movement of the pointer is demonstrated in FIG. 2-62.

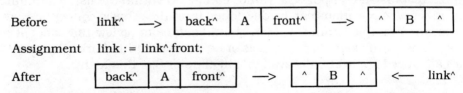

Fig. 2-62. Moving the pointer along the linked list.

The starting point of the list manipulation is always either the start or endd pointers which point to the beginning and end of the linked list. The ending point of the manipulation is the pointer that points to the nil value. This is a special value that is interpreted by Turbo Pascal as pointing to "nowhere" or "infinity." When a pointer contains this value, it has either not been assigned any memory address, or it has purposely been assigned the nil value to indicate the termination of a linked list of records. Remember, when the list was initialized the front and back pointers were purposely set to nil. When new links were added to the list, the back pointer of the new link was set to nil. The while..do loop in FIG. 2-61 performs as long as the current link^.front pointer is not nil.

Each of the individual components of linked list code is essential to the proper generating, maintenance and use of linked lists. After the components procedures are developed, a control procedure must be developed to exercise logical control over the linked list utilities. The control of these procedures to generate a dynamic list of random numbers is demonstrated in FIG. 2-63.

```
Begin (* Main Procedure *)
  (* Initiate the List *)
  Start_Link_List;
  link^.value := RANDOM(1000);
  Printout_Link_Values;

  (* Extend the List to Five Links, Assign Values and Display *)
  for counter := 1 to 4 do
    begin
      New_Link;
      link^.value := RANDOM(1000);
      Printout_Link_Values;
    end;
end.
```

Fig. 2-63. Controlling linked lists.

The first section of the code initiates the list and assigns a number to the value element of the first record. The output procedure is called and the contents of the current list are output to the screen. After initialization, the list is lengthened with the New_Link procedure and the list is then sent to the output procedure. Within the loop in the main section of the program, new records are added to the list and the list sent to the output procedure. As the list grows, the output procedure processes more and more records and outputs the values contained within the list. An infinite number of applications can be developed from these basic concepts. However, the examples in this section should suffice to review the concept of linked lists. An example of the uses of linked lists within Turbo Pascal and an advanced application is available in chapter 8 of this text.

DISCUSSION

The basic elements of the Turbo Pascal language are similar to those found in standard Pascal. However, Turbo Pascal through each of its versions has added to this set of elements. Turbo Pascal provides greater variety for data types and structures. Basic elements of the language such as "case" have been made more robust to allow for unanticipated comparison values.

In addition to these basic elements, Turbo Pascal provides device independent graphics and advanced debugging utilities. Direct access to operating system functions and direct hardware addressing are made easy. Finally, Turbo Pascal 5.5 supports Object Oriented Programming extensions for even more programming power. This chapter has reviewed the basics of Turbo Pascal. The following chapters will expand on this knowledge and introduce the advanced features.

3

The Turbo Pascal Environment Menu

This chapter reviews the Turbo Pascal version 5.0 and 5.5 development environment, and the Turbo Pascal Text Editor.

ENTERING TURBO PASCAL

You enter the version 5.0 integrated environment by typing TURBO ENTER at the DOS prompt. Once entered, the screen shown in FIG. 3-1 is displayed.

Figure 3-1 shows a screen comprised of four main parts: the main menu at the top of the screen, the edit window underneath the main menu, the message window, and the quick reference line at the bottom of the screen.

THE MAIN TURBO PASCAL MENU

The Turbo Pascal menu for version 5.0 contains seven main options: File, Edit, Run, Compile, Options, Debug and Break/Watch. These options may be selected in any of three ways. First, press the F10 key. This action will activate the menu line and allow you to use the LEFT and RIGHT arrow keys to highlight the desired option. Once the appropriate option is highlighted, press the ENTER key to execute that option.

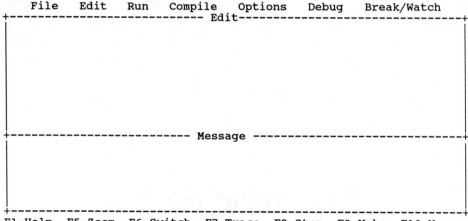

```
     File    Edit    Run    Compile    Options    Debug    Break/Watch
+---------------------------------- Edit-----------------------------------+
|                                                                          |
|                                                                          |
|                                                                          |
|                                                                          |
|                                                                          |
|                                                                          |
|                                                                          |
+------------------------- Message -------------------------+
|                                                                          |
|                                                                          |
|                                                                          |
|                                                                          |
|                                                                          |
|                                                                          |
+--------------------------------------------------------------------------+
 F1-Help   F5-Zoom   F6-Switch   F7-Trace   F8-Step   F9-Make   F10-Menu
```

Fig. 3-1. Opening Turbo Pascal screen.

The second way to select a menu option also begins by pressing the F10 function key. This time, however, instead of using the arrow keys, press the first letter of the option name and that option will be executed. For example if you wish to select the "File" submenu option, press F (in either upper- or lowercase).

The third method of selecting a menu option is by holding down the ALT key and the first letter of the main menu option. The advantage of this alternative is that it can be done directly from the editor without having to activate the menu with F10.

The File Menu

The File menu provides you with the ability to load previously created files, save new files, change the directory and perform other similar activities. Once selected, the File pull-down menu will be displayed. This submenu is shown in FIG. 3-2.

After the above submenu is displayed, the load option will be highlighted. Like the main Turbo Pascal menu, you may select an option on this menu by pressing the UP and DOWN arrow keys to highlight the appropriate option, and then pressing the ENTER key. Alternatively, also like the main menu, you may simply press the first letter of the option you desire and it will be executed. When looking at the File submenu, you will notice that the characters "F3" are on the same line as the word "load," "F2" is the next to "save" and "ALT-X" is next to "quit." These letters list the "hot" keys that may be used to execute that option without going through the menu structure. For example, if you wish to load a file, you may do so just by pressing the "F3" function key.

The Load Option   As explained above, the load option is executed by pressing L from the File menu, or by pressing the F3 function key. Once selected, the window in FIG. 3-3 will be displayed.

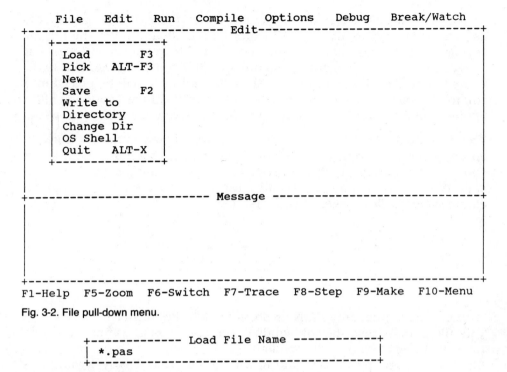

```
      File    Edit    Run    Compile   Options   Debug   Break/Watch
+-------------------------- Edit----------------------------------+
|  +---------------+                                              |
|  | Load      F3  |                                              |
|  | Pick   ALT-F3 |                                              |
|  | New           |                                              |
|  | Save      F2  |                                              |
|  | Write to      |                                              |
|  | Directory     |                                              |
|  | Change Dir    |                                              |
|  | OS Shell      |                                              |
|  | Quit   ALT-X  |                                              |
|  +---------------+                                              |
|                                                                 |
|                                                                 |
+-------------------------- Message ------------------------------+
|                                                                 |
|                                                                 |
|                                                                 |
|                                                                 |
|                                                                 |
+-----------------------------------------------------------------+
F1-Help  F5-Zoom  F6-Switch  F7-Trace  F8-Step  F9-Make  F10-Menu
```

Fig. 3-2. File pull-down menu.

```
      +------------- Load File Name ------------+
      | *.pas                                   |
      +-----------------------------------------+
```

Fig. 3-3. Load file option.

Once displayed, you have three options. First, you may press the ESC key to bring you back to the File menu. Second, you may enter the name of the file you wish to load and press the ENTER key. This action will read the named file from disk, load it into the Turbo Pascal editor and place you in edit mode. Lastly, if you just press the ENTER key without entering a file name, a window will be displayed containing a list of the files in the current directory. Once displayed, use the arrow keys to highlight the appropriate program name and press the ENTER key again. When pressed, the highlighted file will be loaded into the editor and you will be placed in edit mode.

The Pick Option   The Pick option is selected by pressing P from within the File menu, or by pressing the ALT-F3 hot key. Its purpose is to assist you in selecting the file to be loaded. This assistance is provided by displaying the names of the last seven files accessed during the current Turbo Pascal session. An example of this list is shown in FIG. 3-4.

```
      +------------- Recent Files --------------+
      | Prog1.pas                               |
      | Prog2.pas                               |
      | Prog2.pas                               |
      + -- Load File --                         +
      +-----------------------------------------+
```

Fig. 3-4. Recent files option.

Once the file list is displayed, you may either: press the ESC key to exit, use the arrow keys to highlight the appropriate file and press the ENTER key; or highlight and select the line "Load File." If you press ESC, you will be returned to the File menu. If you press ENTER while a filename is highlighted, that file will be loaded into the editor and you will be placed into edit mode. Lastly, if you press ENTER while the "load file" option is highlighted, a window is shown allowing you to enter any file name you wish.

The New Option This option's purpose is to allow you to stop working on the program currently being edited, clear the edit window, and begin entering a new program. When selected, one of two things will happen. If you are currently editing a file and have not saved it since last making changes, you will be asked if you wish to save that file, as shown in FIG. 3-5.

```
+----------------- Verify ----------------+
| c:\prog1.pas not saved. Save? (Y/N) _   |
+-----------------------------------------+
```

Fig. 3-5. New option verify example.

Once displayed, enter Y, N or press the ESC key. Entering Y will save your file on disk, clear the edit window, and place you in edit mode. Entering N will also clear the edit window and place you in edit mode, but the file that you were previously editing will not be saved. Lastly, if you press the ESC key, no action will be performed and you will be returned to the File menu.

The Save Option The Save option is used to save the file currently being edited to disk. When selected, if the file you are editing has a name, your program will be saved. If the program being edited has not yet been given a name, the window shown in FIG. 3-6 will be displayed.

```
+-------------- Rename Noname -------------+
| c:\noname.pas                            |
+------------------------------------------+
```

Fig. 3-6. Rename NONAME example.

Once the window is displayed, you may press ENTER to save your program under the default name of "noname.pas" or you may enter the appropriate filename and press ENTER.

The 'Write to' Option The 'Write to' option is executed by pressing a W from within the File menu. Its purpose is to save the program being edited under a different name. For example, if you wish to edit PROG1.PAS and place your modified program in PROG2.PAS, you could load PROG1. PAS using the Load option, make your changes, and then use the 'Write to' option to save your work under the name PROG2.PAS. Once selected, the window in FIG. 3-7 will be displayed.

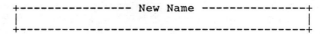

```
+---------------- New Name ----------------+
|                                          |
+------------------------------------------+
```

Fig. 3-7. Write to option example.

When displayed, you may either enter a valid file name or a directory wild card *.pas. If you enter a valid file name, the program will be saved under that name and you will be returned to the File menu. If you enter a directory wild card, a window will appear listing the names of the files that meet your wild card criteria, as well as all directories subordinate to the current directory. An example of this menu is shown below in FIG. 3-8.

```
+---------------------- C:\TP\*.PAS ----------------------+
|   prog1.pas   prog2.pas   prog3.pas   prog4.pas   prog5.pas |
|   prog6.pas   ..            .                             |
|                                                          |
|                                                          |
+--------------------------------------------------------+
```

Fig. 3-8. Example file list.

Using the arrow keys, move to the appropriate program name and press ENTER to select that file. If you wish to save your program to a file that is in a subdirectory, highlight the subdirectory name, and the files in that subdirectory will be displayed. Lastly, note that if you select the ''write to'' file in this manner, Turbo Pascal will ask you if you wish to overwrite the file because it already exists. If you wish to overwrite it, enter Y— if you don't, enter N.

The Directory Option   This option is similar to the DOS command DIR. Its purpose is to list the names of the files contained within your current directory. When selected, the window shown in FIG. 3-9 will be displayed.

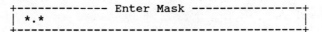

```
+------------- Enter Mask ----------------+
| *.*                                     |
+-----------------------------------------+
```

Fig. 3-9. Directory option example.

When displayed, you may either press ENTER to list all of the files in the directory, or enter the appropriate directory wild cards *.pas. Once the ENTER key is pressed, a window containing the selected file names will be displayed. This window is shown in FIG. 3-10.

If you have more file names than can fit in the window, you may see the remaining files by using the arrow keys to scroll the window up and down. Finally, when you are done reviewing the list of files, press the ENTER key and you will be returned to the File menu.

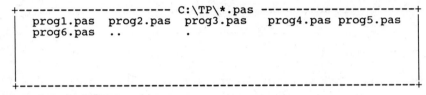

```
+------------------------ C:\TP\*.pas --------------------+
|   prog1.pas  prog2.pas  prog3.pas   prog4.pas prog5.pas |
|   prog6.pas  ..          .                              |
|                                                         |
|                                                         |
|                                                         |
+---------------------------------------------------------+
```
Fig. 3-10. Example file list.

The Change Option   The Change option allows you to change your current default directory, similar to the CD command in DOS. When selected, the window shown in FIG. 3-11 will be displayed.

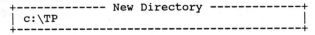

```
+------------- New Directory -------------+
|  c:\TP                                  |
+-----------------------------------------+
```
Fig. 3-11. Directory option example.

Contained within the window will be the current directory. If you wish to change the directory, enter the new name. If you wish to leave the current directory active, just press ENTER.

The OS Option   This option allows you to temporarily return to DOS without exiting Turbo Pascal. When selected, the screen will be cleared and you will be placed in DOS. When you wish to return to the Turbo Pascal environment, type EXIT at the DOS prompt.

The Quit Option   The Quit option may be executed via the File menu, or by pressing the ALT-X hot key, and is used to end your Turbo Pascal session and return you to DOS.

The Edit Option   This option exits you from the Turbo Pascal menu structure and places you in edit mode. The edit commands will be discussed later in this chapter.

The Run Menu

The Run menu provides the user with options for running the current program, as well as tracing through the program one line at a time to determine how specific instructions affect program execution. The Run menu is shown in FIG. 3-12.

The Run Option   This option allows the programmer to run the current program stored in the editor. As long as the selected program does not adversely affect the DOS operating environment, any bug-free program you write should run successfully within the Turbo Pascal environment. If a program is not previously compiled, this option will cause it to compile prior to any attempt at execution.

```
     File    Edit    Run    Compile    Options    Debug    Break/Watch
+-------------------------- Edit------------------------------------+
|                 +----------------------+                          |
|                 | Run            Ctrl-F9|                          |
|                 | Program reset  Ctrl-F2|                          |
|                 | Go to cursor      F4 |                          |
|                 | Trace into        F7 |                          |
|                 | Step over         F8 |                          |
|                 | User screen    Alt-F5|                          |
|                 +----------------------+                          |
|                                                                   |
|                                                                   |
|                                                                   |
|                                                                   |
+-------------------------- Message -------------------------------+
|                                                                   |
|                                                                   |
|                                                                   |
|                                                                   |
+-------------------------------------------------------------------+
 F1-Help  F5-Zoom  F6-Switch  F7-Trace  F8-Step  F9-Make  F10-Menu
```

Fig. 3-12. The "RUN" menu.

The "Program Reset" Option   When selected, this option tells the environment that you have completed debugging the current program. This option also frees up internal memory in case you wish to use the operating system Shell command in the File menu. The use of this option does not preclude you going back into the same program and debugging it again. The advantage of this option is the ability to reset debugging parameters in case the current trace is in an undesirable location in the current program.

The "Go to cursor" Option   This option repositions the editor pointer to where the tracing pointer is. This option allows you to modify code at the location where tracing indicates an unexpected result or difficulty. You may use this option to move current tracing and debugging around within the program.

The "Trace into" Option   This option causes the next command or statement within the current program to be executed. If screen output is created by the program, the output screen receives it. After the command is executed, the tracer pointer returns to the next statement in the current program. If the next step in the program is a reference to an external file or unit, the tracer pointer moves into the indicated procedure and will cause that file or unit to load into memory, if necessary.

The "Step over" Option   This option works similarly to the "Trace into" option except that procedures and functions are treated as single commands. After this command executes, the current point moves to the next statement in the program—or if a procedure is called, to the next statement after the procedure has been executed.

The "User screen" Option   This option causes the screen written to by your program during debugging to display on screen.

The Compile Menu

The Compile Menu is used to make .EXE files, link your programs, recompile all files associated with a program and specify a primary Pascal output file. When selected, the menu window in FIG. 3-13 is displayed.

```
   File    Edit    Run    Compile   Options   Debug   Break/Watch
+---------------------+---------------------------------+-----------+
|                     | Compile            Alt-F9       |           |
|                     | Make                 F9         |           |
|                     | Build                           |           |
|                     | Destinatione     Memory         |           |
|                     | Find Error                      |           |
|                     | Primary File                    |           |
|                     | Get Info                        |           |
|                     +---------------------------------+           |
|                                                                   |
+---------------------------- Message ----------------------------+
|                                                                   |
|                                                                   |
|                                                                   |
|                                                                   |
+-------------------------------------------------------------------+
F1-Help  F5-Zoom  F6-Switch  F7-Trace  F8-Step  F9-Make  F10-Menu
```

Fig. 3-13. Compile menu.

The Compile Option   This option causes the current source code file to be compiled into either a *memory program* capable of being run by Turbo Pascal from memory, or an *executable file* saved in an ".EXE" file on disk.

The Make Option   This option will call MAKE to compile and link your program. If no project "make" file is found, it will attempt to compile the program currently being edited. The name given to the .EXE file will be derived using the following criteria. First, it will try to use the name specified as the Primary File. If none is found, it will use the name of the file currently being edited.

The Build Option   This option causes all of the files specified in your project file to be recompiled even if their source code has not been modified.

The Designation Option   This option allows you to select the destination of the compiled code. The option includes compilation to memory, or .EXE file. Even if the program is compiled to memory, any recompilation of library files through the Build or Make options will be compiled to their .TPU files.

The Find Error Option   This option allows you to search the compiled code for an error discovered at run time. This option locates the run-time error, and places the user back into the editor with the file containing the editor. The editing cursor is placed at the detected location of the error.

The Primary File Option   The Primary option allows you to specify the name of the primary program being compiled. This option is helpful when you are working with a single Pascal program and you are trying to build and debug any include files or libraries. By entering the name of the Pascal program to be compiled, you may perform the compilation without creating a project file and without being forced to move the Pascal program into the edit window.

The Get Info Option   This option brings up an information status window displaying information about the file currently being edited. This information includes the file's name, size, the resulting .EXE file, and available memory on the machine as well as how the code is currently stored and any error messages.

The Options Menu

This menu allows for access to all of the options relating to compilation, environment, run-time parameters, and program options. The Option menu can be seen in FIG. 3-14.

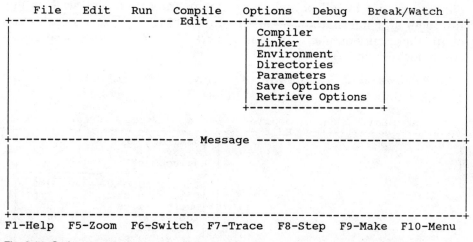

Fig. 3-14. Options menu.

The Compiler Submenu   This option allows you to modify the parameters that affect the way in which your compiled code will run. These options allow you to suspend certain data checks and invoke others. These options give you considerable flexibility in determining how certain aspects of your code will execute. You may choose whether error checking will be performed automatically or through error processing procedures that you might wish to write yourself. The compiler options are discussed in chapter 7 of the Turbo Pascal User's Guide for version 5.0, and Appendix B of the Turbo Pascal Reference Guide for version 5.0.

The Turbo Pascal compiler may be executed in one of several ways. First, through the Compiler menu previously discussed. The second way is by invoking the compiler by typing TPC at the DOS prompt. In addition, the ALT-F9 key combination will activate the compilation process. Regardless of how the compiler is called, the options available to you are the same.

The Linker Submenu   This submenu provides options for creating a map file of the compilation and linking process and a second option, "Linker Buffer" to indicate whether linking information should be stored to a file or in memory as the link is performed.

The "Map File" Suboption   When selected, a selection menu appears describing four options for a map file. These selections include Off, Segments, Publics, and Detailed. The Off option is a toggle which enables or disables the creation of a map file.

The other options can only be selected when the map file is enabled. When Segments is selected, only segment information, name, size, start segment and stop segment, and class information is incorporated into the map file. The Publics choice allows for all segment information as well as symbols, names, addresses and the program's entry points. The Detailed choice provides for all public and segment information as well as line numbers and information about module tables. For more information about these options please consult chapter 7 of the Turbo Pascal User's Guide for version 5.0.

The Environment Submenu   The Environment submenu is broken into six subtopics, and is displayed in FIG. 3-15.

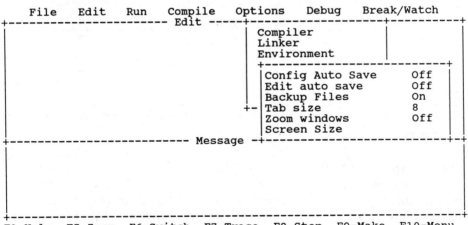

Fig. 3-15. Environment submenu options.

The "Config Auto Save" toggle. This option causes the current compiler and environment setting options to be saved whenever you exit the Turbo Pascal environment.

The "Edit Auto Save" toggle. This option causes Turbo Pascal to automatically save the contents of the current file when you select the Compile, Run or OS options. This toggle should be set with care also. Whenever you run a program, the current source code will be saved to a file. If you compile or run a program two times in succession, the contents of your backup file will be the current source code rather than the previously stored copy.

The "Backup Files" toggle. This option is a toggle that allows the user to enable or disable the saving of previous copies of the current file using the .BAK extension. When enabled, a backup file with a .BAK extension is created when the current file is saved. When disabled, no backup file is created.

The "Tab Size" selection. This option allows you to set the "hard tab" size for the editor from 2 to 16 characters. When in the editor, the "Auto Ident" option must be engaged by using the CTRL-OT command. This key sequence is discussed more fully later in this chapter.

The "Zoomed Window" toggle. This option allows you to turn the split Edit/Message screen on and off. If this option is turned off, you may use the split screen. If this option is turned on, you may only use the zoomed window format (the non-split screen).

The "Screen Size" selection. This option allows you to select how much information may be placed onto the screen at any given time. If you have an EGA or VGA display adapter on your computer, you may specify more than the 25 lines associated with a standard display. The EGA hardware allows for 43 lines to be displayed, while VGA provides 50 lines. The more lines you have displayed, the more information you can see at one time. This makes debugging easier because of the ability to see more of your program at a glance. However, the text for these display modes is smaller and might be more difficult to read.

The Directories Submenu The Directories submenu allows you to define where various portions of your programs, procedures, functions, library and object units are stored. The Directories submenu is shown in FIG. 3-16.

The Directory submenu enables the programmer to specify not only the location from which Turbo Pascal may load information, but also where it may save it.

The Turbo Directory. This directory is used by Turbo Pascal for configuration files, help files, and other associated maintenance files.

The "EXE & TPU" Directory. This directory is used to locate Turbo Pascal "EXE" and "TPU" files needed during compilation to a file, execution of the MAKE command, or execution of the BUILD command.

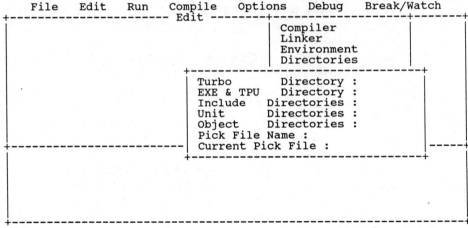

```
      File    Edit    Run    Compile   Options    Debug    Break/Watch
+------------------------ Edit --------+-------------------+-------+
|                                      | Compiler          |       |
|                                      | Linker            |       |
|                                      | Environment       |       |
|                                      | Directories       |       |
|                    +-----------------------------------------+   |
|                    | Turbo      Directory :              |   |
|                    | EXE & TPU  Directory :              |   |
|                    | Include    Directories :            |   |
|                    | Unit       Directories :            |   |
|                    | Object     Directories :            |   |
|                    | Pick File Name :                    |   |
+--------------------| Current Pick File :                 |------+
|                    +-----------------------------------------+   |
|                                                                  |
|                                                                  |
|                                                                  |
|                                                                  |
|                                                                  |
+------------------------------------------------------------------+
 F1-Help   F5-Zoom   F6-Switch   F7-Trace   F8-Step   F9-Make   F10-Menu
```

Fig. 3-16. The Directories submenu.

The Include Directory. This directory is used for your standard library procedures incorporated into your programs using the {$I} compiler directive. A procedure or function that you write, that may be used by more than one program and is stored in source code form, should be stored in this directory.

The Unit Directories. When you have begun to generate procedure and function units, this directory should be used to store them. Units are compiled sections of code that may be linked to your EXE program. Units are discussed in chapter 12 of the Turbo Pascal Reference Guide for version 5.0.

The Object Directories. This directory specifies in which files object code is stored. This directory option enables you to keep object, library and TPU files separate from each other.

The "Pick File Name" and "Current Pick File" options. The "Pick File Name" option allows you to select a specific Pick file and location. The "Current Pick File" option shows the current pick file, if any has been chosen.

The Parameters Option. This option allows you to pass command line arguments to your program, as if you were running the program from the DOS prompt.

The "Load Options" and "Save Options" Options. These options allow you to save and retrieve your previously entered option selections. These files include specific setup information about the Turbo Pascal Environment and any parameter selections you have made that affect it.

THE DEBUG AND BREAK/WATCH MENUS

Turbo Pascal version 5.0 development environment contains two Main Menu options used to control the functions of the integrated debugging utility.

The Debug Menu

This provides the user with a list of options for controlling the method by which the current program can be debugged. The options can be used to display information about the current program as it executes, as well as establish debugging parameters. (See FIG. 3-17.)

```
      File   Edit    Run    Compile   Options   Debug     Break/Watch
+--------------------- Edit --------+-------------------------++
|                                   | Evaluate       Ctrl-F4   |
|                                   | Call Stack     Ctrl-F3   |
|                                   | Find procedure           |
|                                   | Integrated Debugging  ON |
|                                   | Standalone Debugging  OFF|
|                                   | Display swapping    SMART|
|                                   | Refresh Display          |
|                                   +--------------------------+
|                                                              |
|                                                              |
+--------------------------------------------------------------+
|                                                              |
|                                                              |
|                                                              |
|                                                              |
|                                                              |
+--------------------------------------------------------------+
F1-Help  F5-Zoom  F6-Switch  F7-Trace  F8-Step  F9-Make  F10-Menu
```
Fig. 3-17. The Debug menu.

The Evaluate Option   This option is one of the most powerful and versatile of any debugging tool. This option allows the user to determine the value of a variable within the current program as it is executing. The advantage of this option is the ability to determine what values are present within a program without going through the cumbersome process of adding write and writeln statements to the program code.

This option can only be used when integrated debugging is enabled. In addition to displaying the value of a current variable, this option can also be used as an on-line calculator to determine the result of a numeric operation. By entering the equation 13*3 in the evaluation box, a value of 39 will be displayed.

This option normally defaults to the current point of the debugger. You may use the trace or step command to position the current pointer over a variable and then select Evaluate with the CTRL-F4 command to get the value of the variable indicated. Otherwise you may select the variable for evaluation by entering that variable's name within the evaluate box. This can be cumbersome, however, so I recommend the use of the current pointer and the CTRL-F4 command.

The "Call Stack" Option   This option displays the status of the stack at the point in the program indicated by the current pointer. This display includes all functions and procedures on the stack at the current position of the program, as well as parameters for each routine. This option cannot be used when debugging is disabled.

The "Find Procedures" Option   This option allows you to type in the name of a procedure or function. The current pointer is then moved to that location in the program. If the selected procedure is located in an include file or an external unit, these will be loaded as necessary to show the selected routine.

The "Integrated Debugging" Option   This option is a toggle which enables or disables integrated debugging and access to the debugging options described so far in this section. When this option is disabled and the Linker buffer has been placed in memory, ALL debugging tables are trashed and any memory they have occupied is returned to the heap. When the linker buffer has been placed on disk, this will not occur and more memory will be available for program compilation and execution.

The "Standalone Debugging" Option   When activated, this option causes debugging information to be included with the .EXE file created by the compilation of your program to disk. This option allows for debugging away from the Turbo Pascal integrated environment.

The "Display swapping" Option   This option allows the programmer to determine how display swapping will be accomplished. There are three possible states for this option: SMART, ALWAYS, and NEVER. This option allows for intelligent screen management when a program executes and displays information to the screen. In this mode, when a program displays information, the debugger swaps display screens so the information can be displayed, and then swaps back to the debugging screen. When this option is set to SMART, the swap only occurs when a display to the screen is requested. When this option is ALWAYS, a swap occurs regardless of screen display or not. In NEVER mode, this option disables swapping.

The Break/Watch Menu

This menu provides options to aide the programmer in establishing breakpoints in the current program at which debugging should occur. Breakpoints are tokens that indicate to the debugger that current execution should be temporarily suspended so that the user can examine the indicated section of code. The Break/Watch menu is shown in FIG. 3-18.

The first four options of this menu are related to a debugging utility called the *watch window*. Like the evaluate command in the Debug menu, the contents of this window are variables or expressions. The watch window allows you to constantly update any expressions within it based on those expressions within the program. Unlike Evaluate, Watch does not require you to continually reenter the variable name or expression to evaluate.

```
     File    Edit    Run    Compile    Options    Debug    Break/Watch
+--------------------------- Edit --------+-------------------------++
|                                         | Add Watch        Ctrl-F7 ||
|                                         | Delete Watch             ||
|                                         | Edit Watch               ||
|                                         | Remove ALL Watches       ||
|                                         |--------------------------||
|                                         | Toggle BreakPoint Ctrl-F8|
|                                         | Clear ALL Breakpoints    |
|                                         | View Next Breakpoint     |
|                                         +--------------------------+
|                                                                    |
|                                                                    |
|                                                                    |
+--------------------------------------------------------------------+
|                                                                    |
|                                                                    |
|                                                                    |
|                                                                    |
+--------------------------------------------------------------------+
```

F1-Help F5-Zoom F6-Switch F7-Trace F8-Step F9-Make F10-Menu

Fig. 3-18. The Break/Watch menu.

The "Add Watch" Option　　This option allows you to add a variable or an equation to the watch window. As more items are loaded into the watch window, it expands to accommodate them. If you are evaluating a large number of items, the size of the watch window can be modified through the installation program TINST, or you can simply scroll through it with the cursor keys.

The "Delete Watch" Option　　This option allows you to remove watched items from the watch window. When an item is removed, the watch window resizes to accommodate the remaining watched variables and expressions.

The "Edit Watch" Option　　This option allows you to modify an existing watched variable or expression.

The "Remove ALL Watches" Option　　This option clears the current watch window. After removal of all items, the watch window resizes and reduces to its minimum size.

The "Toggle Breakpoint" Option　　This option sets the line in the program indicated by the current pointer as a breakpoint. If the current line is already a breakpoint, this action will remove the breakpoint token.

The "Clear ALL Breakpoints" Option　　This option clears all assigned breakpoints for the current debugging session.

The "View Next Breakpoint" Option　　This option causes the current pointer to relocate to the next assigned breakpoint in the current program. If the current pointer is located at the last breakpoint in the file, it is reassigned to the first breakpoint. When activated, this option will search across include files, and external units if necessary, to bring up the next breakpoint.

The current version of Turbo Pascal provides a large number of hotkeys or shortcuts for execution of a specific task. The version 5.0 hotkeys are shown in FIG. 3-19.

Key(s)	Action
F1	Display the HELP Menu with context sensitive information
F2	Saves the current file in the editor
F3	Load a specified file into the editor
F4	Execute to current cursor location
F5	Zooms and reduces the current window
F6	Switches active window
F7	Traces into subroutines
F8	Steps over subroutine calls
F9	Execute a "MAKE"
F10	Place user in Main Menu
Alt-F1	Retrieve the last HELP menu displayed
Alt-F3	Display current PICK list
Alt-F5	Display saved screen
Alt-F6	Switches the active window
Alt-F9	Compile current program
Alt-F10	Display version screen
Alt-B	Activate BREAK/WATCH menu
Alt-C	Activate the COMPILE menu
Alt-D	Activate DEBUG menu
Alt-E	Activate EDITOR with current file
Alt-F	Activate FILE menu
Alt-O	Activate OPTIONS menu
Alt-R	RUN current program
Alt-X	Terminate Turbo Pascal and return to DOS
CTRL-F1	Gives help with editor
CTRL-F2	Terminate current debug session
CTRL-F3	Display call stack during debugging
CTRL-F4	Evaluate or modify variable
CTRL-F7	Add expression to watch window
CTRL-F8	Toggle break point
CTRL-F9	Run program
Shift-F10	Display version screen

Fig. 3-19. Version 5.0 Turbo Pascal HOTKEYS.

THE TURBO PASCAL TEXT EDITOR

The Turbo Pascal Text Editor allows the programmer to add, delete, or modify the source code of their program. These changes can be made through the use of editing commands which allow the programmer to move through the source code by character, by line or by entire screens. Changes can be made to characters, words, lines or specified sections of source code called *blocks*.

In addition to the add, delete and modify functions, the Turbo Pascal Editor allows the user to move text characters, lines, or blocks from one location in the source code to another. These cut-and-paste functions are usually reserved for word processors, but their availability with the editor enables the programmer to make major modifications to source code with a minimum of keystrokes. The Turbo Pascal Editor commands are displayed in FIG. 3-20.

Cursor Movement

Action	1st Way	2nd Way
Character left	Ctrl-s	Left arrow
Character right	Ctrl-d	Right arrow
Word left	Ctrl-a	Ctrl-Left arrow
Word right	Ctrl-f	Ctrl-Right arrow
Line up	Ctrl-e	Up arrow
Line down	Ctrl-x	Down arrow
Scroll up	Ctrl-w	
Scroll down	Ctrl-z	
Page up	Ctrl-r	PgUp key
Page down	Ctrl-c	PgDn key

Quick Movement

Action	1st Way	2nd Way
Beginning of line	Ctrl-q s	Home key
End of line	Ctrl-q d	End key
Top of edit window	Ctrl-q e	Ctrl-Home
Bottom of window	Ctrl-q x	Ctrl-End
Top of file	Ctrl-q r	Ctrl-PgUp
Bottom of file	Ctrl-q c	Ctrl-PgDn
Beginning of block	CTRL-q b	
End of block	Ctrl-q k	
Last cursor position	Ctrl-q p	

Insert and Delete Commands

Action	1st Way	2nd Way
Insert mode on/off	Ctrl-v	Ins key
Insert line	Ctrl-n	
Delete line	Ctrl-y	
Delete to end of line	Ctrl-q y	

Fig. 3-20. Version 5.0 Edit commands.

Delete character left	Ctrl-h	Backspace key
Delete character right	Ctrl-g	Del key
Delete word right	Ctrl-t	

Block Commands

Action	1st Way	2nd Way
Mark block - begin	Ctrl-k b	F7
Mark block - end	Ctrl-k k	F8
Mark single word	Ctrl-k t	
Copy block	Ctrl-k c	
Delete block	Ctrl-k y	
Hide/display block	Ctrl-k h	
Move block	Ctrl-k v	
Read block from disk	Ctrl-k r	
Write block to disk	Ctrl-k w	

Find and Replace Commands

Action	1st Way	2nd Way
Find	Ctrl-q f	
Find and replace	Ctrl-q a	
Repeat last find	Ctrl-l	

Miscellaneous Commands

Action	1st Way	2nd Way
Abort operation	Ctrl-u	
Autoindent on/off	Ctrl-o i	Ctrl-q i
Control character prefix	Ctrl-p	
Find place marker	Ctrl-q n	
Goto error position	Ctrl-q w	
Insert compiler directives	Ctrl-o o	
Invoke main menu	F10	
Load file	F3	
Optimal fill	Ctrl-o f	
Pair braces forward	Ctrl-o [	
Pair braces backward	Ctrl-o]	
Quit edit and not save	Ctrl-k d	Ctrl-k q
Restore line	Ctrl-q l	
Save and edit	Ctrl-k s	F2
Set place marker	Ctrl-k n	
Tab	Ctrl-i	Tab key
Tab mode	Ctrl-o t	Ctrl-q t
Unindent ON/OFF	Ctrl-o u	

"Fig. 3-20 continued."

The functions available in the Turbo Pascal Editor can be organized into five categories. These categories include: Cursor and Quick Movement, Insert/Delete, Block Functions, Search/Modify and Miscellaneous. There is one command that does not fall into these categories that is the most important editing command of all—how to get out of the editor.

End Edit - ^KD   The end edit command discussed previously is extremely important. It allows the user to successfully terminate execution of the editor and remain within the Turbo Pascal environment to either save, compile or run the program just edited. Without this function, no changes would ever be incorporated into a Turbo Pascal source code file. You can also use the F10 command to perform the same function as ^KD.

Cursor Movement

The indicator of the editing position within source code is called the *cursor*. The cursor can be modified in shape and display type, but it is usually represented by a flashing underline character. The cursor shows the programmer where insertion or deletion of characters will occur. It indicates where the beginning of a block may be placed as well as the end. The cursor is simply the position on the screen where everything happens. The following paragraphs are descriptions of commands that enable the programmer to move the cursor without modification of the source code.

The command descriptions of the cursor movement functions are interpreted as follows. The first word or two of the command description indicates the range or distance the cursor will move. The last word of the command description indicates the direction of the move. The command description is followed by the control key sequence causing the command to be executed.

Character Left - ^S   Allows the user to move the cursor one character position to the left of the current cursor position. This movement may also be accomplished using the LEFT cursor key on the numeric keypad of the keyboard. This cursor key will not work if the NUM LOCK key is activated.

Character Right - ^D   Allows the user to move the cursor one character position to the right of the current cursor position. This movement may also be accomplished using the RIGHT cursor key on the numeric keypad of the keyboard. This cursor key will not work if the NUM LOCK key is activated.

Word Left - ^A   Allows the user to move the cursor one word length to the left of the current cursor position. When called, this function positions the cursor underneath the first character of the current word, if not positioned there already. If the cursor is currently under the first character of the current word, it will be repositioned underneath the first letter of the word to the left of the current word.

Word Right - ^F   Allows the user to move the cursor one word length to the right of the current cursor position. When called, this function positions the cursor underneath the first character of the word to the right of the current word.

Line Up - ^E   Allows the user to move the cursor one line above the current line. This movement may also be accomplished using the UP cursor key on the numeric keypad of the keyboard. This cursor key will not work if the NUM LOCK is activated.

Line Down - ^X   Allows the user to move the cursor one line below the current line. This movement may also be accomplished using the DOWN cursor key on the numeric keypad of the keyboard. This cursor key will not work if the NUM LOCK key is activated.

Page Up - ^R   Allows the user to move the cursor one screen or 20 lines above the current line. If the line above the current line does not contain as many characters as the current line, the new character position becomes the end of the new line. This movement may also be accomplished using the PGUP key on the numeric keypad of the keyboard. This cursor key will not work if the NUM LOCK key is activated.

Page Down - ^C   Allows the user to move the cursor one screen or 20 lines below the current line. If the line below the current line does not contain as many characters as the current line, the new character position becomes the end of the new line. This movement may also be accomplished using the PGDN key on the numeric keypad of the keyboard. This cursor key will not work if the NUM LOCK key is activated.

Scroll Line Up - ^W   Allows the user to move the source code text up one line at a time while maintaining the position of the cursor on the display screen. This is an interesting function because it allows the user to scroll line by line through the source code while apparently maintaining the current cursor position.

Scroll Line Down - ^Z   Allows the user to move the source code text down one line at a time while maintaining the position of the cursor on the display screen. This is also an interesting function because it allows the user to scroll line-by-line through the source code, while apparently maintaining the current cursor position.

Beginning of Line - ^QS   Allows the user to move the cursor to the beginning of the current line. This movement may also be accomplished using the HOME key on the numeric keypad of the keyboard. This cursor key will not work if the NUM LOCK key is activated.

End of Line - ^QD   Allows the user to move the cursor to the end of the current line. This movement may also be accomplished using the END key on the numeric keypad of the keyboard. This cursor key will not work if the NUM LOCK key is activated.

Top of Screen - ^QE   Allows the user to move the cursor to the first character of the first line displayed on the screen.

Bottom of Screen - ^QX   Allows the user to move the cursor to the first character of the second-to-last line displayed on the screen.

Top of File - ^QR   Allows the user to move the cursor to the first character of the file. This corresponds to the first character of the first line of the file.

End of File - ^QC   Allows the user to move the cursor to the last character of the file. This corresponds to the last character of the last line of the file.

Last Cursor Position - ^QP   Allows the user to move the cursor back to the last position. This command reverses the most recent cursor movement, and returns the cursor to its previous position.

Insert/Delete Commands

Character Delete - ^D   Allows the user to delete the character directly above the cursor. The function may also be accomplished with the DEL key on the numeric keypad of the keyboard. This key will not work if the NUM LOCK key is activated.

Character Insert/Overwrite - ^V   Allows the user to choose between INSert and overwrite modes for text entry. Insert mode causes all text after the insertion point to move towards the end of the current line as text is inserted. Overwrite mode allows new text at the cursor location to replace old text as it is written. This command may also be executed using the INSert key on the numeric keypad of the keyboard. This key will not work if the NUM LOCK key is activated.

Word Delete - ^T   Allows the user to delete the current word. When the cursor is positioned below the first character of the word, the entire word is deleted. When the cursor is below a character other than the first, this command deletes all characters to the end of the word including the current character from the word.

Line Delete - ^Y   Allows the user to delete the current line. All characters will be deleted from the current line, including the carriage return and line feed characters. All text below the deleted line fills in the gap left after deletion.

To End or Line Delete - ^QY   Allows the user to delete all characters to the end of the current line, including the character under the cursor. This command does not cause the line below the current line to move up because no gap is created to occupy.

Insert Line - ^N Allows the user to insert a line at the current cursor location. All text on the current line is moved down to the next line. A new blank line appears at the current cursor position.

Block Commands

The *block* commands allow the user to mark a specific section of source code, and then manipulate it as a single entity. The user can copy a block, move it or delete it. A block may be copied into a separate source code file. In addition, a file may be copied into the source code as though it were defined as a block. These functions are usually reserved for more sophisticated word processing software. The addition of these functions to the Turbo Pascal editor makes it one of the most versatile text editors available.

Mark Block Begin - ^KB Allows the user to designate a specific location in the source code as the beginning of a block. When defining a block, the beginning must be defined before the end. Turbo Pascal does not support more than one marked block at a time.

Mark Block End - ^KK Allows the user to define a specific portion of the source code as block providing a Mark Block Begin command has been previously issued. The end mark of a block must come after the begin mark. A block will not be defined unless the end mark occurs later in the source code than the begin mark. Turbo Pascal does not allow more than one marked block at a time.

Mark Word - ^KT Allows the user to perform the Mark Block Begin and Mark Block End commands on a single word with one command. When the cursor is under a word, that word will be marked. If the cursor is under a space in the source code, then the word to the immediate left of the cursor position will be marked as a block. After this command is issued, all block commands are applicable to the block. Turbo Pascal does not allow more than one marked block at a time.

Copy Block - ^KC Allows the user to copy the contents of the currently defined block. The copy is written into the source code after the marked block. All subsequent copies are written to this location. Although the Turbo Pascal editor allows multiple copies of a block to be made, only one marked block may exist at one time.

Move Block - ^KV Allows the user to move a marked block to a location specified by the current position of the cursor. A block is marked using the Mark Block Begin and Mark Block End commands. The cursor is then positioned to a new location. When the Move Block command is called, the block is relocated to the portion of the source code starting at the new cursor position.

Delete Block - ^KY   Allows the user to delete an entire block of code. The user marks the section of code with the Mark Block Begin and Mark Block End commands. The user calls the Delete Block command the block is deleted and the void space filled as if Delete Line or Delete Character commands had been issued.

Read Block from File - ^KR   Allows the user to read source code into the current file from a second file. The user marks the location to start writing the contents of the file into the source code. Turbo then prompts the user for the name of the file with the "READ BLOCK FROM FILE:" question. The user enters the name of the file, and it is written into the source code at the specified location. Unlike the Block Move command, this function requires the user to mark the beginning of the new block location with the Mark Block Begin command.

Write Block to File - ^KW   Allows the user to create a file with a copy of the contents of the currently marked block. This command and the Read Block from File command form the basis for tremendous versatility of manipulation of source code libraries. Complex source code may be moved from one source file to another with only a few keystrokes.

Block Movement

In addition to the normal Turbo Pascal editor commands which allow for a variety of movements, there are some block-specific movements available. These commands allow the user to move directly to the beginning or ending mark positions of a block.

Move to Beginning of Block - ^QB   Allows the user to move the cursor to the beginning mark of the currently defined block.

Move to End of Block - ^QK   Allows the user to move the cursor to the beginning mark of the currently defined block.

Search/Modify Commands

Find Pattern - ^QF   Allows the user to specify a pattern of characters to search for in the current source code text. When the user selects this command, the FIND: question appears. The user enters the pattern to match.

Replace Pattern - ^QA   Allows the user to specify a pattern of characters and replace it with a second pattern. When the user calls the command, the FIND: questions appears. The user enters the pattern to find and replace. The REPLACE WITH: question appears and the user enters the pattern with which to replace the original pattern when found.

Repeat Last Find - ^L   Allows the user to repeat the last Find Pattern command. This command does not allow for any modification of the original search condition or options. It is a simple repeat of the most recently defined Find Pattern.

Miscellaneous Commands

Indentation On/Off - ^QI   Allows the user to set automatic indentation on or off. Automatic indentation causes the cursor to move to the same position on a new line as the first character on the line above. This is a handy feature for maintaining the indentation of statements within loops in source code.

Make a Control Character - ^P   Allows the user to enter control characters directly into source code rather than using the CHR( ) function to convert. The character is generated by pressing the CTRL and P keys simultaneously followed by the letter of the control character desired. To create a ''^L'' the user would press the CTRL and P keys followed by the L key. The value of this function is somewhat dubious because most general programmers would not place control characters in their source code. This causes programs to be less flexible if these characters are Hard Coded.

Restore Line - ^QL   Allows the user to recover the contents of a deleted line, provided the cursor has not been moved from this line. This lament function will not work if you move the cursor to a new line and then back to the original either. Earlier it was stated that the Delete Line command cannot be undone. This is still true because this Restore Line command does not work from anywhere other than the original deleted line.

Abort Operation - ^U   Allows the user to abort the current operation. This includes not only editing commands, such as Find Pattern and Replace Pattern, but also compilation or running of programs in the Turbo Pascal Environment.

DISCUSSION

A thorough knowledge of the editing commands is essential to efficient use of the editor. Until you are completely familiar with all of the editing commands, keep this chapter handy whenever you use The Turbo Pascal Editor.

4

BIOS and Direct Hardware Access

This chapter explains the capabilities of the Basic Input/Output System (BIOS) when accessed with the Turbo Pascal INTR( ) procedure. The user is exposed to system level software and hardware control procedures that enhance the capabilities of the Turbo Pascal development environment.

THE BASIC INPUT/OUTPUT SYSTEM

The Basic Input/Output System, or BIOS, is a layer of software programs running in between the hardware and higher level software on a computer. The BIOS is not read in from a floppy or hard disk. Instead, it is stored in ROM (Read Only Memory) chips which are built into your computer. By virtue of their position in the software layering scheme of the PC, these programs perform the basic functions required to move information from specific devices such as memory, keyboard, or screen to the CPU of the computer.

These programs allow applications such as spreadsheets and databases to open, read from and write to files. They allow graphics procedures to access individual video screen memory locations. Some applications incorporating copy protection use ROM-BIOS software to verify specific sectors on floppy and hard disks and thereby determine that they have not been illegally transferred. The ROM-BIOS services enable the Turbo Pascal user to address specific PC hardware.

Why Use ROM-BIOS?

Turbo Pascal is arguably the best PC Pascal compiler on the market today. Several hundreds of thousands of copies have been purchased. Realistically, there are probably twice as many unlicensed copies in circulation. Turbo Pascal enables the programmer to selectively supercede portions of both the BIOS and DOS Services. These capabilities are explained more fully in the latter portion of this chapter.

Version 5.5 provides graphics services for a wide range of adapters, and file attribute control. Through the use of ROM-BIOS, the user can create applications that make use of all 15 PC specified graphics modes available on the EGA, and even more modes on the new VGA and 8514 display adapters available for the PS/2. The ROM-BIOS services can be used to look into the machinery of the PC and retrieve information about specific equipment on board. The ROM-BIOS services can provide detailed information regarding the format of data on disks. The use of ROM-BIOS provides the programmer with a variety of additional options that are not directly supported by Turbo Pascal.

Most importantly, ROM-BIOS provides a standardized method of accessing PC hardware. International Business Machines (IBM) corporation has taken great pains to adhere to these specifications in as many of its PC models as possible. IBM, as well as other PC manufacturers, adheres to this standard because it enables software written for one PC model to work on other PC models. This is one of the main reasons that a PC standard exists today. It is particularly significant to this book, because if it did not exist, neither would Turbo Pascal, nor this text.

Accessing ROM-BIOS

The ROM-BIOS services are accessed through the Turbo Pascal INTR ( ) or Interrupt procedure. An interrupt is exactly what its name implies: An interrupt in the operation of the program currently running on the PC. This, however, is not a fatal interruption. Instead, during the interrupt, the computer performs a specified operation after which control of the PC returns to the calling program.

Calling an Interrupt

An interrupt is called by using the INTR( ) procedure and a special record structure. Figure 4-1 shows a sample program containing a call to the INTR( ) function and its interpretation.

```
Program Test_intr;
Var
  register : registers;
  number_printers, number_rs232, number_diskettes, video_mode : byte
  math_coprocessor, dma_controller, serial_printer, game_adapter : boole
  video_type : string[15];
  ah, al : byte;

Begin
  with register do
    begin
      INTR($11, register);   (* Interrupt $11 hex (17 decimal) *)
      ah := hi(ax);
      al := lo(ax);
      if ((al AND 1) = 1) then
        number_drives := ((al AND 192) shr 5)
       else
        number_drives := 0;
      math_coprocessor := ((al AND 2) = 2);
      video_mode := ((al AND 48) shr 3);

      dma_controller := ((ah AND 1) = 1);
      number_rs232 := ((ah AND 14) shr 1);
      game_adapter := ((ah AND 16) = 16);
      serial_printer := ((ah AND 32) = 32);
      number_printers := ((ah AND 192) shr 5);
    end;

  writeln('Available disk(ette) drives : ',number_drives);
  writeln('A math coprocessor is installed : ',math_coprocessor);

  case (video_mode) of
      1 : video_type := '40x25 Color';
      2 : video_type := '80x25 Color';
      3 : video_type := '80x25 Monchrome';
    end;

  writeln('Start up video mode : ',video_type);
  writeln('A DMA controller is installed : ',dma_controller);
  writeln('Available RS-232 Ports : ',number_rs232);
  writeln('A game adapter is installed : ',game_adapter);
  writeln('A serial printer is installed : ',serial_printer);
  writeln('Available printers : ',number_printers);
end.
```

Fig. 4-1. Equipment list interrupt call.

The program makes use of the "registers" variable type to retrieve information from 16-bit "word" and 8-bit "byte" systems. The information returned by the second program in FIG. 4-1 could also be generated directly by Turbo Pascal using basic language elements. For an example of this, run the BGIDEMO.PAS program supplied with the Turbo Pascal version 5.0 and 5.5 distribution diskettes.

The register variable is a record structure used by the BIOS and the MSDOS services. It is a standard record structure employed by the hardware of PC and PS/2 computers running MS-DOS. When an interrupt is called, these variables either contain information read by the computer, or receive information and make it available to the program calling the interrupt. As you can see, the version 5.5 record structure is variant depending on the variable "integer." On 16-bit systems, the register is composed of integer or word values as specified in the 0 case. When Turbo Pascal runs on 8-bit systems, the register is composed of byte values. The integer variable is defined by Turbo Pascal version 5.5 at the startup of your program. After initialization, your programs will automatically make use of the proper record format.

The program in FIG. 4-1 calls the BIOS equipment listing service that allows the user to determine what equipment is on board as well as the quantities of that equipment. This particular interrupt also gives the programmer valuable information about the type of video adapter on board, as well as game adapters. The method of interpretation of the information returned by this interrupt is based on a bit map of the AX variable declared in the REGISTERS variable.

The Equipment Services interrupt is called using the value of $11 (hexadecimal) or 17 (decimal). During the call, bit encoded information about the onboard equipment is placed into the AX variable of the REGISTER record variable. The information about the on board equipment was placed into this position by DOS when the computer booted. The AX variable is an integer and can therefore be split up into two bytes (AH and AL) that may be interpreted separately. The interpretation of the bytes is shown in FIG. 4-2.

The AH and AL bytes of the AX portions of the register are both used to report the high and low bytes of the register "integer" or "word." Further interpretation of various bits is accomplished through the use of programming methods to convert the bit information into meaningful data. For the purposes of many of the interrupts, you might want to convert the returned information into either a number or a Boolean value. The program in FIG. 4-1 demonstrates that a byte value can be made to generate a Boolean or numeric value by the use of the AND, SHR and = operators. These are extremely powerful because they allow the user not only to evaluate a condition, but also to change the condition for more convenient evaluation. In the case of the detection of the number of drives available, the program made use of all of these operators. Figure 4-3 demonstrates the use of all of these operators in the determination of the number of disk-(ette) drives available on a PC.

The original AX integer value is broken down into its component byte values. This can be done with any returned integer from an interrupt. It enables the user to recover and evaluate information more readily. High order bytes (8 to 15) are placed into the AH variable, and low order bytes (0 to 7) are placed into the AL variable.

You might want to determine the number of disk drives on board the computer. Because you are only interested in specific bits of each byte, you might wish to eliminate extraneous bit values from consideration. This is accomplished through the use of the AND operator. In FIG. 4-1 you can see how information is selectively eliminated in the line "number_drives := ((al AND 192) shr 5)." The number 192 corresponds to the value of the byte

15	14	13	12	11	10	9	8	7	6	5	4	3	2	1	0	(dec)	
F	E	D	C	B	A	9	8	7	6	5	4	3	2	1	0	(hex)	
1	1	0	0	0	0	0	0	0	0	0	0	0	0	0	0		Number of Printers 00 = 0, 01 = 1, 10 = 2, 11 = 3
0	0	1	0	0	0	0	0	0	0	0	0	0	0	0	0		1 - Serial Printer Installed
0	0	0	1	0	0	0	0	0	0	0	0	0	0	0	0		1 - Game Adapter Installed
0	0	0	0	1	1	1	0	0	0	0	0	0	0	0	0		Number of RS-232 Ports 000 = 0, 001 = 1, 010 = 2, 011 = 3, 100 = 4, 101 = 5, 110 = 6, 111 = 7
0	0	0	0	0	0	0	1	0	0	0	0	0	0	0	0		0 - DMA Chip Installed
0	0	0	0	0	0	0	0	1	1	0	0	0	0	0	0		Number of Diskette Drives 00 = 0, 01 = 1, 10 = 2, 11 = 3
0	0	0	0	0	0	0	0	0	0	1	1	0	0	0	0		1 - Initial Video Mode 01 = 40 × 25 Color 10 = 80 × 25 Color 11 = 80 × 25 Monochrome
0	0	0	0	0	0	0	0	0	0	0	0	1	1	0	0		System Ram 00 = 16k, 01 = 32k, 10 = 48k, 11 = 64k
0	0	0	0	0	0	0	0	0	0	0	0	0	0	1	0		1 - Not Used
0	0	0	0	0	0	0	0	0	0	0	0	0	0	0	1		1 - Disk Drives Present

Fig. 4-2. Interpretation of bit code for equipment service interrupt.

```
if ((al AND 1) = 1) then
   number_drives := ((al AND 192) shr 5);
else
   number_drives := 0;
```
Fig. 4-3. The use of "AND," "SHR" and "=" operators.

if bits 6 and 7 were the only bits with value 1. The construct "(al AND 192)" returns the value 1 in bit positions 6 and 7 if their original values have been 1. Because the number 192 evaluates to the bit positions 0 to 5 containing 0, then the result of the operation will yield values of 1 for bit positions 6 and 7 if they contained that value initially.

From the bit map of the Equipment Services interrupt, you can see that bits 6 and 7 of AX combine to tell you how many disk drives are available. These bits correspond to bits 6 and 7 of AL. Positions 6 and 7 of a byte correspond to the decimal values 64 and 128, respectively. If you took these values without manipulation, you would have either 0, 64, 128, or 192 disk drives available on your PC. If you interpret these bits as bits 0 and 1 of the byte, then you get combinations of 0, 1, 2 and 3 for the number of disk drives. How do you move these bits? You can use the SHR function.

The SHR function allows you to shift the bits of a byte to the right (towards the lower order). An SHR shift of 5 places the original values of bits 6 and 7 into bit positions 0 and 1, respectively. The value of the AL byte after this shift can be placed directly into an output variable and will correspond to the actual number of disk drives available.

You can also use the AND and = operators to return Boolean values when necessary. In FIG. 4-4 you can see how a Boolean value can be generated from the evaluation of a single bit.

```
math_coprocessor := ((al AND 2) = 2);
```

Fig. 4-4. Use of the AND and " = " operators for individual bit evaluation.

The value of bit 1 of the AL variable is combined with value 2 using the AND operator. The value 2 corresponds to bit 1 of a byte having the value 1 and all other bits having the value 0. If the value of bit 1 of AL is 1, then the result of the operation will be bit 1 having value 1—otherwise 0. The logical construction asks whether the result of the AND operation between two "bytes" is the value 2. If the value of bit 1 of AL was 1, then the logical operation will evaluate to TRUE. If bit 1 of AL was not set to 1, then the logical operation evaluates to FALSE.

These examples form the basis of any programmer's method of evaluating information returned from the interrupt services. Just as important, however, is that they represent the basis for evaluating individual bits of any integer or byte variable. This type of bit-by-bit evaluation enables advanced programmers to generate encrypted code, graphical functions, or perform mathematical evaluations of phenomenal complexity. Remember, the byte is the basic memory storage unit upon which all data types are built. If you can manipulate the internal values of this memory unit directly, your ability to control the computer increases greatly.

VIDEO SERVICES INTERRUPTS

Besides retrieving information from the computer, the interrupts may also be used to send information. This capability is most easily demonstrated when you make use of the Video Services ($10 hex, 16 decimal). The ROM-BIOS video services enable the user to go far beyond the video modes offered in version 5.5 of Turbo Pascal. If you have a VGA board, you can write programs that take advantage of resolution such as $640 \times 350 \times 4$-colors, $640 \times 480 \times 16$-colors or even $320 \times 200 \times 256$-colors. This exercise demonstrates some of the power of the BIOS interrupts. You can create graphics programs that are universal to the PC environment without depending upon the use of Turbo Pascal graphics commands. In short, you can generate a complete graphics command library that can make use of ALL of the current and future video modes that are supported by PC compatibles, and PS/2 and compatible computers.

The available video services and their corresponding interrupt numbers are shown in FIG. 4-5.

Service		Action
Dec	Hex	
0	0	Select the Video Mode
1	1	Set Cursor Size
2	2	Set Cursor Position
3	3	Get Cursor Position
4	4	Get Light-Pen Position
5	5	Select Active Display Page
6	6	Scroll Window Up
7	7	Scroll Window Down
8	8	Get Character and Attribute
9	9	Write Character and Attribute
10	A	Write Character
11	B	Set Color Palette
12	C	Write Pixel
13	D	Read Pixel
14	E	Write Character as TTY
15	F	Get Current Video Mode

Fig. 4-5. Video services interrupts.

These video services ($10 hex, 16 decimal) enable you to control the display on your computer in both text and graphics mode. You can select colors, or black and white. You can generate memory screens that contain a full 25 lines of text, and have them display instantaneously by selecting the active display page. Rather than being limited to $320 \times 200 \times 4$-colors or shades and $640 \times 200 \times 2$-color graphics, you can explore higher resolution and greater color through pixel graphics manipulation. The video services are only a small part of the capability of the ROM-BIOS services, but a representative one.

Video Service 0 - Set Video Mode

The Set Video Mode subservice of the ROM-BIOS video services provides the Turbo Pascal programmer with the capability to select from all available video modes, rather than those provided by Turbo Pascal. This capability is particularly valuable when the programmer has a Virtual Graphics Array (VGA) or an Enhanced Graphics Adapter (EGA) on board rather than the standard Color Graphics Adapter (CGA). Any mode accessible with a CGA can be found in an EGA. Any mode accessible with a CGA or EGA can be found in a VGA. The additional modes available with an EGA or VGA, however, provide greater resolution as well as a greater

Video Mode	Dimensions	Adapter
0	40 × 25 Black and White Text	CGA, EGA and VGA
1	40 × 25 × 16 Color Text	CGA, EGA and VGA
2	80 × 25 Black and White Text	CGA, EGA and VGA
3	80 × 25 × 16 Color Text	CGA, EGA and VGA
4	320 × 200 × 4 Color Graphics	CGA, EGA and VGA
5	320 × 200 × 4 Shade Graphics	CGA, EGA and VGA
6	640 × 200 × 2 Color Graphics	CGA, EGA and VGA
10	640 × 200 × 64 Color	EGA and VGA
13	320 × 200 × 16 Color	EGA and VGA
14	640 × 200 × 16 Color	EGA and VGA
15	640 × 350 × 16 Color	EGA and VGA
16	640 × 480 × 2 Color	VGA
17	640 × 480 × 16 Color	VGA
18	320 × 200 × 256 Color	VGA

Fig. 4-6. BIOS video modes available from CGA, EGA and VGA graphics adapters.

variety of color. The standard video modes and the adapters supporting them are listed in FIG. 4-6.

Figure 4-6 shows only those modes supported by CGA, EGA, and VGA graphics adapters. Mode 7 is 80 × 25 black and white monochrome text, and is only supported through Monochrome and Hercules adapters. Modes 8 and 9 are available on the adapter for the discontinued PCjr, and the Tandy line of color and PC compatible computers. Modes 11 and 12 are reserved for use with later versions of PC display adapters.

Listed with these modes are the entirely new set of modes available with the Personal System 2 computers recently made available from International Business Machines. The model 50, 60, 70 and 80 incorporate a VGA adapter board that provides extremely high resolution with up to 256 colors displayed simultaneously. The PS/2 line of computers also support the 8514 adapter and monitor which can provide resolution of 1024 × 768 × 256-colors. The 8514 adapter and monitor are supported with version 5.5 of Turbo Pascal. A listing of these modes is available in the Turbo Pascal User's Guide and the Reference Guide for version 5.5.

How are these modes called? If you recall from the demonstration program in FIG. 4-1, the number of the ROM-BIOS service is placed into the first argument position of the interrupt call, and the REGISTER variable is placed into the second argument slot. The number of the subservice, in this case 0, is placed into the high order bit of the AX portion of the REGISTER variable. The desired video mode is placed into the low order byte of the AX variable. A typical mode selection is shown in FIG. 4-7.

It is important to note that each time the video mode is reset, the screen is cleared and the contents of the screen are lost. Use this proce-

Fig. 4-7. A typical video mode selection procedure utilizing the INTR( ) interrupt procedure.

```
Procedure Set_Video_Mode(mode : byte);
Var
   register : registers;
   ah, al : byte;
Begin
   ah := 0;
   al := mode;
   with register do
      begin
         ax := (ah shl 8) + al;
         INTR($10, register);
      end;
end;
```

dure wisely in your programs. If you change the video mode too often you will frustrate your users greatly. Finally, on some computers this mode change causes a short, but noticeable, delay. If you decide to use this method to clear your display, be aware of this fact.

Video Service 1 - Set Cursor Size

This subservice allows the user to modify the size of the cursor on your video screen. The user places the video service number into the high order byte of the AX portion of the REGISTER variable. The starting scan line of the cursor is placed into the high order byte of the CX portion of the REGISTER variable, and the ending scan line of the cursor is placed into the low order byte of CX. The values for the scan line can range from 0 to 7 with a CGA adapter, and 0 to 13 with an EGA and VGA.

The programmer can make the cursor disappear by setting bit 5 of the high order byte of CX to 1. This is done automatically when you select a graphics mode, but it can be implemented in text modes to eliminate a distracting, flashing cursor. The usefulness of this subservice is questionable at best. However, if it's there, some programmer will likely make use of it.

Video Service 2 - Set Cursor Position

For the experienced programmer who wishes to have the user enter a value at a specific location, this subservice is extremely useful. Specific entry screens such as Form Entry Screens benefit immensely from this subservice. This procedure also opens up the possibilities of multiple screen entry in text modes. When the programmer uses this subservice, he specifies the row and column of the placement of the cursor, as well as the video page into which the cursor will be placed.

In standard text mode, the user has 80×25 characters in a variety of color combinations. A full screen of characters represents 2000 bytes of memory. In addition, another 2000 bytes is used to hold color and additional attribute information. This means that a text screen at most requires 4000 bytes of memory. Video modes 0 to 3 and 7 allow the user to specify which page of video memory to set the cursor. For the 40 column modes, there are eight pages of memory available numbered from 0 to 7. For the 80 column modes, there are four pages of memory numbered from 0 to 3.

Figure 4-8 shows a typical cursor placement using this interrupt.

```
Procedure Set_Cursor(row,col,page : byte);
Var
   register : registers;
   dh,dl : byte;
Begin
   dh := row;
   dl := col;
   with register do
     begin
       ax := (2 shl 8) + 0;
       bx := (page shl 8) + 0;
       dx := (dh shl 8) + dl;
       INTR($10, register);
     end;
end;
```

Fig. 4-8. A typical cursor placement procedure using the INTR( ) interrupt procedure.

The DX portion of the REGISTER variable holds the position of the cursor. The high order byte of BX holds the page number onto which the cursor will be placed. The high order byte of AX, as usual, holds the value of the subservice number to be called by the video services interrupt.

Video Service 3 - Read Cursor Position

This video service allows the programmer to obtain information about the current cursor position and size from the computer. Information is received into the various portions of the REGISTER variable as it was sent using Video Services 1 and 2. The current page number is returned into the high order byte of the BX portions of the REGISTER variable. The current row number and column number are returned in the high and low order bytes, respectively, of DX. The starting and ending scan lines of the cursor are returned into the high and low order bytes, respectively, of CX. A typical decoding procedure for this video service is shown in FIG. 4-9.

In the video service call to set the cursor size, the size of the cursor was specified in the CX portion of the REGISTER variable. In the video service call to set the cursor position, it was specified in CX and the page number in the high order byte of BX. As you can see in FIG. 4-9, the placement of information is uniform for most interrupts, whether they are sending or receiving information.

Video Service 4 - Read Light Pen Position

At this time, the validity of this utility is somewhat in question. I have never used this interrupt, and I would not presume to present information about a topic for which I have no familiarity. It might be worth noting that

```
Procedure Get_Cursor;
Var
   register : registers;
   bh,bl,ch,cl,dh,dl : byte;
Begin
   with register do
     begin
       ax = (3 shl 8) + 0;
       INTR($10, register);
       bh := hi(bx);
       ch := hi(cx);
       cl := lo(cx);
       dh := hi(dx);
       dl := lo(dx);
     end;

   writeln('Current page number : ',bh);
   writeln('   Cursor starting scan line : ',ch);
   writeln('   Cursor ending scan line   : ',cl);
   writeln('   Cursor row (in characters) : ',dh);
   writeln('   Cursor col (in characters) : ',dl);
end;
```

Fig. 4-9. A typical cursor information retrieval procedure using the INTR( ) interrupt procedure.

with the advent of pointer devices such as the mouse, track ball, and joystick, the use of light pens has decreased dramatically. Along with devices such as touch-screens, light pens have an inherent inexactness for keeping track of and reporting positions. These services might be included in future versions of ROM-BIOS, but most pointer devices now have their own memory-resident device drivers and do not make use of this interrupt.

Video Service 5 - Set Active Display Page

As discussed for video service 2, additional display screens exist in video memory that allow the user to generate more than a single page of text at any given time. The ability to select the active display page is provided by video service 5. As usual, the video service number is placed in the high order byte of the AX portion of the REGISTER variable. The number of the desired display page is placed into the low order byte of AX. A typical page selection procedure is shown in FIG. 4-10.

Fig. 4-10. A typical page selection procedure using the INTR( ) interrupt procedure.

```
Procedure Set_Page(page : byte);
Var
   register : registers;
   ah, al : byte;
Begin
   ah := 5;
   al := page;
   with register do
     begin
       ax := (ah shl 8) + al;
       INTR($10, register);
     end;
end;
```

The programmer should make certain which display pages contain which information. There is no interrupt which retrieves the current display page directly. For video modes 0 and 1 there are eight available display pages number 0 to 7. For video modes 2, 3 and 7 there are four available display pages numbered 0 to 3.

Video Services 6 and 7 - Window Scrolling

These video services are particularly useful for creating a scrolling window effect with a portion of the display screen. Turbo Pascal incorporates window definition procedures, which allow insert and deletion of lines within these windows or for the entire screen. The reader is encouraged to look through the WINDOW.PAS program included in his Turbo Pascal disk to find out more about these procedures.

These services differ only in the direction in which they move the selected portion of the screen. Video service 6 causes the specified window to scroll up, but service 7 causes the selected window to scroll down. The arguments for these functions and their meanings are shown in FIG. 4-11.

Argument	Contents
AH	Video service number
AL	Number of lines to scroll
BH	Display attribute for blank lines
CH	Top row of scrolling window
CL	Left column of scrolling window
DH	Bottom row of scrolling window
DL	Right column of scrolling window

Fig. 4-11. Argument lists for video services 6 and 7.

When you scroll a window, you will likely wish to replace the newly created blank lines with predefined text. Because you had previously specified the outline of the window to the scrolling functions, you can simply reset the cursor to the new line's location using either the interrupt procedure or the Turbo Pascal GOTOXY( ) procedure. There really is no right or wrong way to use the interrupt functions in place of predefined Turbo Pascal procedures. In most cases, the Turbo procedures call these very same interrupts. The main difference is speed of execution. Remember, your program is written in Turbo Pascal, and the Turbo Pascal function is written in either the C or assembly language. The difference in the speed of execution can substantially favor the Turbo Pascal function. If you want more control over what is actually happening inside the computer, you might wish to use the interrupt call. The choice with any program you write is, as always, up to you.

Video Service 8 - Read Character

This procedure is particularly interesting in that it provides the user with the capability to store information in a display screen rather than a declared variable. The read character video service allows the programmer to retrieve information about a character from both text and graphics screens. A sample procedure that uses this interrupt is shown in FIG. 4-12.

```
Procedure Get_Character(X,Y,page : byte;
                        var character : char;
                        var attribute : byte);
Var
  register : registers;
  ah,al,bh,bl,ch,cl : byte;
Begin
  (* Set the cursor to the desired location *)
  bh := page;
  dh := Y;
  dl := X;
  with register do
    begin
      ax := 2 shl 8;
      INTR($10, register);
    end;

  (* Read the character at the current cursor location *)
  with register do
    begin
      ax := 8 shl 8;
      INTR($10, register);
      character := chr(lo(ax));
      attribute := hi(ax);
    end;
end;
```

Fig. 4-12. A typical read character procedure using the INTR( ) interrupt procedure.

The procedure defined in FIG. 4-12 demonstrates the combination of two interrupts to supply information about a specific area of the computer. The read character video service retrieves information about the current position pointed to by the cursor. The advantage of the procedure displayed above is the capability to specify, to a single procedure, all of the requirements of information retrieval, and to have it return the character at the specified position. This procedure is not part of the Turbo Pascal library, but should have been included.

The interrupt procedure not only retrieves information about the character displayed in a text mode, but also in graphics mode as well. This enables the programmer to detect recognizable characters on any video screen supported by the ROM-BIOS video service 0. The advantages of standardized BIOS interrupt services have become important to systems and applications programmers because of this capability to write one set of code for a variety of equipment.

Video Service 9 - Write Character

This service allows the programmer to generate one of more copies of a character starting at a specified cursor location and written to the screen with a display attribute. Display attributes include high or low intensity, reverse video or blinking text. For color text mode, this attribute also includes the foreground color of the character. The sample program in FIG. 4-13 demonstrates the use of this interrupt.

```
Program Write_Character(X,Y : byte;
                        character : char;
                        attribute,page,copies : byte);
Var
  register : register;
  ah,al,bh,bl,cj,cl,dh,dl byte;
Begin
  (* Set current cursor position to specified location *)
  bh := page;
  dh := Y;
  dl := X;
  with register do
    begin
      ax := 2 shl 8;
      dx := (dh shl 8) + dl;
      bx := bh shl 8;
      INTR($10, register);
    end;

  (* Write specified character to current cursor location *)
  ah := 9;
  al := character;
  bl := attribute;
  with register do
    begin
      ax := (ah shl 8) + al;
      bx := (bh shl 8) + bl;
      cx := copies;
      INTR($10, register);
    end;
end;
```

Fig. 4-13. A typical character writing procedure using the INTR( ) interrupt procedure.

For the write character procedure, the lower order byte of the AX portion of the REGISTER variable contains the character to be written to the screen. The lower order portion of BX holds the display attribute or color of the character. If the specified color has a value greater than $80 hex (128 decimal) then the specified attributes will be combined with the existing colors at that location in a manner consistent with the XOR bitwise operator.

The high order byte of BX holds the value of the page number to which the character will be written. This number is set to 0 in graphics modes. The CX variable is used for direct transfer of the number of copies of the character that should be written. In text mode, the character will wrap from line to line, if that many copies are specified. In graphics mode, no line wrap will occur.

Video Service 10 - Write Character

There is some redundancy in the ROM-BIOS system which provides two similar functions: Video services 9 and 10. There is no effective difference between these services, except that service 9 can specify a change in character color in text and graphics mode, and service 10 only affects graphics modes. The logic behind having both functions is elusive.

Video Service 11 - Set Color Palette

Turbo Pascal version 3.0 has a PALETTE( ) procedure that is limited to the selection of colors for the $320 \times 200 \times 4$-color graphics mode. It also allows the user to select the foreground color for $640 \times 200 \times 2$-color graphics. The "set palette" video service enables the user to specify these as well as palette selections required in higher video modes. Turbo Pascal version 5.5 offers superior palette selection capabilities with the SET-PALETTE( ) procedure described in the User's Guide. A BIOS based palette selection procedure is shown in FIG. 4-14.

```
Procedure Set_Palette(palette, color : byte);
Var
  register : registers;
  bh, bl : byte;
Begin
  bh := palette;
  bl := color;
  with register do
    begin
      ax := 11 shl 8;
      bx := (bh shl 8) + bl;
      INTR($10, register);
    end;
end;
```

Fig. 4-14. A typical palette setting procedure using the INTR( ) interrupt procedure.

The palette procedure places the value of the palette type selected into the high order byte of the BX portion of the REGISTER variable. The low order byte of BX is used for the color or palette determination based on the value of the high order byte. In text modes, if BH is set to 0 then BL is interpreted as the color of the border around the text area. In graphics modes, if BH is 0 then BL specifies the background color as well as the border color. In graphics modes, if BH is set to 1, then BL is used to identify the palette to be used.

Video Services 12 and 13 - Write and Read Pixel Dot

Originally, Turbo Pascal had the capability to read and write pixel information to three of the seven graphics modes supported by the Enhanced Graphics Adapter. If only these modes were required, then this section would not be necessary. However, since the advent of EGA and

VGA boards and graphical interfaces, this repertoire of graphics modes has been extensively expanded. These BIOS subservices can provide for graphics in modes not supported by the Turbo Pascal 5.5 drivers. The ROM-BIOS Video Service interrupts for writing and reading pixel dots are the basis for a general graphics driver for your Turbo Pascal programs.

The video services 12 and 13 can form the basis for such a general drive. As long as the equipment aboard the user's computer can be recognized by ROM-BIOS, your driver will function correctly. Of course, this does not account for other graphics adapters, such as the Hercules and Professional Graphics adapters. However, because VGA is becoming the industry standard for the serious PC user, you can be reasonably certain that your graphics program will operate on most personal computers.

Video services 12 and 13 use the high order byte of the AX portion of the REGISTER variable to hold the video service call. In service 12, the low order byte of AX contains the pixel color code for the point to be written. In service 13 the low order byte of AX also holds this value, but as a returned value. The DX and CX portions of the register hold the value of the Y and X coordinates of the point, respectively. In graphics modes, the top left corner of the screen is the origin or (0,0). With a resolution of 640×200 the points of the screen are addressed as 0 to 639 for the x-axis, and 0 to 199 for the y-axis. A typical pixel setting and verification procedure is shown in FIG. 4-15.

```
Procedure Write_Pixel(X,Y : integer; Color : byte;
                      var success : boolean);
Var
  register : registers;
Begin
  (* Write pixel to screen *)
  with register do
    begin
      ax := (12 shl 8) + color;
      dx := Y;
      cx := X;
      INTR($10, register);
    end;

  (* Verify the point just written *)
  with register do
    begin
      ax := (13 shl 8);
      dx := Y;
      cx := X;
      INT($10, register);

      (* If the returned value is equal to the specified color *)
      (* the pixel was set to the specified color correctly *)
      success := (color = (lo(ax)));
    end;
end;
```

Fig. 4-15. A typical pixel setting procedure using the INTR( ) interrupt procedure.

Using line and form drawing algorithms, the programmer can develop an extensive library of graphics commands for shapes and shadings. A number of critics of this method claim that it is too slow. They are correct in observing that this method is slow in comparison to assembly language drivers. It is worth noting, however, that this method is also more widely applicable than many assembly language routines, is very easy conceptually, and represents a starting point for the beginning and intermediate graphics programmer.

Video Service 14 - Write Character as TTY

This video subservice allows the user to generate character output for the screen in much the same way as printing to a simple printer. This video service does not require the use of a cursor location for positioning the text. Instead, it uses the current position and advances the cursor one position to the right, or to the next line, after the specified character is written.

As usual, the subservice number is placed in the high order byte of the AX portion of the register variable. The code value of the ASCII character to be written is placed in the low order byte of AX. In graphics modes, the foreground color of the character to be written is placed in the low order byte of BX. In text modes, the display page may be specified in the high order byte of BX. The major difference between this service and subservice 9 is the capability to specify both position and color in 9.

Video Service 15 - Get Current Video Mode

Unlike the startup video mode returned by the equipment services interrupt ($11 hex, 17 decimal), this procedure can be used to determine the current video mode. This type of procedure would be used for the generic video driver as part of a procedure to exactly determine the capabilities of the video adapter on board the computer.

This interrupt returns the number corresponding to the current video mode in the low order byte of the AX portion of the REGISTER variable. The number of characters per line is returned in the high order byte of AX. The active display page is returned in the high order byte of the BX portion of the REGISTER variable. As usual, the interrupt is called with the sub-service number (15) in the high order byte of AX. A video board identification procedure is shown in FIG. 4-16.

The value of the procedure in FIG. 4-16 is obvious. With it, you can determine the type of video adapter you have on board the computer. By creating programs that take advantage of this information, you can create applications that are hardware independent. Because of the wide variety of hardware available for the PC, you would have to create dozens, perhaps hundreds, of versions of your software to accommodate every variation. By incorporating general equipment determination procedures, such as FIG.

```
Procedure Video_Adapter(adapter : char);

(*
  This procedure determines the current video adapter by
  testing what video mode is returned by the video mode
  subservice. When a determination of the video mode is made
  the value returned into the ADAPTER variable will be a
  single letter code based on the key below:

        Code          Meaning
        ====          =======
        M             Monchrome or Hercules Video Adapter
        C             CGA - Color Graphics Adapter
        E             EGA - Enhanced Graphics Adapter
        V             VGA - Virtual Graphics Array
*)
Var
  register : registers;
  ah,al,original : byte;
Begin
  (* Determine the original video mode *)
  with register do
    begin
      ax := 15 shl 8;
      INTR($10, register);
      original := lo(ax); (* original video mode *)
    end;

  if (original <> 7) then
    begin
      (* Try Settings Adapter to a VGA Mode *)
      with register do
        begin
          ax := 15;
          INTR($10, register);
        end;

      (* Determine the current video mode *)
      with register do
        begin
          ax := 15 shl 8;
          INTR($10, register);
          original := lo(ax); (* original video mode *)
        end;

      if (original = 17) then
        adapter = 'V' (* VGA, because only VGA supports this mode *)
      else
        begin
          (* Try Setting the Video Mode to an EGA Mode *)
          with register do
            begin
              ax := 15; (* Try to set adapter to an EGA mode *)
              INTR($10, register);
            end;
      (* Determine the current video mode *)
      with register do
        begin
          ax := 15 shl 8;
          INTR($10, register);
          original := lo(ax); (* original video mode *)
        end;

      if (original = 15) then
        adapter = 'E' (* EGA, because only EGA supports these modes
      else
        adapter = 'C' (* We already know its not Monochrome *)
                      (* VGA or EGA, so it must be a CGA     *)
```

Fig. 4-16. A procedure to determine the current video adapter on board the computer using the INTR( )
interrupt procedure.

"Fig. 4-16 continued."

```
        end;
     end
   else
     adapter = 'M';  (* Only Monochrome and Hercules cards *)
                     (* support this video mode *)
 end;
```

4-16, into your programs, you can determine what your applications are executing on at run time. The current Turbo Pascal implementation provides for functionality beyond the example in FIG. 4-16. This example is provided as a demonstration of the uses of the interrupt capabilities of the personal computer.

DIRECT MEMORY ACCESS

As has been seen previously, the Turbo Pascal INTR( ) functions allow the programmer to access specific memory locations and services through the ROM-BIOS routines. You have seen the capability to retrieve specific equipment information as well as direct manipulation of video services. There are many more functions available—only some of which will be discussed in this section. You are strongly encouraged to seek out more information about these services, because the ROM-BIOS services are available on ALL personal computers.

There are two other ROM-BIOS services about which you should have knowledge. These include the Print Screen $05 hex (05 decimal) and the Available Memory $12 hex (18 decimal) functions. The Available Memory service is called using $12 as the interrupt number. The available memory, in kilobytes, is returned in the AX portion of the REGISTER variable. If there were 640,000 bytes of RAM memory available, then this service would return the number 640 in AX. The use of this interrupt is demonstrated in FIG. 4-17. Unlike the MAXAVAIL and MEMAVAIL functions, this BIOS function call enables the programmer to determine the total amount of memory on the computer. The integer variable would be able to report up to 32767 kilobytes of RAM, and the word variable would be able to report up to 65535 kilobytes of RAM.

```
Procedure Available_Memory;
Var
  register = register;
Begin
  with (register) do
    begin
      intr($12, register);
      writeln('The available RAM memory is ',ax,' Kbytes.');
    end;
end;
```

Fig. 4-17. The memory available ROM-BIOS function accessed using the INTR( ) interrupt function.

This function provides valuable information concerning the amount of memory available on the machine where the programmer's applications are running. For more sophisticated applications, such as Spreadsheets and Databases, this information is necessary for proper data storage, retrieval and manipulation.

The Print Screen utility is extremely useful for the programmer who might wish to give the user a quick method for printing both text and graphical information. The call to this interrupt is made by using the value $05 hex (05 decimal) to the INTR( ) function. If the current video mode is text, then the resulting output will be text to the default printer. If the current video mode is graphics, and the program GRAPHICS.COM has been loaded previous to the current application, then a graphics output will be printed.

If the printer is related to the IBM proprinter or EPSON FX series of printers, and the video mode is 4, 5 or 6, then a graphics output will be produced. However, if a mode of 8 or greater is selected, only recognizable text characters will be printed. A recognizable text must be both a known pattern of pixels, and it must be situated on a character boundary. The obvious advantage of this utility is the ability to produce text and graphical output, quickly and efficiently, with a minimum of program code. Version 3.3 of DOS, and lower, support only graphics from a CGA graphics adapter. With the release of version 4.0 of DOS, the GRAPHICS.COM supports all modes for the EGA and VGA adapters. Some examples of printouts of VGA graphics screen can be seen in chapter 8.

MEM( ) and MEMW( ) Functions

Direct memory access using the MEM( ), MEML( ), and MEMW( ) functions allows the user to send information to, and retrieve information from, the memory of the computer. The basic difference between these functions is that MEM( ) operates with bytes, MEML( ) operates with long integers, and MEMW( ) allows the user to manipulate words. A byte is the smallest discrete memory unit of a computer's memory. A word is composed of two bytes, or in data type terms it is an integer. Because these functions are similar, I will review the workings of the MEM( ) function.

The MEM( ) function enables the programmer to send information to, and receive information from, specific memory locations. The programmer specifies the memory location using two 16-bit integers that are used by the MEM( ) function to generate an even larger memory address. The two integers are called the base and offset addresses. The use of the MEM-( ) function is shown in FIG. 4-18.

The MEM( ) function is really nothing more than a specialized array variable that can take array indexes based on two 16-bit integers rather than a single 16-bit value. As you know, a 16-bit integer usually ranges from −32768 to 32767. When the 16-bit integer is used as a hexadecimal number, it ranges from $0000 to $FFFF (or 0 to 65535 decimal). When the

```
Function Demonstrate_Mem;
Var
  mode : byte;
  base, offset : integer;
Begin
  base := $0000; (* This corresponds to 0 decimal *)
  offset := $0449; (* This corresponds to 713 decimal *)
  mode := MEM[base:offset];
  Initial_Video_Mode := mode;
end;
```

Fig. 4-18. Using the MEM( ) function.

MEM( ) function combines two 16-bit integers constructed from the base and offset variables, it can accommodate numbers from 0 to greater than four billion.

Each subscript of the MEM( ) function points to a specific byte in RAM. Using the proper base and offset, the MEM( ) function can create an address capable of reaching any portion of the computer's memory. This is particularly useful for transferring information between two programs, or from the operating system to an application and back. One of the specific memory locations which I have found useful in my programs is the byte located at $0000:$0449. This address holds the initial video mode. This location is accessed by the Equipment Services Interrupt to provide the programmer with the startup video mode. If you are only interested in this information rather than the entire equipment survey, then you need only access this location. The use of this particular location is demonstrated in FIG. 4-19.

```
Function Initial_Video_Mode;
Var
  mode : byte;
  base, offset : integer;
Begin
  base := $0000; (* This corresponds to 0 decimal *)
  offset := $0449; (* This corresponds to 713 decimal *)
  mode := MEM[base:offset];
  Initial_Video_Mode := mode;
end;
```

Fig. 4-19. Determining the initial video mode for the computer using the MEM( ) function.

This is different than the Get Video Mode subservice of the INTR( ) Video services, because it returns the startup video mode of the computer. The INTR( ) call returns the current video mode. There are a variety of other locations that return information about the computer. The programmer is encouraged to investigate these with the aid of a reference text that provides more detailed information about these locations and their uses.

DIRECT HARDWARE ACCESS - THE PORT ( ) FUNCTION

One of the more interesting functions available in Turbo Pascal is the PORT( ) function. The PORT( ) function allows the user to access specific hardware locations. Unlike the MEM( ) and MEMW( ) functions, the PORT( ) function makes use of a single 16-bit integer as an index variable.

This variable, which can range from $0000 to $FFFF, allows you to reference specific locations such as the CRT, floppy, or Hard Disk controllers. This type of control allows you to manipulate equipment that is not standard to the PC.

One of the most useful aspects of the PORT( ) with version 3.0 of Turbo Pascal and previous versions is the capability to provide the user with a method to activate a HERCULES graphics adapter. The HERCULES graphics adapter is supported directly by Turbo Pascal, beginning with version 4.0. The HERCULES activation sequence is based on the programming of specific hardware registers that may be accessed through the PORT( ) function. The sequence requires the user to program the CRT ports and their related registers in a stepwise fashion. This sequence, and the Turbo Pascal code necessary to activate a HERCULES graphics adapter for graphics mode, are shown in FIG. 4-20.

```
Procedure Activate_HERCULES;
{
  This procedure accesses the necessary display and adapter ports
  to cause the HERCULES adapter to shift into graphics mode
}
Var
  counter;
Begin
  (* Enable software switch for graphics and page one *)
  port[$03BF] := $03;

  (* Set screen to inactive display *)
  port[$03B4] := $F7;

  (* Display ports are programmed *)
  (* with HERCULES display information *)
  port[$03B4] := 0;      port[$03B5] := $35;
  port[$03B4] := 1;      port[$03B5] := $2D;
  port[$03B4] := 2;      port[$03B5] := $2E;
  port[$03B4] := 3;      port[$03B5] := $07;
  port[$03B4] := 4;      port[$03B5] := $5B;
  port[$03B4] := 5;      port[$03B5] := $02;
  port[$03B4] := 6;      port[$03B5] := $57;
  port[$03B4] := 7;      port[$03B5] := $57;
  port[$03B4] := 8;      port[$03B5] := $02;
  port[$03B4] := 9;      port[$03B5] := $03;
  port[$03B4] := 10;     port[$03B5] := $00;
  port[$03B4] := 11;     port[$03B5] := $00;

  (* Screen is set blank *)
  for counter := 0 to $7FFF do mem[$B800:counter] := 0;

  (* Adapter is programmed for screen *)
  (* one and screen is activated *)
  port[$03B8] := $8A;
end;
```

Fig. 4-20. Activation of HERCULES graphics adapter using Turbo Pascal PORT( ) and MEM( ) functions.

The activation of the HERCULES adapter board requires several steps in a procedure. The board must first be set to the desired page and display mode. The HERCULES board comes with 64K of memory. Because a typical HERCULES display yields a 720×348-pixel resolution, 32K of memory is required per display. This allows the user to program both the active display as well as a memory display screen. This means that two full screens of information may be made available to you at any given time.

The act of switching display screens takes significantly less time than actually writing two sets of information to the same screen. If the programmer fills screen page 0 with some information and then fills page 1 with more information, he can program the HERCULES adapter to switch between the two screens almost instantaneously. This enables you to design some really professional displays as well as giving you an animation capability.

After the display page has been chosen, the procedure must then set the display to inactive so that PORT( ) manipulations will not cause erratic behavior on the display screen. After the adapter has been set up to accept page one input, the procedure begins to program the CRT registers. The programming sequence proceeds stepwise through 11 of the 16 registers associated with the CRT controller. Each register is selected by entering its index into the PORT[$03B4] function. The actual value to be used is then inserted into the PORT[$03B5] function.

The values assigned to the CRT registers specify scan rates, resolutions for graphics and text, as well as other vital information. After this information is placed into the CRT registers, the memory associated with the display page chosen must be set to $00. This is necessary because the information from the previous use of the HERCULES adapter might still be present. It's also good programming and basic housekeeping practice. After the memory page has been reset, the adapter is reset to active display, and the chosen application, if it possesses a HERCULES graphics card, may perform.

The design of a basic graphics driver is left to you. However, because the procedure in FIG. 4-20 shows how to access specific portions of the screen memory using the MEM( ) function, and because the literature accompanying the HERCULES display explains how specific picture elements (*pixels*) are modified, this exercise should be feasible. A text driver is unnecessary because, in text mode, the HERCULES driver is identical to a Monochrome Display Adapter which is accessed by Video Mode 7.

This is merely an example of how you might use the PORT( ) procedure. However, Turbo Pascal version 5.5 already has an extremely advanced Hercules driver. Another example of the PORT( ) procedure is presented in chapter 5 of this book.

In a previous section the INTR function, in conjunction with the Video Services, allowed the programmer to access any recognized pixel or character position. Because the HERCULES adapter is not a standard ROM-BIOS recognized adapter, special drivers must be created to accommodate it. Version 3.0 of Turbo Pascal has no such driver. However, the devices drivers of versions 4.0 and 5.0, accommodate the HERCULES graphics adapter.

MsDos SERVICES

In addition to the range of services offered by the ROM-BIOS system, any PC running DOS has access to a set of DOS functions. These functions enable the user to perform operations that are usually reserved for operating systems from within a Turbo Pascal program.

The MsDos( ) function uses the same record structure as the INTR( ) function to send and receive information. This function differs from the INTR( ) function because the number used to specify the service is specified in the high order byte of the AX portion of the REGISTER variable. The values that the user wishes to send to DOS are placed in the BX, CX and DX variables. Any returned values may be retrieved from the AX, BX, CX and DX variables. A typical MsDos( ) function is shown in FIG. 4-21.

```
Procedure Set_Drive(drive);
Var
  record : registers;
Begin
  with register do
    begin
      ax := $0E shl 8;
      dx := drive;
      MsDos(register);
    end;
end;
```

Fig. 4-21. A procedure to modify the default disk drive specifier base on the MsDos( ) DOS access function.

The procedure in FIG. 4-21 allows the user to specify which disk drive will be used as the default for reading and writing files. The function is called by placing the function number $0E hex (14 decimal) into the high order byte of the AX portion of the REGISTER variable. The drive to change to is a byte value. The number corresponding to the A drive is 0, B corresponds to 1, C to 2, and so on. Drive specifiers need not be letters. For instance, drive 27 is [, and 28 is /. Turbo Pascal provides the CHDIR procedure to accomplish this task as well as modify the default directory. In this respect, the MS-DOS service would limit the capability of your program. However, this MS-DOS function provides an additional piece of data not available through CHDIR.

This MS-DOS function, besides allowing you and the user to select the default drive, also returns a value into the low order byte of the AX portion of the REGISTER variable. This value corresponds to the number of drives available on the computer. Because many of the newer PC configurations include a hard disk and a single floppy disk drive, DOS creates a second logical floppy disk drive. This function will recognize this logical driver; hence, even though a computer might only have one hard disk and one floppy disk driver, this function will return the value 3.

Other MsDos( ) functions available include file allocation information, clock access, drive information access, and keyboard control. The full capabilities of this function are beyond the bounds of this text. Some of the more useful, and less complex, functions are described here.

Get Current Drive

Figure 4-21 demonstrates the use of the Select Current Drive function available from the MsDos( ) function. A complementary function is the Get Current Drive function, $19 hex (25 decimal). This function allows you or the user to verify that the Select Drive function has indeed performed correctly, or merely to determine the default disk drive.

The Get Drive function requires the service number $19 to be placed in the high order byte of the AX portion of the REGISTER variable. When the MsDos( ) function is called with this service number, the value of the current drive is returned in the low order byte of the AX portion of the REGISTER variable. Unlike the ROM-BIOS interrupt functions that have standard return locations within the REGISTER variable, the MsDos( ) functions return and send values seemingly in a random fashion. In the Select Drive service the low order byte of AX returned the number of drives, while in the Get Drive function this variable holds the value of the current drive. Once again, drive A corresponds to the value 0, drive B to 1, C to 2, and so on.

Get and Set Date Functions

The Get and Set Date functions $2A and $2B (42 and 43 decimal) allow you and the user to retrieve and modify the date as it is stored by the computer's clock. This capability allows you to generate date stamps for specific pieces of information, to modify erroneous information stored in the computer, or to simply display the date to the user. These functions are superseded by the GETDATE, GETTIME, SETDATE, and SETTIME procedures in version 5.5 of Turbo Pascal. For more information on these procedures, consult the Turbo Pascal User's Guide for versions 5.0 and 5.5.

These functions are called by placing the service number in the high order byte of the AX portion of the REGISTER variable. When setting the date, the number of the month (1 to 12) is placed in the high order byte of DX. The day of the month (1 to 28, 29, 30 or 31) is placed in the low order byte of DX. The year, which can assume values between 1980 and 2099, is placed in the CX portion of REGISTER. When getting the date, these variables hold the same type of information. In addition, the Get Date function returns the day of the week (0 to 6, where 0 = Sunday and 6 = Saturday) in the low order byte of AX. Typical Get and Set Date functions are shown in FIG. 4-22.

These functions, along with the GETTIME and SETTIME functions, allow the programmer and user to have full access to the time keeping capabilities of the PC.

The GETTIME and SETTIME functions $2C and $2D (44 and 45 decimal) utilize the high order byte of AX to hold the service number requested. The high order byte of CX holds the hour (0 to 23), and the low

```
Procedure Get_Date(var month,day,year : integer;
                   var day_of_week : string[9]);
Var
  register : registers;
Begin
  with register do
    begin
      ax := $2A shl 8;
      MsDos(register);
      month := hi(dx);
      day := lo(dx);
      year := cx;
      case (lo(ax)) of
          0 : day_of_week := 'Sunday';
          1 : day_of_week := 'Monday';
          2 : day_of_week := 'Tuesday';
          3 : day_of_week := 'Wednesday';
          4 : day_of_week := 'Thursday';
          5 : day_of_week := 'Friday';
          6 : day_of_week := 'Saturday';
      end;
    end;
end;

Procedure Set_Date(month,day,year : integer);
Var
  register : registers;
Begin
  with register do
    begin
      ax := $2B shl 8;
      dx := month shl 8 + day;
      cx := year;
      MsDos(register);
    end;
end;
```

Fig. 4-22. Typical get and set date functions using the MsDos( ) function call and DOS services.

order byte of CX holds the minutes (0 to 59). The high order byte of DX holds the seconds (0 to 59) and the low order byte of CX holds hundredths of seconds (0 to 99). When the Get Time function is called, these values are returned into the specified variables. When the Set Time function is called, these values must be present in the specified variables, or an incorrect time will be sent to the computer's clock.

The final function presented is extremely useful for applications that might require large amounts of disk space. This function, Get Disk Free Space $36 (54 decimal), allows the user to determine not only the amount of free disk space available on the specified drive, but also the total disk capacity. For applications that might be required to generate large disk files, this function is invaluable for telling the user how to establish the necessary environment for proper execution.

This function, as do other MsDos( ) function calls, requires that the user place the service number in the high order byte of the AX portion of the REGISTER variable. The value of the number of sectors per disk cluster are returned in AX. The number of available clusters is returned in BX. The number of bytes per sector is returned in CX. And the total clusters on the chosen drive are returned in DX.

When you combine the returned values, you can generate some useful numbers that describe the utilization of the current drive. For example, by multiplying the Sectors/Cluster by Bytes/Sector by Total Clusters you can generate a number, in bytes, which is the total capacity of the current drive. When you multiply Sectors/Cluster by Available Clusters by Bytes/Sector you can generate a second number, in bytes, which is the available or free space in the current drive. By dividing the second number by the first and multiplying by 100, you can generate a percentage representation of the amount of free space compared to the total capacity of the drive. A Get Free Space procedure is shown in FIG. 4-23 demonstrating how to use this MsDos( ) function.

```
Procedure Get_Free_Space(drive : byte;
                         var total,free,percent_free : integer);
Var
  register : registers;
  old_drive : byte;
Begin
  (* Get the current drive *)
  with register do
    begin
      ax := $19 shl 8;
      MsDos(register);
      old_drive := lo(ax);
    end;

  (* Select the specified drive *)
  with register do
    begin
      ax := $0E shl 8;
      dx := drive;
      MsDos(register);
    end;

  (* Call The Get Disk Space Function *)
  with register do
    begin
      ax := $36 shl 8;
      MsDos(register);
      total := ROUND((CX / 1000)*AX*DX);
      free := ROUND((CX / 1000)*AX*BX);
      percent_free := 100*(free/total);
    end;

  (* Reset Default Drive to original drive *)
  with register do
    begin
      ax := $0E shl 8;
      dx := old_drive;
      MsDos(register);
    end;
end;
```

Fig. 4-23. A function to return basic and calculated values describing the total capacity and available free space on a specified drive.

The procedure in FIG. 4-23 takes four arguments and returns three values. The variable DRIVE is the drive for which the information will be retrieved. The variable TOTAL is the value, in kilobytes, of the total amount of storage capacity available on the specified drive. The variable

FREE is the value, in kilobytes, of the amount of storage space NOT currently used to store files on the specified drive. The variable PERCENT_FREE is the amount of free space available as a percentage of the total storage capacity of the selected drive.

This function is particularly useful because it makes use of three MsDos( ) functions to generate useful information about the PC on which an application is running. The application can then check the setup before using anything that's not ready—or not there at all. The DISKSIZE and DISKFREE functions in version 5.5 of Turbo Pascal provide the same capabilities.

DISCUSSION

This chapter emphasizes the video services because they are the most user-oriented of all the ROM-BIOS services. With the new graphical interfaces and video adapters available, you must consider many adapter types when designing the output screens for an application. By making use of the ROM-BIOS routines, this task can be performed at run time by the application, rather than by you at compile time. From a practical perspective, this requires much less programming effort.

5

TSR Programs and the "KeyClick" Application

Beginning with version 4.0 of Turbo Pascal, advanced capabilities were provided to facilitate the creation of *Terminate-but-Stay-Resident* (TSR) applications. This chapter demonstrates the use of several of the more advanced capabilities of Turbo Pascal version 5.5. In addition, new BIOS access routines are introduced that enable you to replace BIOS routines with your own to provide even more control over the data input capabilities of the computer.

WHAT A TSR APPLICATION IS

A *Terminate-but-Stay-Resident* (TSR) program can load into memory, perform an action, and terminate. This definition can apply to about any program running under DOS. Unlike other programs which are removed from memory after they terminate their activities, a TSR remains in memory. Because it remains in memory after termination, a TSR can be called at any time without have to be reloaded from disk. TSRs will execute when specific keyboard input or display output conditions are met. Thus, TSRs perform seemingly "parallel" or "multi-tasking" functions within the DOS environment.

The term *multi-tasking* simply means the ability to perform more than one task at a time. In the computer's case, this means two programs can appear to execute simultaneously. I emphasize the words "appear to" because TSR programs do not allow for simultaneous execution of two programs. TSRs provide for interruption of the current program to perform a task, and then they cause the computer to rejoin the suspended program at the point where the TSR was called. Chapter 4 of this text introduced and reviewed the use of the Basic Input/Output System(BIOS) of the personal computer. The functioning of the Terminate-but-Stay-Resident application is exactly analogous to the use of interrupt procedures. In fact, many TSR applications are centered around the replacement of a specific BIOS procedure with an interrupt procedure of their own.

Turbo Pascal provides two procedures that allow programmers to substitute their own procedures for standard BIOS routines. These procedures are called getintvec and setintvec. They allow you to obtain and establish information about specific BIOS routines. These procedures are described later in this chapter. For now, it is more educational to introduce the BIOS routine that is most often replaced or enhanced by TSR programs.

THE BIOS KEYBOARD SERVICES

Unlike the BIOS video services, which control the display of information, the keyboard services control how information gets from the keyboard to your program. The keyboard services enable your applications to detect any keyboard activity. The standard Turbo Pascal keypressed function provides this same functionality by taking advantage of this service. In addition, information from the keyboard can be read into your applications one character at a time. The ReadKey function provides a similar function. Finally, the keyboard services enable your programs to determine whether noncharacter keys such as CTRL, left-shift, right-shift and others are being pressed. This last service is called the "Shift Status" subservice, and it is one of the most versatile and informative of the services offered through BIOS.

Like the video services, the keyboard services are called using the Turbo Pascal intr function. As you might recall, the intr function takes two arguments, the interrupt service number ($16) and a special record structure called the "register." A typical call to the BIOS keyboard services is shown in FIG. 5-1.

The procedure in FIG. 5-1 is an extremely simple example of some of the uses of the keyboard services. More advanced capabilities enable you to create your own ReadKey function. In addition, you can create a KeyStatus procedure that indicates whether CTRL, ALT, left-shift, right-shift, SCROLL LOCK, NUM LOCK, CAPS LOCK or the INS keys were pressed or activated. The advantages of these subservices will become apparent as I describe each of them in depth.

```
procedure TestKeyBoard;
Var
   register : registers; (* The REGISTERS type is predefined *)
   charvar  : integer;
   ah, al   : byte;
begin
   (* Initialize the FLAG variable *)
   register.flag := 1;

   (* Read the keyboard until a key is pressed *)
   while (register.flag = 1) do
     begin

       (* Call the REPORT CHARACTER READY Subservice *)
       ax := $00FF; (* 256 *)
       intr($16, register);
     end;

   (* When a key is pressed, read the return code *)
   with register do
     begin
       (* Call the GET KEYBOARD CHARACTER Subservice *)
       ax := $0000; (* 0 *)
       INTR($16, register);

       (* Translate returned integer register into bytes *)
       ah := hi(ax);
       al := lo(ax);
     end;

   (* If AH = 1 then the returned code is an extended code *)
   if (ah = 1) then
     writeln('The returned code is an extended code ',al)
   else
     writeln('The keyboard character is ',chr(al));
end;
```

Fig. 5-1. Calling the BIOS keyboard services.

Subservice 0 - Read Character

The Read Character subservice enables the programmer to read the keyboard buffer directly. It can distinguish between regular keyboard keys such as "A" or "2." It can also report extended codes such as "right-cursor" or "CTRL-HOME." When a key is pressed, the scan codes for that key are then made available in the AX register variable for decoding.

The high order byte of AX is a flag indicating whether the returned code is to be taken at face value (AH = 0), or whether the returned code is extended (AH = 1). The low order byte of AX contains the actual keyboard return value of the character. This value is in integer form, and must be converted to ASCII to be used as a char or string value. The example program in FIG. 5-1 shows how subservice 0 might be used.

Subservice 1 - Character Ready

The Character Ready subservice performs essentially the same function as service 0. Each subservice enables the programmer to read the keyboard buffer directly. Each can distinguish between regular keyboard keys such as "A" or "2." Each service can also report extended codes such as "right-cursor" or "CTRL-HOME." The difference between the two functions is the use of the REGISTER.FLAG variable. When a key is pressed, the flag variable is set to 1 to indicate that a character is waiting within the keyboard buffer ready to be read. The scan codes for that key are then made available in the AX register variable for decoding.

Like subservice 0, the high order byte of AX is a flag indicating whether the returned code is to be taken at face value (AH = 0), or whether the returned code is extended (AH = 1). The low order byte of AX contains the actual keyboard return value of the character. This value is in integer form and must be converted to ASCII to be used as a char or string value.

Subservice 2 - Get Shift Status

The Get Shift Status subservice is one of the more valuable BIOS services available through the INTR function. This service enables the programmer to determine whether certain functional keys on the keyboard are in their active or inactive position, such as the CAPS LOCK and SCROLL LOCK keys. In addition, specific information about which SHIFT key, left or right can be retrieved. Finally, this service enables you to determine the status of special keys such as CTRL or ALT. All of this information can be invaluable for advanced applications that might make use of exotic key combinations to initiate an action.

The "Shift Status" subservice is called by assigning the value 2 to the high order byte of the AX register portion of the REGISTER structure. When the keyboard services are called, status information for specific keys is returned in the low order byte of AX. Each bit corresponds to a different key. The specific keys, and the bits to which they correspond, are shown in TABLE 5-1.

Bit Location	Corresponding Key
0	Right-Shift Key
1	Left-Shift Key
2	CTRL Key
3	ALT Key
4	SCROLL Lock (active)
5	NUM Lock (active)
6	CAPS Lock (active)
7	INSERT State (active)

Table 5-1. The GET SHIFT STATUS Reporting Byte

The first four bits of the low order byte of AX represent the depressed status of the keys for which they report. The last four bits correspond to active/inactive flags indicating whether the key is in its active locked state or inactive unlocked state. You know that the SCROLL, NUM, CAPS, and INS keys are more like switches that are turned ON and OFF. The last four bits of the low order byte of AX reports the status of these switches. The first four bits simply indicate whether the key is currently depressed. An example of a special key status reporting procedure is shown in FIG. 5-2.

```
          procedure ShiftStatus(var RShift, LShift, Ctrl,
                                    Alt, Scroll, Num,
                                    Caps, Insert : Boolean);
          var
            register : registers;
            AL : byte;
          begin
            (* Get the current status key report *)
            with register do
              begin
                ax := $0200;
                intr($16, register);

                (* Extract the low order byte into AL *)
                al := lo(ax);

                (* Decode the Report *)
                RShift := ((al AND $01) = $01);
                LShift := ((al AND $02) = $02);
                Ctrl   := ((al AND $04) = $04);
                Alt    := ((al AND $08) = $08);
                Scroll := ((al AND $10) = $10);
                Num    := ((al AND $20) = $20);
                Caps   := ((al AND $40) = $40);
                Insert := ((al AND $80) = $80);
              end;
          end;
```

Fig. 5-2. Using the GET SHIFT STATUS subservice.

The procedure shown in FIG. 5-2 returns the status of several keys using the "call by reference" method of defining arguments. Whenever this procedure is called, each of the arguments must be a Boolean variable. The values of these variables can then be used in other procedures for a variety of activities. The use of the bitwise AND operator allows for the creation of a Boolean value to be assigned directly to a specific key-status Boolean variable. More information about the types of variables that may be defined for a procedure or function is available in chapter 2 of this book. Additional reference information about Turbo Pascal procedure definitions is available in the Turbo Pascal User's Guide and Reference Manual.

You might have noticed that the assignment of TRUE and FALSE to any of the Boolean arguments is made using an unusual Boolean expression, like "Insert := (al AND $80);." This evaluates to "If the result of bitwise addition of the values in AL and $80 (128 decimal) is equal to $80 then the expression is TRUE, otherwise it is FALSE." The generic construct "var := ((var AND val) = val)" is used frequently in C programs. However, it is also a valid logical assignment in Turbo Pascal, and more efficient than the corresponding "If ((var AND val) = val) Then var := TRUE" expression.

The difference between the use of the "var := ((var AND val) = val)" construct and "If ((var AND val) = val) Then var := TRUE" is also a good example of beginning or intermediate programming versus advanced. Both constructs can be used in a variety of applications. The executable code generated by the first construct is considerably more efficient than that generated by the second. However, there are drawbacks to the use of this method. The "var := ((var AND val) = val)" ALWAYS changes the value of the assigned Boolean variable (VAR). The "If ((var AND val) = val) Then var := TRUE" only changes the value of VAR when the expression is TRUE. So, if you always want to reassign the value of the evaluation of the expression to VAR, then use the C-like construct. However, if your control logic does NOT require reassignment of FALSE as well as TRUE values, then use the "If..Then" construct.

You might wish to consider the use of control logic carefully when designing an application. If you make your control logic too complex, another programmer might not be able to understand it. This might be your goal, but good programming style dictates that other programmers of equal or greater skill should be able to comprehend what you have written. An interesting addition to Turbo Pascal, not available in the standard Pascal, is the "Logic Short-Circuit" compiler directive. This compiler directive allows your programs to evaluate only as many Boolean expressions as necessary to get a result. An example of this type of logical control is shown in FIG. 5-3.

Boolean Short Circuit Logic Activated

{$B – } – This is the default Boolean logical evaluation system
{$B + } = Complete evaluation of ALL Boolean expressions
{$B – } = Short-Circuit evaluation of leading Boolean expressions

Examples

---

1) VAR := (A = TRUE) AND (B = TRUE);
2) VAR := (A = TRUE) OR (B = TRUE);

Explanations

---

1) If A = FALSE then (B = TRUE) is NEVER evaluated
2) If A = TRUE then (B = TRUE) is NEVER evaluated

Fig. 5-3. Boolean short-circuit logic.

The examples in FIG. 5-3 demonstrate how more efficient code can be generated by use of the {$B – } directive. The first example in FIG. 5-3 shows a simple Boolean expression composed of two Boolean evaluations. Because it is an AND expression, then the elements on both sides of the

AND must evaluate to TRUE for the entire expression to be TRUE. If the first element "A = TRUE" is NOT TRUE, then you do NOT need to continue with the evaluation of the second element. The second example in FIG. 5-3 shows another simple expression using the OR operator. Because it is an OR, only one of the two elements connected by the OR needs to evaluate to TRUE for the entire expression to be TRUE. If the first element "A = TRUE" is TRUE, then you do NOT need to evaluate further.

If fewer evaluations need to be performed, and the same control results are obtained, then the code is more efficient. Of course, this type of short circuit logic is NOT always applicable, and can change the intended control logic of the program. As always, care should be taken with enhancements such as these. You might wish to test your application with this directive in both states to see if there is a difference. This directive and others are explained in more detail in appendix B of the Turbo Pascal reference guide for version 5.5.

The keyboard services provide programmers with direct access to keyboard input and status. This information can be used to create applications capable of reading keys directly without the need for pressing the ENTER key. Applications can be constructed to react differently to input if a specific status key is depressed. This gives programmers the ability to extend the range of values that may be input from the keyboard. Several of the functions available within Turbo Pascal provide this capability already. With access to the keyboard services, your applications can perform the work of keypressed and readykey along with accessing keyboard status information within a single procedure. As you will see in the next section, the keyboard services play a vital role in the access of any TSR application.

WHY TO REPLACE THE BIOS KEYBOARD SERVICE

When you call a TSR program like Borland's SideKick application, you normally press the CTRL and the ALT keys simultaneously. This combination of keys is detected by the program and causes SideKick to activate and provide you with some interesting and useful utilities. This program also provides an alternate method for activation: The pressing of both the left-shift and right-shift keys simultaneously. The application, when installed, enhances the BIOS keyboard service with a specific control statement that says "If the CTRL and ALT keys are pressed at the same time, or the left-shift and right-shift keys are pressed simultaneously, then call the menu procedure of the application." Virtually all TSR programs function using this form of control logic to cause themselves to activate.

Assuming you had defined your applications to read the keyboard and determine that your activation sequence had been entered, how would DOS know to call your application? With programs that are NOT TSR applications, the procedure to detect the key sequence is not running unless the application is already running. If this is the case, then you DO NOT NEED an activation sequence.

So how do you teach the keyboard services to recognize your activation sequence? You guessed it; you substitute your own keyboard services procedure for the original BIOS keyboard service. The original keyboard services cannot be reprogrammed, but they can be circumvented. Now you might be asking yourself: "Are the original services lost if I replace them?" or "Do I have to rewrite the BIOS code for ALL of the subservices?" The answer to both questions is NO. Turbo Pascal provides two procedures getintvec and setintvec that allow you to modify the interrupt services tables within DOS to replace a specific procedure or set of procedures.

The getintvec procedure is used to retrieve the memory location of a DOS interrupt procedure. This procedure takes two arguments: The interrupt number for which a pointer will be returned, and a pointer variable into which the location of the specified interrupt procedure will be placed. The setintvec procedure is used to assign a procedure into the interrupt table so that subsequent calls to that interrupt will cause the NEW procedure to execute. The setintvec procedure also takes two arguments: The interrupt number into which the location of the new procedure will be written, and the pointer location of the new procedure to be installed. A typical interrupt procedure replacement is shown in FIG. 5-4.

```
var
   oldkey, newkey : pointer;

procedure my_readkey;

procedure initialize_my_readkey;
begin
   (* Initialize Keyboard Service Pointers and Reroute *)
   (* Interrupt $16 to the used BIOS Interrupt $88     *)
   getintvec($16, oldkey);
   setintvec($88, oldkey);

   (* Assign the location of the procedure MY_READKEY *)
   (* as the new $16 keyboard interrupt procedure     *)
   newkey := @my_readkey;
   setintvec($16, newkey);
end;
```

Fig. 5-4. Replacing an interrupt procedure.

The procedure in FIG. 5-4 does NOT discard the old keyboard services procedures. In fact, the original keyboard services are preserved to provide their original functionality. The original interrupt $16 is replaced with the my_readkey procedure. The original keyboard services procedure is reassigned to interrupt $88. The interrupt number ($88) is not currently used by DOS.

THE KEYCLICK APPLICATION

The information presented so far is simply an introduction into some of the elements of TSR programming. The remainder of this chapter is dedicated to the examination and explanation of a simple TSR program called KeyClick.

The KeyClick program is a utility for audio verification of keyboard entry. When entering data into an application from the keyboard or a numeric keypad, it can be reassuring to hear a "click" or tone, verifying that a key has been pressed. Many of the more expensive terminal display devices available have this capability as do many applications available for the personal computer. However, as with many facets of the personal computer industry, this is NOT standard among applications. If you use the standard Turbo Pascal read or readln procedures for data input, a "click" does not occur during data entry.

You could create your own procedures to take the place of read and readln, but these would not be available to applications other than your own. In addition, once these procedures had been compiled, the pitch and duration of the "click" could NOT be modified. Finally, you would need to recreate ALL of the functionality of the read procedures including file read/write/append access. In general it is NOT cost effective to try and replace existing functionality. Most TSR programs don't replace existing capabilities—they enhance them.

The KeyClick application uses TSR programming techniques to enhance the standard BIOS keyboard services to generate a tone each time a key is pressed. The pitch and duration of the "click" tone can be set using DOS command arguments. In addition, specific key sequences are defined to allow you to interactively modify the pitch and duration of the "click" from within the DOS application. The enhancement of the BIOS keyboard services is necessary to provide this capability. The source code for the KeyClick application is shown in FIG. 5-5.

```
Program KeyClick;

uses DOS, CRT;

{
   This memory allocation is necessary for any TSR program to
   insure that all CODE and DATA for the program is saved when
   the KEEP command is issued.
}

{$m $2000,$2000,$2000}

var
   dummy : string;
   errorcode, frequency, duration : word;
   oldkey, newkey : pointer;
   init_frequency, init_duration : word;

{
   The SOUND, NOSOUND and DELAY Procedures could not be used because
   of an incompatability between TSR programs which incorporated the
   CRT unit. The initial load is successful, but subsequent calls
   to the program circumvent the Installation Detection Scheme used
   in most TSR programs.

   The FREQUENCY Variable is used to determine which frequency to
   use for the sound generated.
```

Fig. 5-5. The complete KeyClick application.

The DURATION Variable is the time, in HUNDREDTHS of SECONDS to make the sound.
"Fig. 5-5 continued."

```pascal
}
procedure create_sound(frequency, duration : word);
var
  temport : byte;
  counter : word;
begin
  (* Prepare Speaker for Output *)
  port[67] := 182;

  (* Load Sound Frequency *)
  port[66] := lo(frequency);
  port[66] := hi(frequency);

  (* Get Current Speaker Condition *)
  temport := port[97];

  (* Turn Speaker On *)
  port[97] := temport OR $03;

  (* Pause for DURATION counting *)
  for counter := 1 to duration do;
    begin
    end;

  (* Restore Original Speaker Condition *)
  port[97] := temport;
end;


{
  Specialized character readin procedure. This procedure replaces the
  current BIOS character waiting, detection and special key status
  procedure as $16. The original procedure is reassigned to interrupt
  $88.
  The original procedure is called regardless of starting registers.
  Calls are made to CREATE_SOUND when keyboard characters are selected.
  This procedure also processes specific key combinations to modify
  the TONE and LENGTH of the 'click'.
}
procedure my_readkey(Flags,CS,IP,AX,BX,CX,DX,
                     SI,DI,DS,ES,BP : WORD); interrupt;
var
  old_char2, old_char1, current_char, extended_char, counter : word;
  hi_ax, lo_ax : byte;
  register : registers;
begin
  (* Generate the HI and LO byte portions of AX *)
  hi_ax := hi(ax);
  lo_ax := lo(ax);

  (* Copy Current Registers *)
  register.Flags := Flags;
  register.ax := ax;
  register.bx := bx;
  register.cx := cx;
  register.dx := dd;
  register.si := si;
  register.di := di;
  register.ds := ds;
  register.es := es;
  register.bp := bp;


  (* Determine if this is a CHARACTER READ or CHARACTER READY Call *)
  if (hi_ax = 0) or (hi_ax = $7F) then
    begin
      (* Determine is this is a maintenance cost *)
      if (hi_ax = $7F) then
        begin
          (* Return the Proper Detection Code *)
          ax := 136;
        end
      else
        begin
          (* Call the Original Keyboard Action Interrupt Service *)
          intr($88, register);
```

"Fig. 5-5
continued."

```
                       (* Get the current Character and Extended Character Code *)
                       extended_char := hi(register.ax);
                       current_char  := lo(register.ax);

                       (* Create a predefined tone to indicate a key was pressed *)
                       (* and it is neither and extended code nor ESC           *)
                       if (current_char <> 0) then
                         begin
                           create_sound(frequency, duration);
                         end;

                         (* UP arrow *)
                         if (extended_char = 132) then frequency := frequency + 250
                          else
                         (* DOWN arrow *)
                         if (extended_char = 118) then frequency := frequency - 250
                          else
                         (* LEFT arrow *)
                         if (extended_char = 115) then duration  := duration  - 1000
                          else
                         (* RIGHT arrow *)
                         if (extended_char = 116) then duration  := duration  + 1000
                          else
                         (* HOME key - Reset to Original FREQUENCY and DURATION *)
                         if (extended_char = 119) then
                           begin
                             frequency := Init_Frequency;
                             duration  := Init_Duration;
                           end;

                         if (frequency < 0) then frequency := 200;
                         if (duration < 0) then duration := 10;

                         (* Call Create Sound to Demonstrate NEW Parameters *)
                         for counter := 1 to 10 do;
                           begin
                             create_sound(frequency,duration);
                           end;
                    end;
             end
           else
            begin
              (* Call the Original Keyboard Action Interrupt Service *)
              intr($88, register);
            end;

      (* Reassign Registers for Calling Program *)
      Flags := register.Flags;

      (* If DETECTION was NOT used then return the NEW AX code *)
      if (hi_ax <> $7F) then ax := register.ax;

      bx := register.bx;
      cx := register.cx;
      dd := register.dx;
      si := register.si;
      di := register.di;
      ds := register.ds;
      es := register.es;
      bp := register.bp;

      (* Save old Character Values *)
      old_char2 := old_char1;
      old_char1 := current_char;
    end;


    {
     This procedure initializes all variables for use in 'click'
     generation.
     The GETINTVEC and SETINTVEC procedures install the MY_READKEY
     procedure as Interrupt $16, replacing the original interrupt
     procedure. The original $16 procedure is reassigned to interrupt
     $88. The reassigned procedure is used by the new $16 interrupt
     to process keyboard interrupt values properly.
     Initial values for FREQUENCY and DURATION are read-in from
     command line. If valid variables are not available, default
     values are substituted.
```

"Fig. 5-5 continued."

```
    }
procedure initialize_my_readkey;
begin
  (* Initialize Video Service Pointers and Reroute *)
  (* Interrupt $16 to the used BIOS Interrupt $88  *)
  getintvec($16, oldkey);
  setintvec($88, oldkey);

  newkey := @my_readkey;
  setintvec($16, newkey);

  (* Initialize Frequency and Duration Variables *)
  (* for sound generation TONE and LENGTH         *)
  if (paramcount > 1) then
    begin
      (* Convert First Argument into a usable number *)
      VAL(paramstr(1), Init_Frequency, ErrorCode);
      if (ErrorCode <> 0) then Init_Frequency := 3000;

      (* Convert Second Argument into a usable number *)
      VAL(paramstr(2), Init_Frequency, ErrorCode);
      if (ErrorCode <> 0) then Init_Duration := 2100;
    end
  else
    begin
      Init_Frequency := 3000;
      Init_duration  := 2100;
    end;
  Frequency := Init_Frequency;
  Duration := Init_Duration;
end;


{
   Determine if the TSR has been previously installed.
}
function my_readkey_installed : boolean;
var
  register : registers;
begin
  (* Determine if the Program is Already Installed by Sending *)
  (* A known Code $7F which will be interpretted as a Query   *)
  (* by the Video_Interrupt Procedure.                        *)

  with register do
    begin
      ax := $7F shl 8;
      intr($16, register);
      my_readkey_installed := (lo(ax) = 136);
    end;
end;


{ main }
Begin
  (* Determine if the NEW MY_READKEY interrupt is installed *)
  if (my_readkey_installed = True) then
    begin
      (* Indicate previous installation *)
      writeln('KeyClick ALREADY Installed');
    end
  else
    begin
      (* Initialize the NEW keypressed interrupt *)
      initialize_my_readkey;

      (* Indicate Key Click Program Installed *)
      writeln('KeyClick Application Installed');

      (* Terminate Program and make it TSR *)
      keep(errorcode);
    end;
end.
```

The Components of a TSR Application

Virtually every TSR application available has three basic components that enable it to perform its designed function. These portions are the Installation, Detection, and Action code sections. These sections may be composed of one or more functions or procedures, but each section performs a specific action needed to ensure proper execution of the application as a TSR program.

The Action portion for the KeyClick application is a single procedure used to generate a tone. This procedure makes use of direct hardware access routines available within Turbo Pascal. The procedure is a merging of the actions of the sound, nosound and delay procedures currently available within Turbo Pascal. These procedures have been ignored to provide an example of direct hardware address programming techniques.

The CRT unit contains the compiled code for the sound and nosound procedures. Version 4.0 of the Turbo Pascal compiler does NOT allow for implementation of a TSR program that uses the CRT unit. This limitation required the creation of a new procedure that accessed the sound generating capabilities of the PC without the use of the CRT unit. Even though this limitation does NOT exist with version 5.0 and 5.5 of Turbo Pascal, I have made use of this single procedure to reduce unnecessary procedure and function calls to sound, nosound and delay.

The Detection portion of this application is used to detect the TSR activation sequence. After this sequence is detected and verified, the Detection code causes the Action code to execute. The KeyClick application uses a single procedure to cause the Action code to execute. For any TSR application, the Detection code detects a specific key sequence. When the initialization sequence is detected, a set of predefined actions are initiated based on the logical flow control of the code. For the KeyClick program there are several command sequences. These sequences are used to manipulate the pitch and the duration of the generated tone. If a simple key is pressed, then a tone is generated. If one of the predefined key sequences is selected, then the generated tone can be modified.

The Installation portion of the KeyClick application is used to install the TSR program into memory, permanently. This code is also used to detect possible previous installations of the program code. If you did not detect previous installations then it would be possible to load copy after copy of the KeyClick program into memory until no memory was left. If there is no remaining memory, then no other applications may be executed. In addition, if memory is filled, then the computer will likely freeze. The KeyClick application has an extensive set of installation routines which enable it to detect itself in memory and terminate installation procedures before additional memory is occupied by duplicate copies.

I have tried to make the Installation procedures and functions as generic as possible. You should examine the source code for these routines to make sure you understand their workings completely. You may also use the source code for these routines as the basis for an installation and detection scheme for your own TSR programs. Even though these routines perform their functions well, you might wish to continue developing your own code for the Installation section of your TSR.

From a functional perspective, the Detection code is what makes a TSR application's existence possible. This is the section of code that senses and verifies the data entered from the keyboard. This section of code is used by the Installation section to determine if previous installations of the application have been performed. Without this code, the enhancements available with your TSR application will NEVER be made available to ALL applications running on the PC.

The Action code must be made compatible with TSR techniques in order for the desired functionality to be available. The Installation code serves the dual purpose of installing the application in memory and making sure that other copies of the code do NOT get installed on top of the first program. The interactions of these sections of code provide the basis for a majority of the TSR applications currently available.

The create_sound Procedure

This procedure replaces three existing procedures offered by Turbo Pascal. When this TSR was originally designed, there were some basic incompatibilities between the CRT unit of version 4.0 and TSR programming techniques. These difficulties have since been resolved by Borland with versions 5.0 and 5.5 of Turbo Pascal. I still use the create_sound procedure because of its ease of use, and its ability to manipulate hardware directly. The size of the create_sound application is small relative to the CRT unit, but larger than the amount of memory required for the sound, nosound and delay procedures. It could be argued that the create_sound application is less efficient than using the Turbo Pascal procedures, because its code is larger. It could also be argued that the create_sound procedure is more efficient because it does NOT require three procedure calls as sound, nosound and delay would. The ultimate choice of which routines to use is yours. I know I had more fun writing and using my own sound generator.

The size of a TSR application is extremely important, because the code size along with the data is the amount of memory that will be permanently occupied. In this case, "permanently" simply means "until the computer is rebooted." The amount of memory taken up by a TSR is no longer available to other applications running on the machine. Remember, standard DOS allows for 640,000 bytes of active memory. All other memory beyond 640K falls into two categories: Extended RAM, and expanded RAM. For this application, and any other TSR program, you should assume that you are occupying some portion of the usable 640K of memory. The source code for the create_sound procedure is shown in FIG. 5-6.

```
{
  The SOUND, NOSOUND and DELAY Procedures could not be used because
  of an incompatability between TSR programs which incorporated the
  CRT unit. The initial load is successful, but subsequent calls
  to the program circumvent the Installation Detection Scheme used
  in most TSR programs. This limitation is version 4.0 specific.
  Subsequent versions such as 5.0 and 5.5 do NOT possess this
  limitation.

  The FREQUENCY Variable is used to determine which frequency to
  use for the sound generated.

  The DURATION Variable is the time, in HUNDREDTHS of SECONDS to
  make the sound.
}
procedure create_sound(frequency, duration : word);
var
  temport : byte;
  counter : word;
begin
  (* Prepare Speaker for Output *)
  port[67] := 182;

  (* Load Sound Frequency *)
  port[66] := lo(frequency);
  port[66] := hi(frequency);

  (* Get Current Speaker Condition *)
  temport := port[97];

  (* Turn Speaker On *)
  port[97] := temport OR $03;

  (* Pause for DURATION counting *)
  for counter := 1 to duration do;
    begin
    end;

  (* Restore Original Speaker Condition *)
  port[97] := temport;
end;
```

Fig. 5-6. The CREATE_SOUND procedure.

The `create_sound` procedure is the primary Action procedure available for the KeyClick program. This procedure accesses ports 66, 67 and
97 directly to control the computer's speaker. The information needed to
create this application is available from any technical reference manual for
the personal computer.

Port 67 is used to prepare the speaker for sound generation. The specific action of this port is not clear. However, several technical manuals
that I have examined have noted the necessity of sending information to
this port. After the proper codes have been sent to the port, the speaker is
ready to be programmed. It could be argued that this step is a primer for
the generation of sound, however, the specific actions intitiated by this
step are not clear.

Port 66 controls the frequency or pitch of the tone created by the
speaker when active. The frequency is loaded into port 66 using two individual byte values. The upper and lower bytes of the frequency argument
are sent to port 66 as the two individual byte values. Each byte is loaded

separately using an assignment to the `port` function. After the new frequency is loaded into the port, the sound may be turned on to generate the selected tone.

Port 97 is used to control the activity of the speaker. For this port, activity refers to whether the speaker is ON or OFF. The procedure in FIG. 5-6 assumes that the speaker is OFF when first accessed. The original value contained within this port is stored in a temporary variable. Port 97 is simply an ON/OFF switch used to control speaker activity.

It is NOT required that you turn the speaker OFF, change the frequency, and then turn the speaker ON again. Situations requiring modification of sound with continuous sound generation are bound to come up at some time. The only difficulty that might arise is a momentary aberration in the generated sound as the frequency is modified. Remember, a new frequency is loaded as two byte variables in two separate call assignments to port 66. If these assignments are not made in a timely manner, or if an interruption occurs during the modification of the tone, then an unexpected tone might be generated. Another possibility is that a tone could be generated continuously and not be silenced appropriately. This possibility could be described as the audio equivalent of a continuous loop. Remember, the frequency of the tone does NOT control the activity of the speaker.

The `create_sound` procedure takes two arguments: `frequency`, and `duration`. The `frequency` variable contains an integer value corresponding to the frequency of the tone to be generated. Frequency is defined as the number of cycles of sound completed for each second. The scientific term for a cycle of sound is a "hertz."

The higher the frequency the higher the *pitch*. The lower the frequency, the lower the pitch. The standard scale of musical notes ranges from about 15 to 4200 hertz (Hz). Other tones can be heard for several hundred hertz above 4000 Hz. Any tones with frequencies above that can be heard by your dog, cat or pet gerbil. Some examples of frequencies and their corresponding musical tones are shown in TABLE 5-2.

Frequency	Note
27.5	A0
55	A1
110	A2
220	A3
440	A4
880	A5
1760	A6
3520	A7

Table 5-2. Some Frequencies and Corresponding Musical Notes

The frequency scale for musical notes is NOT a linear scale. The function to generate valid tones is based on an exponential increase of frequency of the speaker. The function to generate values for an A note is "$(27.5 * (2**X))$" where X is the octave for which you wish to generate an A note, and 27.5 is the starting frequency for that note's letter. The starting frequencies for other notes in octave 0 are shown in TABLE 5-3.

Table 5-3. Starting Frequencies for Notes in Octave 0

Frequency	Note
C	16.35
C#	17.32
D	18.35
D#	19.45
E	20.60
F	21.83
F#	23.12
G	24.50
G#	25.96
A	27.50
A#	29.14
B	30.87

One of the major discrepancies of the PC sound generating system, and Turbo Pascal's access to it, is the inability to accept real number data. Currently the speaker, the PORT function, and the SOUND procedure can only accept integer values. This means that any tone you generate, other than A, will be sharp or flat. For higher frequencies that number in hundreds or thousands of cycles per second, this problem is not as noticeable.

The duration variable is used to control the length of time the tone sounds. Although the duration variable is used to time the length of the tone, it is NOT based on clock ticks. Instead a simple for..do loop counts the number of integer values between 1 and the number specified by duration. The rate at which these counts are made is dependent on the processor type of your computer and its clock speed. Because KeyClick enables you to modify the duration of the "click" at start-up time and during operation, you can tailor this parameter as necessary.

The my_readkey Procedure

The my_readkey procedure for the KeyClick application is used to detect the activation key sequence. The Installation code section replaces the BIOS keyboard services interrupt procedure with the my_readkey procedure. The argument list for any "interrupt" procedure is predefined to include ALL of the known register variables associated with the `regis-ters` data type. For more information about this data type, please consult the User's Guide and Reference Manual for Turbo Pascal 5.5.

Because the `my_readkey` procedure will be replacing a BIOS interrupt service, it must be defined as an "interrupt" procedure. The procedure is defined as an interrupt routine by the use of the `interrupt;` string following the procedure header declaration. This `interrupt` declaration modifier, like `forward`, causes the generation of extra code to provide for additional functionality.

When installed, this procedure replaces the BIOS keyboard services interrupt procedure. Any keyboard action results in the calling of the keyboard interrupt services and this procedure. Normally when the keyboard services are called, a specific subservice is called such as detecting keyboard action, reading a character or determining the status of the toggle and special action keys. The `my_readkey` procedure provides for all of these actions by intercepting keyboard action, determining if it or the original keyboard service can provide the service, and then calling the appropriate action. The `my_readkey` procedure is shown in FIG. 5-7.

```
{
    Specialized character read-in procedure. This procedure replaces the
    current BIOS character waiting, detection and special key status
    procedure as $16. The original procedure is reassigned to interrupt
    $88.
    The original procedure is called regardless of starting registers.
    Calls are made to CREATE_SOUND when keyboard characters are selected.
    This procedure also processes specific key combinations to modify
    the TONE and LENGTH of the 'click'.
}
procedure my_readkey(Flags,CS,IP,AX,BX,CX,DX,
                          SI,DI,DS,ES,BP : WORD); interrupt;
var
    old_char2, old_char1, current_char, extended_char, counter : word;
    hi_ax, lo_ax : byte;
    register : registers;
begin
    (* Generate the HI and LO byte portions of AX *)
    hi_ax := hi(ax);
    lo_ax := lo(ax);

    (* Copy Current Registers *)
    register.Flags := Flags;
    register.ax := ax;
    register.bx := bx;
    register.cx := cx;
    register.dx := dx;
    register.si := si;
    register.di := di;
    register.ds := ds;
    register.es := es;
    register.bp := bp;


    (* Determine if this is a CHARACTER READ or CHARACTER READY Call *)
    if (hi_ax = 0) or (hi_ax = $7F) then
        begin
            (* Determine is this is a maintenance cost *)
            if (hi_ax = $7F) then
                begin
                    (* Return the Proper Detection Code *)
                    ax := 136;
                end
```

Fig. 5-7. The MY_READKEY keyboard control procedure.

"Fig. 5-7 continued."

```
            else
              begin
                (* Call the Original Keyboard Action Interrupt Service *)
                intr($88, register);

                (* Get the current Character and Extended Character Code *)
                extended_char := hi(register.ax);
                current_char  := lo(register.ax);

                (* Create a predefined tone to indicate a key was pressed *)
                (* and it is neither and extended code nor ESC            *)
                if (current_char <> 0) then
                begin
                  create_sound(frequency, duration);
                end;

                (* UP arrow *)
                if (extended_char = 132) then frequency := frequency + 250
                  else
                (* DOWN arrow *)
                if (extended_char = 118) then frequency := frequency - 250
                  else
                (* LEFT arrow *)
                if (extended_char = 115) then duration  := duration  - 1000
                  else
                (* RIGHT arrow *)
                if (extended_char = 116) then duration  := duration  + 1000
                  else
                (* HOME key - Reset to Original FREQUENCY and DURATION *)
                if (extended_char = 119) then
                  begin
                    frequency := Init_Frequency;
                    duration  := Init_Duration;
                  end;

                if (frequency < 0) then frequency := 200;
                if (duration < 0) then duration := 10;

                (* Call Create Sound to Demonstrate NEW Parameters *)
                for counter := 1 to 10 do;
                  begin
                    create_sound(frequency,duration);
                  end;
            end;
        end
      else
        begin
          (* Call the Original Keyboard Action Interrupt Service *)
          intr($88, register);
        end;

  (* Reassign Registers for Calling Program *)
  Flags := register.Flags;

  (* If DETECTION was NOT used then return the NEW AX code *)
  if (hi_ax <> $7F) then ax := register.ax;

  bx := register.bx;
  cx := register.cx;
  dx := register.dx;
  si := register.si;
  di := register.di;
  ds := register.ds;
  es := register.es;
  bp := register.bp;

  (* Save old Character Values *)

    old_char2 := old_char1;
    old_char1 := current_char;
end;
```

The my_readkey procedure performs three basic actions. Its primary purpose is to process calls to the keyboard services. The specific keyboard subservice is defined in the high order byte of the AX register variable. This procedure does NOT access keyboard hardware directly. Instead, anytime my_readkey is called it passes on the specific subservice call to the original keyboard services interrupt procedure. my_readkey then uses the information returned in the register record to determine the next task to perform.

When a character key is pressed, a tone is generated. This occurs with the alphanumeric characters, the function keys, the cursor keys, the punctuation characters and the ENTER key. When a special key combination such as CTRL-LEFT is selected, the my_readkey procedure interprets the individual key combination and modifies the duration of the "click" so it lasts for a shorter period of time. Pressing the CTRL-RIGHT key increases the duration of a click. When the CTRL-PGUP key combination is selected, the frequency or "pitch" of the tone rises. The CTRL-PGDN key combination reduces the frequency of the generated tone. The CTRL-HOME key causes the frequency and the duration of the tone to return to their default settings. The default values for these variables can be those values hard-coded into the initialization procedure. The default values might be the values passed to it as command arguments during the initial installation of the KeyClick application.

The actions of the my_readkey procedure are fairly straightforward. However, certain guidelines must be observed to assure proper functioning of the TSR program. When first called, my_readkey copies all register values passed to it into a local register variable. This enables the procedure to call other interrupt-based procedures and services without losing track of interrupt values. After my_readkey has finished executing, the values returned for called interrupts are passed back into the register variables.

Through this calling scheme, the register variables containing stack and heap information are preserved. However, by calling other procedures that use interrupts, but do NOT take register variables as arguments, this stream of information and services is NOT maintained. When stack and heap information is NOT maintained between procedure calls, the computer will likely freeze. A prime example of this problem is the use of write from within a TSR application.

The Turbo Pascal write procedure makes use of the video service interrupt $0E (14 decimal) to write a character to the screen. This interrupt can be called from my_readkey using the INTR procedure. If write was used, then the register variable would not be passed, and modifications to the register values would be passed back to the application that called my_readkey originally. If the stream of register values is NOT preserved then, at some point within the chain of interrupt calls, the computer would lose track of what task it is performing. When this happens the computer usually freezes.

The initialize_my_readkey Procedure

The initialize_my_readkey procedure performs two functions. Its primary purpose is to replace the existing keyboard services interrupt procedure $16 (decimal 22) with the my_readkey procedure. In addition, the command line arguments are examined to determine if an initial value for the pitch and duration of the "click" has been supplied. If initial values have been supplied, they are converted to integer values for use in the create_sound procedure.

The importance of this procedure cannot be overstated. The initialize_my_readkey procedure determines where the new keyboard services will be installed. The procedure also creates a link to the original keyboard services by installing them as a new interrupt service $88 (136 decimal). The interrupt $88 is currently not used by the standard BIOS services. The source code for the initialize_my_readkey procedure is shown in FIG. 5-8.

```
{
  This procedure initializes all variables for use in 'click'
  generation.
  The GETINTVEC and SETINTVEC procedures install the MY_READKEY
  procedure as Interrupt $16, replacing the original interrupt
  procedure. The original $16 procedure is reassigned to interrupt
  $88. The reassigned procedure is used by the new $16 interrupt
  to process keyboard interrupt values properly.
  Initial values for FREQUENCY and DURATION are read-in from
  command line. If valid variables are not available, default
  values are substituted.
}
procedure initialize_my_readkey;
begin
  (* Initialize Video Service Pointers and Reroute *)
  (* Interrupt $16 to the used BIOS Interrupt $88  *)
  getintvec($16, oldkey);
  setintvec($88, oldkey);

  newkey := @my_readkey;
  setintvec($16, newkey);

  (* Initialize Frequency and Duration Variables *)
  (* for sound generation TONE and LENGTH        *)
  if (paramcount > 1) then
    begin
      (* Convert First Argument into a usable number *)
      VAL(paramstr(1), Init_Frequency, ErrorCode);
      if (ErrorCode <> 0) then Init_Frequency := 3000;

      (* Convert Second Argument into a usable number *)
      VAL(paramstr(2), Init_Frequency, ErrorCode);
      if (ErrorCode <> 0) then Init_Duration := 2100;
    end
  else
    begin
      Init_Frequency := 3000;
      Init_duration  := 2100;
    end;
  Frequency := Init_Frequency;
  Duration := Init_Duration;
end;
```

Fig. 5-8. The INITIALIZE_MY_READKEY procedure.

The get i ntvec procedure is used to obtain the pointer location of the original keyboard service interrupt. This value is assigned into a local pointer variable. The pointer location of the my_readkey procedure is then determined using the @ operator. The set i ntvec procedure is used to assign that location as the new keyboard services interrupt. Finally, the location of the original keyboard services is assigned into a new interrupt location using the set i ntvec procedure.

The i n i t i a l i ze_my_readkey procedure performs one of the most important functions of any of the TSR routines. It installs the new keyboard services interrupt procedure and maintains a pointer to the original services. This pointer can then be used to reinstall the original keyboard services into an unused interrupt number. Interrupt numbers can range from 0 to 255 ($00 to $FF hexadecimal). When reinstalled, the original keyboard services can be accessed by other procedures such as my_readkey.

This form of interrupt procedure reorganization is ideal for enhancement of existing functionality. Access to original procedures can be provided as if the replacement never took place. Access to the enhanced features of the new interrupt service procedure is built into the BIOS system. The new interrupt procedure does NOT need to emulate the original interrupt services, because it can call them as necessary.

The my_readkey_installed Function

The my_readkey_i nsta l l ed function provides an important service for the KeyClick program. During the installation of the TSR, memory which might be used for other applications is reserved. This memory cannot be reused for other applications after the TSR is installed. If a new copy of the TSR program is installed into memory each time the program is executed from DOS, the computer will eventually run out of memory.

It's like stacking empty boxes, that only open from the top, on top of each other; you take up space with each box, but you can only add or remove objects to or from the top box. A TSR uses memory in a similar fashion. As you load a copy of the application into memory, a previous copy becomes a closed box which takes up memory, but cannot perform its action.

If a new copy of the KeyClick program gets installed over a previous copy, then the original copy of the keyboard services will be lost. The reason for this is that copy A, when it is installed, places the original keyboard services into interrupt $88. When copy B gets loaded, it places what it thinks is the original keyboard services into interrupt $88. However, what copy B doesn't know is that the procedure it is installing at interrupt $88 is actually the my_readkey procedure for copy A of the KeyClick program. And the pointer to the original keyboard services procedures is destroyed. The source code for the my_readkey_i nsta l l ed function is shown in FIG. 5-9.

```
{
  Determine if the TSR has been previously installed.
}
function my_readkey_installed : boolean;
var
  register : registers;
begin
  (* Determine if the Program is Already Installed by Sending *)
  (* A known Code $7F which will be interpretted as a Query   *)
  (* by the Video_Interrupt Procedure.                        *)

  with register do
    begin
      ax := $7F shl 8;
      intr($16, register);
      my_readkey_installed := (lo(ax) = 136);
    end;
end;
```

Fig. 5-9. The MY_READKEY_INSTALLED function.

In order for the my_readkey procedure in FIG. 5-7 to function, it must be able to determine which subservice to call. Besides the predefined subservices 0, 1 and 2, the my_readkey procedure also defines an additional subservice, $F7 (127 decimal). This subservice is designed specifically for use in conjunction with the my_readkey_installed function. This subservice returns a specific number to the calling routine if the my_readkey procedure is installed. If the original keyboard services receive a subservice request, they will return a number other than the specific code required.

When an improper code is returned by the call to interrupt $16, the my_readkey_installed function returns a value of FALSE indicating that the keyboard services have NOT been circumvented by the KeyClick program. If the value 136 is returned, then the my_readkey_installed function returns a value of TRUE. A returned value of TRUE indicates prior installation of the my_readkey procedure and the KeyClick program. This information can then be used by the main procedure to determine if the current program should be installed as Terminate-but-Stay-Resident, or simply halted and not installed at all.

This function, as well as the interrupt replacement procedure, must be defined to be compatible. Each must understand what the other procedure expects. When a well-defined installation determination procedure such as this is created, it can be used by other TSR applications as well. Other programs can be defined to detect NOT only themselves, but also other TSR applications. This information can be used by any TSR to determine exactly what programs are running on the computer, what procedures have been replaced, and what TSR installation options are available.

The main Program Procedure

The main procedure provides the logical control needed to determine whether to install the TSR program or halt the process. If the value returned by the my_readkey_installed function is TRUE, then a message indicating previous installation is displayed and the program terminates normally. None of the initialization procedures, or a call to the Turbo Pascal KEEP procedure, are made. If the value returned by my_readkey _installed is FALSE, all of the predefined installation procedures are executed. A message indicating the "NEW" installation is displayed. Finally, a call to the standard Turbo Pascal keep procedure is made using the errorcode variable.

The value contained within the errorcode variable is supplied by the keep procedure during the call. This value is used by DOS for error detection and processing. The source code for the main procedure is shown in FIG. 5-10.

```
Begin (* main *)
    (* Determine if the keypressed interrupt is installed *)
    if (my_readkey_installed = True) then
      begin
        (* Indicate previous installation *)
        writeln('KeyClick ALREADY Installed');
      end
    else
      begin
        (* Initialize the NEW keypressed interrupt *)
        initialize_my_readkey;

        (* Indicate Key Click Program Installed *)
        writeln('KeyClick Application Installed');

        (* Terminate Program and make it TSR *)
        keep(errorcode);
      end;
end.
```

Fig. 5-10. The MAIN installation control procedure.

The getintvec, setintvec and keep procedures are documented in the Turbo Pascal User's Guide and Reference Manual. These procedures form the basis of any high level attempt to modify or enhance the BIOS capabilities of the PC. Other facilities exist, but they are rooted with the BIOS itself. A unique interrupt procedure is defined to create TSR applications. Other interrupt and DOS services exist to insert a new interrupt services procedure into an existing interrupt location. For more information on the use of the BIOS and BIOS service offerings, you should consult a low-level programming guide for the PC.

Debugging

The Turbo Pascal version 5.0 and 5.5 application development environments provide the programmer with access to an integrated program debugging facility. This debugger is a set of tools that enable the programmer to see "inside" an application as it is running. Unfortunately, the presence of the keep procedure to create a TSR program precludes the use of the debugging utility. The best way to get around this is to comment out the keep procedure until the program is debugged. In its place, substitute a call to the read procedure to get a string variable. This way you can test your Detection and Action code sections within the Turbo Pascal environment. However, you CANNOT test the Installation code sections of your application within Turbo Pascal version 5.5.

Notes

Special care must be taken when designing and implementing TSR programs. Because the TSR techniques demonstrated here require the replacement of existing BIOS services, care must be taken to prevent the elimination of vital functionality. The KeyClick program makes use of existing functionality with enhancements put into place by adding a new interrupt services procedure. If several TSR programs need to use the original keyboard services, it is best to maintain access to the circumvented routine to provide access for ALL applications.

Well-designed and implemented TSR programs provide for access to the basic services replaced, even if their unique activation key sequences are not called. Some applications provide programmable options enabling the user to modify the key sequence for activation. The user-defined activation sequences can then be read into a file and recalled at installation time. Several of the currently available TSR applications make use of this customizing option to provide flexibility, and avoid conflicting with other TSRs.

Some of the more advanced TSR applications provide graphics output. However, many of the Turbo Pascal graphics routines contain references to dynamic memory data structures. You likely noticed the code "{$m $2000,$2000,$2000}" in the beginning section of the source for the KeyClick program. This statement is used to specify the amount of stack and heap needed to be saved by the keep procedure. If the memory size specified within this compiler directive is inadequate, then an error will occur and the computer will likely freeze. If you are going to use graphics in your TSR applications, please be aware of the limitations and restrictions of these techniques.

It is important to keep track of the memory used by a TSR application during usage. The ultimate goal of TSR programming is to enhance current functionality without sacrificing performance. Many TSR applications enhance system performance by providing disk caching or intelligent file buffer handling capabilities. These applications take up space in memory, but provide better performance of specific tasks. Your TSRs must be able to provide some form of enhancement that makes the loss of some memory equitable to the user.

DISCUSSION

Each component of a typical TSR program provides a specific function. The three most important aspects of any TSR program are its Installation, Detection and Action procedures and functions. The Installation procedures provide the program with the ability to install itself in memory, as well as detect previous copies and prevent multiple installations. The Detection procedures tell the program when to activate and terminate activity. And finally, the Action procedures execute specified tasks to provide the desired functionality.

The TSR programs provide extensions to the DOS operating system. Many TSR applications provide advanced file listing, sorting, and other access utilities not available from any version of DOS. The makers of the DOS language try to discourage the use of TSR applications because they can conflict with certain DOS utilities. However, it is these utilities which have been enhanced and replaced by the TSR programs. Future versions of DOS, or perhaps even OS/2, might circumvent the need for TSR programs. However, for the present Terminate-but-Stay-Resident applications can provide the functionality missing from DOS.

6

DOS Shell and
the Command Line
Recall "Shell" Program

This chapter presents the SHELL.PAS program. This program allows users to enter DOS commands, and then makes use of the standard Turbo Pascal Exec procedure to cause these commands to be executed as though they were entered at the DOS prompt. In addition, the Shell program enables users to recall and edit up to 20 previously entered commands. Finally, commands can be recalled in their entirety and executed using only the number of the command as it appears in the listing.

THE "SHELL" PROGRAM

The Shell program is an example of a DOS shell environment. Within the environment, specific functionality that enhances DOS is available. Outside of this environment, these enhanced capabilities are NOT available. Unlike a TSR program, Shell is NOT memory-resident. This enables users to move from one shell program to another without having to reboot their computers—which is what changing TSRs would require.

You might recall from chapter 5 that the KeyClick application makes a modification to the Basic Input/Output System (BIOS). The Shell application does NOT require such a modification, because it does not provide its functionality within ALL applications. Instead, Shell is designed to execute as though its command prompt is the DOS command prompt for operating system commands.

The Exec Procedure

Turbo Pascal provides a specific procedure called Exec that enables programmers to cause DOS commands to be executed as though they were entered at the DOS prompt. The commands can be generated from predefined command strings. Commands can also be generated interactively using the Read procedure to get a string of characters. The string of characters can then be passed to the Exec procedure and executed. The Exec procedure can cause DOS commands, utilities, and even other applications to execute from inside of the Turbo Pascal program.

What the "SHELL" Program Does

The Shell program uses the Exec procedure to provide transparent access to DOS, its utilities and other applications. Besides access to existing functionality, the Shell application provides additional capabilities not provided by DOS. These capabilities include a command-line history recall capability similar to that offered by the UNIX operating system. The Shell program also provides a command-line editing functionality similar to that offered by the VMS operating system.

The Shell program can be loaded and tested within the Turbo Pascal Application Development Environment. Unlike the KeyClick Terminate-but-Stay-Resident application presented in Chapter 5, the Shell program does NOT replace any interrupt procedures or modify any portion of DOS. Because the program creates a shell to DOS, Turbo Pascal can handle all operations within the shell while the environment is active. This enables you to debug applications such as the Shell program using the Turbo Pascal Integrated Debugger.

Starting the "SHELL" Program

The source code for the Shell program is presented in its entirety in FIG. 6-1. The program can be called by entering SHELL at the DOS prompt and pressing the ENTER key. The Shell program takes an optional argument that enables the user to specify the prompt that appears to the user when a command can be entered. The specified prompt cannot include any spaces. It may be upper- or lowercase characters, or a combination of both. If a user-specified prompt is not passed to Shell during the call, then a default prompt of Yes Master> is used.

```
{
  This application demonstrates how a DOS emulation program
  can be created using the basic components of the Turbo
  Pascal language.

  Specific DOS commands are executed using the EXEC command
  which passes command text to the DOS command interpreter
  COMMAND.COM.

  Normally, commands entered at the DOS prompt are immediately
  intepreted by COMMAND.COM. This application enables you
  to use the cursor keys to recall up to 20 previous commands
  and execute them.

  In addition, selected commands can be edited using the cursor
  keys. The specific actions of cursors keys are shown below:

  UP - Recall previous command
  DOWN - Recall subsequent command. This enables you to move
         backwards and forwards through the list of previous
         commands.
  LEFT - Move editing cursor one character Left
  RIGHT - Move editing cursor one character Right
  HOME - Move editing cursor to the first character of the command
  END - Move editing cursor to the last character of the command
  INSERT - Toggle editing between, INSERT and OVERSTRIKE modes.
           The default value for editing is INSERT
  BACKSPACE - Delete one character to the left of the editing cursor
  RETURN - Accept and execute the entered or edited command

                        ** Note **
  Command length is limited to 72 characters. Longer strings
  can be accepted if the STR72 data type is modified.
}
program Shell;

{
  Make sure memory is left over for the commands or
  applications that may be called from this shell
}
{$M $4000,$2000,$2000}

uses Dos, Crt;
type
  str72 = string[72];
var
  xline, yline : integer;
  insert_mode : boolean;
  prompt : str72;


{
  Initialize prompt and display location values. The shell's
  prompt can be specified by command line argument to the
  program.

  Display location variables are determined from the current
  cursor location and the character length of the PROMPT text
```

Fig. 6-1. The complete source code for the SHELL program.

"Fig. 6-1 continued."

```
          Warning: Only the first word of multiple word prompts will
                   be accepted for the prompt. DOS and Turbo Pascal
                   treat spaces as command line argument separators
}
procedure Initialize_Prompt(var xline, yline : integer; var prompt
                            : str72);
begin
  (* Determine if a prompt was specified *)
  if (paramcount = 1) then
    prompt := paramstr(1)
   else
    prompt := 'Yes Master';

  (* Add a 'Greater Than' symbol to the prompt *)
  prompt := prompt + '> ';

  (* Generate the value of the current line *)
  yline := WhereY;
  xline := length(prompt);

  (* Reposition Cursor if Necessary - If the current cursor *)
  (* location is not on the left most portion of the screen *)
  if (WhereX > 1) then writeln;
end;


{
  Remove Edited Text from the screen in case a previous command
  of longer or shorted length is created or selected
}
procedure Remove_Text(Command : str72; xline, yline : integer);
var
  counter : integer;
  blank_text : str72;
begin
  (* Initialize Blank Text *)
  Blank_Text := ' ';

  (* Create a blank line the same length as the displayed text *)
  for counter := 1 to length(Command) do
    begin
      Blank_Text := Blank_Text + ' ';
    end;

  (* Display Blank Text at the current location *)
  gotoxy(xline, WhereY);
  write(Blank_Text);
end;


{
  Display Text function for displaying edited text
}
procedure Display_Text(Command : str72;
                       xline, yline, char_count : integer);
begin
  (* Display the entire text at the specified location *)
  gotoxy(xline, WhereY);
  write(Command);

  (* Redisplay the character at the current location *)
  (* so that the editing cursor can be seen at the   *)
  (* current character location                      *)
```

"Fig. 6-1
continued."

```
      gotoxy(xline + char_count - 1, WhereY);
      write(copy(command, char_count, 1));
end;


{
    Returns the selected character, or a DIRECTION or a special
    function key descriptive label.

    This function returns the selected character or key pressed
    by the user.

    This function uses READKEY to get an entered key value and
    then translates it into a more easily recognized text. This
    is less efficient than using READKEY directly, however it
    provides for easy extension to include function keys, as
    well as Control, or Alternate key combinations.

    For a complete list of extended key code for the PC and Turbo
    Pascal see Appendix C.2 on page 424 of the Turbo Pascal version
    5.0 Reference Guide.
}
function GetKey : str72;
var
    command_char : char;
begin
    (* Get a Character from the KeyBoard *)
    command_char := ReadKey;

    (* If an EXTENDED Character is Entered process it *)
    if (command_char = #0) then
      begin
        (* Call ReadKey for Extended Character Code *)
        command_char := ReadKey;

        (* UP arrow *)
        if (command_char = #72) then GetKey := 'UP'
         else
        (* DOWN arrow *)
        if (command_char = #80) then GetKey := 'DOWN'
         else
        (* LEFT arrow *)
        if (command_char = #75) then GetKey := 'LEFT'

         else
        (* RIGHT arrow *)
        if (command_char = #77) then GetKey := 'RIGHT'
         else
        (* INS insert key *)
        if (command_char = #82) then GetKey := 'INSERT'
         else
        (* DEL delete key *)
        if (command_char = #83) then GetKey := 'DELETE'
         else
        (* HOME key *)
        if (command_char = #71) then GetKey := 'HOME'
         else
        (* END key *)
        if (command_char = #79) then GetKey := 'END'
         else
        (* PGUP pageup key *)
        if (command_char = #73) then GetKey := 'PAGEUP'
         else
        (* PGDN pagedown key *)
        if (command_char = #81) then GetKey := 'PAGEDOWN';
```

"Fig. 6-1
continued."

```
      end
    else
      begin
        (* Not an Extended Character *)

        (* RETURN key *)
        if (command_char = #13) then GetKey := 'RETURN'
         else
        (* BS backspace key *)
        if (command_char = #8) OR
           (command_char = #127) then GetKey := 'BACKSPACE'
         else
           (* Assign COMMAND_CHAR to GETKEY function return *)
           GetKey := command_char;
      end;
end;


{
  Get characters and assemble a command string. When RETURN
  is pressed, pass the assembled string back to the calling
  procedure

  This function polls the GETKEY function for keyboard input.
  When a character is entered, a determination is made to
  see if it is a cursor key or RETURN. If the character does
  not have a special function, it is concatenated to the current
  command string at the location specified by the CHAR_COUNT
  variable. CHAR_COUNT tracks the editing cursor location, not
  the length of the command string. This enables you to edit
  in the middle of the command rather than just the end.

  When the RETURN, UP, or DOWN is pressed, the current command
  text is returned to the calling procedure for execution or
  special interpretation.
}
function GetCommand(command, prompt : str72;
                    xline, yline : integer;
                    var direction : str72) : str72;
var
  char_count : integer;
  command_text, original_command : str72;
begin
  (* Display prompt *)
  gotoxy(1, WhereY);
  write(prompt);

  (* Initialize variables *)
  original_command := command;
  command_text := ' ';
  direction := ' ';
  char_count := length(command);

  (* Display the default command *)
  Display_Text(command, xline, WhereY, char_count);

  (* Loop until the RETURN key is pressed *)
  while (command_text <> 'RETURN') do
    begin
      (* Get a Character from the KeyBoard *)
      command_text := GetKey;

      (* Decode or interpret the returned character *)
```

"Fig. 6-1
continued."

```
(* UP arrow *)
if (command_text = 'UP') then
  begin
    direction := 'UP';
    command_text := 'RETURN';
    command := original_command;
  end
 else
(* DOWN arrow *)
if (command_text = 'DOWN') then
  begin
    direction := 'DOWN';
    command_text := 'RETURN';
    command := original_command;
  end
 else
(* LEFT arrow *)
if (command_text = 'LEFT') then
  begin
    char_count := char_count - 1;
    if (char_count < 0) then char_count := 0;
  end
 else
(* RIGHT arrow *)
if (command_text = 'RIGHT') then
  begin
    char_count := char_count + 1;
    if (char_count > length(command)) then
        char_count := length(command);
  end
 else
(* INS insert key *)
if (command_text = 'INSERT') then Insert_mode := NOT(Insert_mode)
 else
(* HOME key *)
if (command_text = 'HOME') then char_count := 0
 else
(* END key *)
if (command_text = 'END') then char_count := length(command)
 else
(* BACKSPACE and DELETE *)
if (command_text = 'BACKSPACE') OR
   (command_text = 'DELETE') then
  begin
    (* Remove the text *)
    Remove_Text(command, xline, WhereY);

    (* If the length of the command text  *)
    (* is greater than one character then *)
    (* you can delete characters from it  *)
    if (length(command) > 1) then
      begin
        (* If the current character is NOT      *)
        (* the first character in the command   *)
        (* text then delete it from the string *)
        if (char_count > 1) then
          begin
            command := concat(
                          copy(command, 0, char_count - 1),
                          copy(command, char_count + 1,
                               length(command)));
            char_count := char_count - 1;
            if (char_count < 0) then char_count := 0;
          end
```

"Fig. 6-1
continued."

```
            else
              begin
                (* If the current character IS the first    *)
                (* character in the string then simply       *)
                (* copy everything from the second character *)
                (* to the last into the command variable     *)
                command := copy(command, 1, length(command));
                char_count := char_count - 1;
                if (char_count < 0) then char_count := 0;
              end;
          end
        else
          begin
            command := '';
          end;
      end
    else

    (* If RETURN was pressed or a special key not  *)
    (* allowed for in this application is selected *)
    if (command_text = 'RETURN') OR (length(command_text) > 1) then
      begin
      end
    else
      begin
        (* Neither BACKSPACE nor DELETE were specified     *)
        (* Add the new character into the current command *)
        (* string                                          *)
        if (insert_mode) then
          begin
            (* INSERT character addition mode *)
            if (char_count >= length(command)) then
              begin
                command := concat(command, command_text);
                char_count := char_count + 1;
              end
            else
              begin
                command := concat(copy(command,0,char_count),
                                  command_text,
                                  copy(command,char_count + 1,
                                       length(command)));
                char_count := char_count + 1;
              end;
          end
        else
          begin
            (* OVERSTRIKE character addition mode *)
            if (char_count >= length(command)) then
              begin
                command := concat(command, command_text);
                char_count := char_count + 1;
              end
            else
              begin
                command := concat(copy(command,0,char_count),
                                  command_text,
                                  copy(command,char_count + 2,
                                       length(command)));
                char_count := char_count + 1;
              end;
          end;
      end;
  end;
```

"Fig. 6-1
continued."

```
                    (* Redisplay the Edited Text *)
                    Display_Text(command, xline, WhereY, char_count);
                end;

            GetCommand := command;
        end;


        {
            Process returned command strings. This procedure calls the
            GETCOMMAND function to read in characters from the keyboard
            and assemble them into a text. The text is then interpreted
            as follows:

            If the UP key is returned then a command previous to the
            current command is retrieved from the PREV_COMMANDS array
            and placed into the COMMAND variable.

            If the DOWN key is returned and you have previously used UP,
            then the command called after the current command is retrieved
            from the PREV_COMMANDS array and placed into the COMMAND
            variable.

            Neither UP nor DOWN cause the retrieved command to execute.
            Instead they pass the retrieved command to the command line
            editing function (GetCommand) to allow you to modify the text.
            After modification or entry of data simply press RETURN to
            accept and Execute the current command string.

            The 'H' command lists the 20 commands previously executed

            Entering a NUMBER between 1 and 20 will cause the command
            corresponding to that number in the PREV_COMMANDS array to
            be executed. You will also notice that the text of the
            command gets placed into the PREV_COMMANDS array in its
            entirety rather than as a number.

            If a text other than those described above is entered, it will
            be passed to the EXEC command to be executed as though it were
            typed at the DOS prompt.
        }
        procedure Process_Commands(xline, yline : integer;
                                        prompt : str72);
        type
            string_array = array[0..19] of str72;
        var
            direction, command : str72;
            prev_commands : string_array;
            command_count, count, code : integer;
        begin
            (* Initialize the Command Counter and Previous Commands Array *)
            for count := 0 to 19 do
                begin
                    prev_commands[count] := ' ';
                end;
            command := ' ';
            command_count := 0;
            insert_mode := True;

            (* Loop until LOGOUT is entered *)
            while (command <> 'LOGOUT') do
                begin
                    (* Clear the DIRECTION variables *)
                    direction := ' ';
```

"Fig. 6-1
continued."

```
(* Get a command text from the Getcommand Function *)
command := GetCommand(command, prompt, xline, WhereY, direction);

(* Trim out leading spaces from the command *)
while (copy(command,1,1) = ' ') do
  begin
    command := copy(command,2,length(command));
  end;

(* If the returned command can be converted into an  *)
(* integer, between 1 and 20, assign that command to *)
(* the COMMAND variable for immediate execution      *)
VAL(command, count, code);
if (code = 0) then
  begin
    if (count >= 1) AND (count <= 20) then
      begin
        command := prev_commands[count - 1];
        direction := ' ';
      end
    else
      begin
        command := ' ';
        direction := 'PASS';
      end;
  end;

(* Process the UP command *)
if (direction = 'UP') then
  begin
    (* Remove the OLD command string *)
    Remove_Text(command, xline, WhereY);
    command := ' ';

    command_count := command_count + 1;
    if (command_count > 19) then
      command_count := 20
     else
      command := prev_commands[command_count];
    direction := 'PASS';
  end;

(* Process the DOWN command *)
if (direction = 'DOWN') then
  begin
    (* Remove the OLD command string *)
    Remove_Text(command, xline, WhereY);
    command := ' ';

    command_count := command_count - 1;
    if (command_count < 0) then
      command_count := -1
     else
      command := prev_commands[command_count];
    direction := 'PASS';

  end;

(* Special Commands *)
(* H - History *)
(* This command causes the 20 previous commands to be displayed *)
if ((command = 'H') OR (command = 'h')) AND
   (direction <> 'PASS') then
```

"Fig. 6-1
continued."

```
              begin
                writeln;
                (* Push H command onto command stack *)
                for count := 19 downto 1 do
                  begin
                    prev_commands[count] := prev_commands[count - 1];
                  end;
                prev_commands[0] := command;
                command_count := -1;
                command := ' ';

                (* Call History Listing Command *)
                for count := 20 downto 1 do
                  begin
                    writeln(count:2,') ',prev_commands[count-1]);
                  end;
                writeln;

                (* Do NOT execute the H command *)
                direction := 'PASS';
              end;


          (* If the command is a variant of LOGOUT *)
          (* convert it to the text = 'LOGOUT'      *)
          if (command = 'logout') OR
             (command = 'LO') OR
             (command = 'lo') then command := 'LOGOUT';

          (* If a LOGOUT command was NOT issued and a special *)
          (* internal command was not issued (PASS) then       *)
          (* execute the specified command string              *)
          if (command <> 'LOGOUT') AND
             (direction <> 'PASS') then
              begin
                (* Execute the Selected command *)
                SwapVectors;
                Exec(GetEnv('COMSPEC'), '/C ' + command);
                SwapVectors;

                (* Push the NEW command onto command array *)
                for count := 19 downto 1 do
                  begin
                    prev_commands[count] := prev_commands[count - 1];
                  end;
                prev_commands[0] := command;
                command_count := -1;
                command := ' ';
              end;
        end;
    end;

{ Main Procedure }
begin
  (* Initialize the Line Editing Prompting Variables *)
  Initialize_Prompt(xline, yline, prompt);

  (* Call the Program-Flow Controlling Procedure *)
  Process_Commands(xline, yline, prompt);
end.
```

As you might have noticed, the text "Yes Master" does contain a space. The default prompt is a hard-coded text string built into the Shell application's source code. Because you have the source code for application, you can modify the prompt to be whatever text you desire. The Shell program automatically adds a greater-than symbol to the specified prompt to ensure that the user knows where the prompt terminates.

Once the Shell program has been started, it may be terminated by entering either LOGOUT or LO at the Shell program's prompt. The termination command can be either upper- or lowercase. When the termination command is issued, the program terminates and the memory it used is returned to DOS. Remember, Shell is not a TSR application, so when it terminates it returns all memory to the operating system.

One final note before examining the capabilities of the Shell program. The KeyClick application possesses a method by which previous installations of the program could be detected and halted. The Shell program does NOT possess such a scheme. Because the Shell program can call DOS functions, utilities, and other programs, it can call itself. This means that several copies of the Shell program can be loaded into memory simultaneously. As an exercise you might consider how to prevent one copy of Shell from loading another.

Using the "Shell" Program

The primary function of the Shell program is to prompt the user for DOS commands. These commands are then passed to the DOS interpreter where they are executed as if they were entered at the DOS prompt.

The Shell program enables users to recall and execute up to 20 previous commands. When a command is entered at the Shell program prompt, it is executed by the Exec function. After the command is executed, the string is stored in a list of character strings. This list is composed of an array of 20 character strings of 72 characters in length. When a new command is entered, it is placed into the first slot in the list. As more commands are entered they are placed into the first position on the list also. As more commands get entered, the command string in position one is moved to position two. The text in position two is moved to position three and so on. The Shell application enables users to see the list by entering H at the prompt and pressing ENTER. A typical command list is shown in FIG. 6-2.

You might have noticed that the H command actually gets stored in the history listing. When a new command is entered, the previous commands in the list get pushed back by one position in the command string array. Figure 6-3 shows a history listing of the previous commands after the DIR command has been entered.

```
                                        20
                                        19
                                        18
                                        17
                                        16
                                        15
                                        14
                                        13
                                        12
                                        11
                                        10
Fig. 6-2. A typical HISTORY listing.     9
                                         8 dir
                                         7 cls
                                         6 copy shell.pas newshell.pas
                                         5 dir *.pas
                                         4 turbo c:\programs\shell.pas
                                         3 cd c:\programs
                                         2 dir shell.*
                                         1 h
```

```
                                        20
                                        19
                                        18
                                        17
                                        16
                                        15
                                        14
                                        13
                                        12
Fig. 6-3. The HISTORY listing after a new 11
command is executed.                    10
                                         9 dir
                                         8 cls
                                         7 copy shell.pas newshell.pas
                                         6 dir *.pas
                                         5 turbo c:\programs\shell.pas
                                         4 cd c:\programs
                                         3 dir shell.*
                                         2 h
                                         1 dir
```

As more and more commands are entered, the list eventually fills up. If the list is filled and a new command is entered, it is placed into position one in the array. The command that resided in position 1 previously moves to position 2, position 2 to 3, and so on. The command in position 20 simply falls off the list to accommodate the new command in position 1. The number of commands that can be stored by Shell is limited by available memory. You can increase the number of commands in the list as far as you desire; but remember, each element in the list takes up memory for the Shell program. The more memory that Shell uses, the less memory is available for your applications.

Commands can be recalled using the UP and DOWN arrow keys. The recalled command can then be executed by pressing the ENTER key. Alternatively, commands can be recalled and executed in one step by entering a number from 1 to 20. The command at this number position is then recalled and executed. When you use the UP and DOWN arrow keys to recall a command, you have the option of reviewing the command before it is executed.

In addition to the review capabilities, the UP and DOWN arrow keys enable you to recall a command so that it may be edited. The editing commands and their basic functions are shown in FIG. 6-4.

LEFT	Move editing cursor one character Left
RIGHT	Move editing cursor on character Right
HOME	Move editing cursor to the first character of the command
END	Move editing cursor to the last character of the command
INSERT	Toggle editing between, INSERT and OVERSTRIKE modes. The default value for editing is INSERT
BACKSPACE	Delete one character to the left of the editing cursor

Fig. 6-4. The basic line editing commands.

The Shell application's line editing commands enable you to edit recalled commands, as well as the command you are currently entering. You can use the LEFT and RIGHT cursor keys to move the cursor to a position in your command text. You can use the BACKSPACE key to delete characters from the current cursor position. In addition, you can use the INS key to allow for insert or overstrike of new characters at the current cursor position. Finally, if you want to move to the beginning or ending of the current command without pressing the cursor keys over and over, Shell provides for the HOME and END keys. The HOME key enables you to move the cursor to the beginning of the current command. The END key moves the cursor to the end of the current command.

The advantage of the application is its ability to provide command recall, and command editing, at the DOS level.

Why the "Shell" Program Isn't a TSR Application

If Shell is such a useful utility, why not make it into a TSR program? The Shell program is extremely useful for DOS level activities, but it might not be welcome inside applications. Some applications already provide their own command recall and editing services. Some applications do not use command lines at all—instead, they use menus. Menu based applications don't use command strings because they have key command sequences. The Turbo Pascal Application Development Environment is a prime example of such a menu system. Many applications have "hot-key" and "menu" command sequences that do not have specific separator characters such as the Return string that command lines use.

Without some form of standardized command delimiter, a TSR based command recall program would NOT know where to begin and end a command string. In fact, several different key combinations and commands might be captured as if they were a single command. Obviously, a TSR based command line recall and editing procedure is impractical. Until DOS, OS/2 or some other form of PC operating system becomes more structured and standardized, command line recall and editing across applications will be unlikely. In addition, differentiating between commands in separate applications would be impossible.

INNOVATIVE PROGRAMMING

Although the Shell application is designed to highlight the use of the Exec command, it also demonstrates some extremely useful procedures. The GetKey function is particularly interesting because it provides interpretation of the alpha-numeric keyboard, as well as the arrow and some extended and function key combinations. The GetCommand function provides a method of prompting the user for input at a specific location on the display screen. The source code for the GetKey function is shown in FIG. 6-5.

The GetKey function uses ReadKey to get an entered key value, and then translates it into a more easily recognized text. This is less efficient than using ReadKey directly. However, it provides for easy extension to include function keys. The GetKey function can also be extended to interpret control and alternate key sequences. For a complete list of extended key codes for the PC and Turbo Pascal, see appendix C.2 on page 424 of the Turbo Pascal version 5.0 reference guide.

The advantage of using the GetKey function over ReadKey is the ability to eliminate the need for calling ReadKey twice. When an extended key is selected, ReadKey first returns the value 0. This indicates that ReadKey needs to be called a second time to get the extended code. If you program this logic into every code location requiring interpretation of the keyboard, your application will quickly become unmanageably large. The GetKey function encapsulates the interpretation of character sequences so that a single call can be used to obtain either the entered character or a string representation of special character string. It provides a centralized method of interpreting extended key sequences, and an easily extended procedure for interpreting additional key sequences.

Enhancing GetKey

Some possible extensions you might wish to make to this function include the use of a case statement in place of the sequence of If..Then..Else statements currently implemented. The addition of function key interpretation would give the GetKey routine greater range of use. Finally, the use of shortened extended key code words, and a shortened return string variable, would improve the general efficiency of the application.

```
      function GetKey : str72;
      var
        command_char : char;
      begin
        (* Get a Character from the KeyBoard *)
        command_char := ReadKey;

        (* If an EXTENDED Character is Entered process it *)
        if (command_char = #0) then
          begin
            (* Call ReadKey for Extended Character Code *)
            command_char := ReadKey;

            (* UP arrow *)
            if (command_char = #72) then GetKey := 'UP'
              else
            (* DOWN arrow *)
            if (command_char = #80) then GetKey := 'DOWN'
              else
            (* LEFT arrow *)
            if (command_char = #75) then GetKey := 'LEFT'
              else
            (* RIGHT arrow *)
            if (command_char = #77) then GetKey := 'RIGHT'
              else
            (* INS insert key *)
            if (command_char = #82) then GetKey := 'INSERT'
              else
            (* DEL delete key *)
            if (command_char = #83) then GetKey := 'DELETE'
              else
            (* HOME key *)
            if (command_char = #71) then GetKey := 'HOME'
              else
            (* END key *)
            if (command_char = #79) then GetKey := 'END'
              else
            (* PGUP pageup key *)
            if (command_char = #73) then GetKey := 'PAGEUP'
              else
            (* PGDN pagedown key *)
            if (command_char = #81) then GetKey := 'PAGEDOWN';
          end
        else
          begin
            (* Not an Extended Character *)

            (* RETURN key *)
            if (command_char = #13) then GetKey := 'RETURN'
              else
            (* BS backspace key *)
            if (command_char = #8) OR
               (command_char = #127) then GetKey := 'BACKSPACE'
              else
                (* Assign COMMAND_CHAR to GETKEY function return *)
              GetKey := command_char;
          end;
      end;
```

Fig. 6-5. The GetKey function.

The GetCommand function is used to accept data from the user at a specific line of the display screen. When called, GetCommand calls the GetKey continually for characters. When a key or extended key sequence is pressed, GetKey returns this information to GetCommand. The GetCommand function works like a text editor for a single line of text. The command text can be a maximum of 72 characters in length. The cursor keys can be used to move the cursor backwards and forwards along the current command text. Additional keys such as HOME, END, and BACKSPACE also have special functions. The INS key enables the user to select the method of addition of text characters to the current command line. When Insert is ON, new characters are added into the text at the current cursor position. Any text to the right of the cursor is pushed to the right to make space for the new characters. The length of the command text increases with each new character. When Insert is OFF (Overstrike Mode), new characters replace previous characters. The command string does not increase in length, but its character composition changes. Figure 6-6 demonstrates the difference between Insert and Overstrike modes of character addition when the word NEW is added.

```
INSERT Mode

    Original Text  : This is the_Text
    Resulting Text : This is theNEW_Text


OVERSTRIKE Mode

    Original Text  : This is the_ Text
    Resulting Text : This is theNEWext
```

Fig. 6-6. Comparing Insert and Overstrike modes.

The underline character shows the position of the cursor. When Insert is ON, new characters are added and characters to the right of the cursor are displaced. When Insert is OFF, new characters are added into the text and characters to the right of the cursor are replaced. The source code for the GetCommand function is shown in FIG. 6-7.

```
function GetCommand(command, prompt : str72;
                    xline, yline : integer;
                    var direction : str72) : str72;
var
   char_count : integer;
   command_text, original_command : str72;
begin
   (* Display prompt *)
   gotoxy(1, WhereY);
   write(prompt);

   (* Initialize variables *)
   original_command := command;
   command_text := ' ';
   direction := ' ';
   char_count := length(command);

   (* Display the default command *)
   Display_Text(command, xline, WhereY, char_count);

   (* Loop until the RETURN key is pressed *)
   while (command_text <> 'RETURN') do
      begin
```

Fig. 6-7. The GetCommand function.

"Fig. 6-7
continued."

```
         (* Get a Character from the KeyBoard *)
         command_text := GetKey;

         (* Decode or interpret the returned character *)
         (* UP arrow *)
         if (command_text = 'UP') then
           begin
              direction := 'UP';
              command_text := 'RETURN';
              command := original_command;
           end
          else
         (* DOWN arrow *)
         if (command_text = 'DOWN') then
           begin
              direction := 'DOWN';
              command_text := 'RETURN';
              command := original_command;
           end
          else
         (* LEFT arrow *)
         if (command_text = 'LEFT') then
           begin
              char_count := char_count - 1;
              if (char_count < 0) then char_count := 0;
           end
          else
         (* RIGHT arrow *)
         if (command_text = 'RIGHT') then
           begin
              char_count := char_count + 1;
              if (char_count > length(command)) then
           char_count := length(command);
   end
 else
(* INS insert key *)
if (command_text = 'INSERT') then Insert_mode := NOT(Insert_mode)
 else
(* HOME key *)
if (command_text = 'HOME') then char_count := 0
 else
(* END key *)
if (command_text = 'END') then char_count := length(command)
 else
(* BACKSPACE and DELETE *)
if (command_text = 'BACKSPACE') OR
   (command_text = 'DELETE') then
   begin
     (* Remove the text *)
     Remove_Text(command, xline, WhereY);

     (* If the length of the command text  *)
     (* is greater than one character then *)
     (* you can delete characters from it  *)
     if (length(command) > 1) then
       begin
         (* If the current character is NOT     *)
         (* the first character in the command  *)
         (* text then delete it from the string *)
         if (char_count > 1) then
           begin
             command := concat(
                             copy(command, 0, char_count - 1),
                             copy(command, char_count + 1,
                                  length(command)));
             char_count := char_count - 1;
             if (char_count < 0) then char_count := 0;
           end
          else
           begin
             (* If the current character IS the first  *)
             (* character in the string then simply    *)
```

"Fig. 6-7
continued."

```
                            (* copy everything from the second character *)
                            (* to the last into the command variable     *)
                            command := copy(command, 1, length(command));
                            char_count := char_count - 1;
                            if (char_count < 0) then char_count := 0;
                          end;
                      end
                    else
                      begin
                        command := '';
                      end;
                  end
                else
                (* If RETURN was pressed or a special key not  *)
                (* allowed for in this application is selected *)
                    if (command_text = 'RETURN') OR (length(command_text) > 1) then
                      begin
                      end
                    else
                      begin
                        (* Neither BACKSPACE nor DELETE were specified  *)
                        (* Add the new character into the current command *)
                        (* string                                        *)
                        if (insert_mode) then
                          begin
                            (* INSERT character addition mode *)
                            if (char_count >= length(command)) then
                              begin
                                command := concat(command, command_text);
                                char_count := char_count + 1;
                              end
                            else
                              begin
                                command := concat(copy(command,0,char_count),
                                                  command_text,
                                                  copy(command,char_count + 1,
                                                       length(command)));
                                char_count := char_count + 1;
                              end;
                          end
                        else
                          begin
                            (* OVERSTRIKE character addition mode *)
                            if (char_count >= length(command)) then
                              begin
                                command := concat(command, command_text);
                                char_count := char_count + 1;
                              end
                            else
                              begin
                                command := concat(copy(command,0,char_count),
                                                  command_text,
                                                  copy(command,char_count + 2,
                                                       length(command)));
                                char_count := char_count + 1;
                              end;
                          end;
                      end;
                (* Redisplay the Edited Text *)
                Display_Text(command, xline, WhereY, char_count);
              end;

  GetCommand := command;
end;
```

The GetCommand function offers several advantages over the read or readln commands. The GetCommand function allows for command line editing above and beyond control key sequences that simply enable single-character deletion, or removal of the entire command text. These command line capabilities of read and readln are documented on pages 335 through 338 of the Turbo Pascal reference guide for versions 5.0 and 5.5. The GetCommand function can be modified for specific data entry purposes. Finally, because GetCommand uses a detached procedure for display of text, Display_Text, modifications can be made to the procedure to allow for entry within graphics as well as text screens.

Enhancing GetCommand

The GetCommand function can be modified to allow for even greater versatility. You might consider how to limit the command string to a specific character length. The limiting length could be determined by a calling procedure using an additional argument. The left side of the entry string could be modified to be a user specified location on the screen. As I noted previously, the Display_Text procedure called by the GetCommand function can be modified to display text on a graphics screen as well as text.

Enhancing the "Shell" Program

Most of the possible enhancements that could be made to the Shell program have been outlined previously for the GetKey and GetCommand programs. Additional modifications might include options for the command prompt itself. You might consider a function that would determine the current directory, and then display it each time the GetCommand function prompted for a command text. In addition, you might consider increasing the number of commands that can be saved by increasing the size of the string array used to store them. Finally, because the Shell program stores DOS commands in an array, it could just as easily write these commands to a file. In such a case, a series of DOS commands could be stored to a file and copied to a batch file. This type of command storage is called a "log" file, because it is a permanent record of the commands executed through the Shell application. Finally, you might consider programming special tasks into functions keys such as generating a directory listing, changing directories, or listing a file's contents.

DISCUSSION

The Shell program enables users to recall and edit DOS commands. The command prompt can be modified using an argument to the Shell program when it is first called. In addition to the program itself, the GetKey and GetCommand functions provide generic functionality that may be incorporated into other applications.

The Shell application provides functionality not available in the DOS operating system. This functionality allows for easier construction of commands. If you need to construct one command similar to a previous command, simply recall it and modify only those portions needed to be changed. You do NOT need to retype the entire command to execute it.

7

The "SlideShow" Graphics Display Program

This chapter introduces and explains the SlideShow graphics display application. The SlideShow program enables users and programmers to create graphics display slide shows through files containing SlideShow commands. The slide shows can be composed of graphs, charts, tables or simple demonstrations of Turbo Pascal graphics routines.

THE "SlideShow" APPLICATION

The SlideShow application provides access to the Turbo Pascal Graphics Environment for non-Turbo Pascal programs. SlideShow is a utility application that accepts a filename as a command argument. The file is simply an ASCII-based file, in which each line is a specific command to the SlideShow application to perform an action. Actions can include drawing points, lines, circles, texts and other objects. An action can also be the selection of the graphics driver and mode, text style, text size, the current color and fill pattern. In short, an action is a call to any of the Turbo Pascal graphics routines supported in the SlideShow program.

In its most basic form, SlideShow is a graphics based "script" interpreter. As stated before, SlideShow takes a filename argument as part of its call. The file contains a series of commands that are interpreted by

SlideShow into calls to Turbo Pascal's graphics routines. These calls are then transformed into the desired graphical image by Turbo Pascal's BGI graphics unit.

Many graphics presentation applications use files containing complex structures in which images are stored. When the application runs, the images are recalled from the file and placed in part, or in their entirety, on the display screen. The commands to manipulate these images are hard-coded into a compiled application. A *hard-coded* command is simply a command written in Turbo Pascal, or whatever language you are using. The command is compiled into executable code. Because the command is compiled and executable, it is NOT modifiable from outside the application. The difference is similar to that of a variable to a constant. Once you have created a constant within a program, you CANNOT change its value. With a variable, the value within the variable can be changed. Hard-coded commands cannot be changed unless you recompile the program using them. These applications are usually very efficient, generate excellent graphics, and are entirely dedicated to a SINGLE purpose.

SlideShow overcomes the limitations of dedicated graphics applications by providing a system of graphics commands accessible from anywhere. The user or programmer can create ASCII files manually from a text editor. A file can also be created from an entirely separate application written in either Turbo Pascal or another language. If another application is used, script files can be generated automatically. No compilation of the graphics commands is necessary, because SlideShow is an interpreter that can read in, interpret and display a specified graphics image from a text file.

The use of a series of commands, rather than images, is referred to as *vector* or *object-oriented* graphics. The implementation of object graphics in Turbo Pascal has existed since the release of version 4.0. The Turbo Pascal graphics environment provides for the access of graphics routines using simplified graphics calls. These calls contain only the basic information needed to place and size an image. Specific attributes such as color, shade, text height and width or style are specified separately.

Graphics images are typically stored as a series of picture elements, or *pixels*, on the screen or in a file. SlideShow and the Turbo Pascal graphics environment relate specific commands to graphics generating routines. A circle is created by passing the center position and the radius to the `circle` procedure. A pie slice is created by passing the center position, the radius and the starting and end angles to either the `pieslice` or `slice` procedures. Colors for objects are established using the `setcolor` command. Other graphics environment parameters—like font type, font size, and filling pattern for filled objects—are selected and specified using the `set...` procedures.

VECTOR GRAPHICS

When images are stored as a series of commands rather than sets of pixels, the graphics are usually referred to as "vector." A *vector* is simply a line. Vectors are usually defined to be drawn from point A to point B. The locations of points are described using Cartesian coordinates. *Cartesian* coordinates are based on the use of X and Y values to describe position. A sample Cartesian location is shown in FIG. 7-1.

```
        0   1   2   3   4   5   6
                                        + (5,0)
    0 -                         +
    1 -                                 * (1,3)
    2 -
    3 -    *                            . (2,5)
    4 -
    5 -         .
    6 -

        0   1   2   3   4   5   6
```

Fig. 7-1. Sample Cartesian point locations.

The points in FIG. 7-1—plus-sign at (5,0), asterisk at (1,3) and period at (2,5)—demonstrate the basic features of a Cartesian system. The horizontal, or X, position is shown first separated from the vertical, or Y, position by a comma. Any point within the Cartesian space can be defined using the coordinates. Any point can be located as long as the "origin" is known. The *origin* is the point at which both the X and Y positions are equal to zero, or (0,0). A typical Cartesian origin is normally located on the bottom left corner of the display screen. Positive directions are defined as left to right for the X direction, and bottom to top for the Y.

For the Turbo Pascal graphics environment, the origin is located at the top left corner of the screen. Positive movement in the X or horizontal direction results in a change in location from left to right on the display screen. Positive movement in the Y, or vertical, direction results in a change in location from top to bottom on the display screen. The SlideShow application uses the bottom left corner of the screen as the origin to be conventional. The SlideShow origin is more consistent with the original ideas of the Cartesian system. This change of origin means that positive Y movement results in a change in position from bottom to top on the display screen.

The term "Vector Graphics" was originated to describe a method of generating graphics using only lines. Any object could be created using a combination of lines of varying lengths. A point is a VERY short line. A triangle is the result of combining three lines such that the ends of one line connect to one end of each of the other two. A square is generated from four lines. A circle is the combination of many short lines drawn around a specific point. Text characters could be generated using long, medium or short lines. Because Cartesian coordinates allow for the definition of line locations using only two coordinates per line, complex objects could be created based on relative distances between their components. Examples of vector objects in the SlideShow application can be seen in the putsymbol procedure. The source code for SlideShow is shown in FIG. 7-2.

```
Program SlideShow;
uses CRT, DOS, GRAPH, DRIVERS, FONTS;

{
  Generic Screen Control Plotter Emulation Program

  Special TEXT-based Vector Graphics Interpretation Program
  for use with VGA, EGA, CGA, HERCULES, ATT400, IBM 8514 and
  IBM 3270 Graphics Drivers

  Based on a special Command Line Graphics Language, this program
  will interpret the contents of a TEXT (ASCII) file to produce
  graphics for the current and/or specified graphics device and
  graphics mode.
}


Type
  charsizetype = 1..10;
Var
  comline : string;
  regs : registers;

  GraphDriver, GraphMode, Code : integer;
  Path : string;
  MaxX, MaxY : word;
  MaxColor : word;
  I_found : boolean;

  current_color, current_style, current_font,
                 current_shade, current_linetype : word;
  current_size : charsizetype;
  current_highlight, current_replace, current_bar : word;


  {
  Initialize the SPECIFIED Graphics Driver, Mode and Path.
  This procedure translates the Graphics Driver and Mode
  variables into valid integer values to be used in the
  INITGRAPH procedure.

  If the specified codes cannot be converted properly into
  integers, then the DRIVER variable is assigned the value
  '0' to detect the current adapter and the available graphics
  modes.

  Since the GRAPHICS DRIVERS and FONT files are actually linked
  into the program, the path variable is NOT used.
  }
```

Fig. 7-2. The SlideShow graphics display application.

"Fig. 7-2 continued."

```
procedure initialize_driver(command : string);
var
   code : integer;
begin
   (* Convert Initialization Information into GRAPH DRIVER *)
   VAL(COPY(command,1,4),graphdriver,code);
   if (code <> 0) then graphdriver := 0;

   (* Convert Initialization Information into GRAPH MODE *)
   VAL(COPY(command,5,4),graphmode,code);

   (* Load Selected Graphics Driver or Detect and Load *)
   (* based on the value of the GRAPHDRIVER variable    *)
   initgraph(graphdriver, graphmode, path);

   (* Establish Maximums for X and Y Directions *)
   maxx := GETMAXX;
   maxy := GETMAXY - 10;

   (* Establsh Text Justification Parameters *)
   (* (X,Y) is the BOTTOM LEFT corner of the *)
   (* Text to be Displayed                   *)
   settextjustify(0,0);

   (* Establish BAR Type *)
   current_bar := 0;
end;


{
   This procedure is used to pause for input between SLIDES.
   After an image is displayed, the PROGRAM_PAUSE procedure
   is called.

   The procedure displays the message 'press any key to continue'
   in reverse video.

   The procedure then waits for any key to be pressed. After the
   key is pressed the procedure terminates.

   The display of graphics images does not need to be terminated
   after the call to PROGRAM_PAUSE. However, it can supply a
   convenient pause in the action of your 'show'.
}
procedure program_pause;
var
   ch : char;
begin
   (* Set FillStyle to SOLID and the current color to 'WHITE' *)
   setfillstyle(1,getmaxcolor);

   (* Create a 'WHITE' bar around the area to be written to *)
   bar(0,getmaxy-10,maxx,getmaxy);

   (* Set current color to 'BLACK' for text *)
   setcolor(0);

   (* Establish text settings for the smalled default font *)
   settextstyle(0,0,1);
   settextjustify(1,0);
   (* Write the PAUSE text to screen *)
   outtextxy((maxx + 1) DIV 2,GETMAXY,'press any key to continue');

   (* Wait for any key to be pressed *)
   ch := READKEY;
end;
```

"Fig. 7-2 continued."

```
{
  Draw a LINE in the Current Color and Line Style. The line's
  end points are defined by (X1,Y1) and (X2,Y2). The values
  for the locations of these points are supplied within the
  command string.

  Specific locations within the command text represent specific
  numbers. These numbers are stored in the command string as a
  text representation. The text must be converted into a number
  using the VAL function.

  The VAL function REQUIRES that the text to be converted into a
  number contain only numeric characters. The string cannot contain
  any punctuation characters, not even spaces.

                         ** NOTE **
          You may wish to created your own function which first
          replaces space characters in the command string with
          zeros (0) and then calls the VAL procedure to convert
          the command string into a number.
}
procedure draw_line(command : string);
var
  x1,x2,y1,y2,code : integer;
begin
  (* Convert TEXT Values to INTEGER Values *)
  VAL(copy(command,1,4),x1,code);
  VAL(copy(command,5,4),y1,code);
  VAL(copy(command,9,4),x2,code);
  VAL(copy(command,13,4),y2,code);

  (* Convert Y1 and Y2 to Lower Left Origin *)
  Y1 := maxy - Y1;
  Y2 := maxy - Y2;

  (* Call LINE Procedure with X1,Y1,X2,Y2 Coordinates *)
  line(x1,y1,x2,y2);
end;




{
  Set Line Type for Line Drawing Procedures. This procedure
  uses a specific code supplied in the COMMAND string variable
  to select a line drawing style.
}
procedure set_linetype(command : string);
var
  code : integer;
begin
  VAL(command,current_linetype,code);
  case (current_linetype) of
      0 : setlinestyle(0,0,1);        (* Single Line *)
      1 : setlinestyle(0,0,3);        (* Thick Single : Double *)
      2 : setlinestyle(1,0,1);        (* Dotted Line *)
      3 : setlinestyle(3,0,1);        (* Dashed Line *)
      4 : setlinestyle(4,16140,1);    (* Dot/Dash Line *)
      5 : setlinestyle(4,64716,1);    (* Dot/Dot/Dash Line *)
    end;
end;




{
  Move the Current Pointer(CP) to the Specified Cursor Position.
```

"Fig. 7-2
continued."

This procedure is normally used to move the CP to the location
at which text will be displayed. The CP is marked off in PIXEL
units rather than CHARACTER units.

```
}
procedure move_cursor(command : string);
var
  x1,y1,code : integer;
begin
  (* Convert TEXT Values to INTEGER Values *)
  VAL(copy(command,1,4),x1,code);
  VAL(copy(command,5,4),y1,code);

  (* Convert Y1 to Lower Left Origin *)
  Y1 := maxy - Y1;

  (* Move Graphics Cursor to New Positon *)
  moveto(x1,y1);
end;


{
  Draw an ARC around (X,Y) with radius R along a specific arc
  defined by a starting and ending angle. This procedure is
  used to produce a simple arc without shading.
}
procedure draw_arc(command : string);
var
  x1,y1,code : integer;
  sd,ed,rad : word;
begin
  (* Convert TEXT Values into INTEGER Values *)
  VAL(copy(command,1,4),x1,code);
  VAL(copy(command,5,4),y1,code);
  VAL(copy(command,9,4),rad,code);
  VAL(copy(command,13,4),sd,code);
  VAL(copy(command,17,4),ed,code);

  (* Convert Y1 to Lower Left Origin *)
  Y1 := maxy - y1;
  ed := sd + ed;

  (* Call The ARC Procedure with X1,Y2,SD,ED,R Arguments *)
  arc(x1,y1,sd,ed,rad);
end;


{
  Draw a BAR in the Current Color and fill it with the Current
  Shade.

  This procedure uses the X1 and Y1 variables to define the top
  left corner of the bar. The X2 variable holds the value of the
  width of the bar. The Y2 variable holds the value of the height
  of the bar.

  A global value CURRENT_BAR set within another procedure determines
  what type of bar to draw. If CURRENT_BAR is 0 then a 2D bar is
  drawn. If CURRENT_BAR is 1 then a 3D bar is drawn using the
  parameters.
}
procedure draw_bar(command : string);
var
  x1,x2,y1,y2,code : integer;
```

"Fig. 7-2 continued."

```
begin
  (* Convert TEXT Values to INTEGER Values *)
  VAL(copy(command,1,4),x1,code);
  VAL(copy(command,5,4),y1,code);
  VAL(copy(command,9,4),x2,code);
  VAL(copy(command,13,4),y2,code);

  (* Convert Y1 and Y2 to Lower Left Origin *)
  Y1 := maxy - Y1;
  Y2 := Y1 - Y2 + 1;
  X2 := X1 + X2 - 1;

  (* Call BAR Procedure with X1,Y1,X2,Y2 Coordinates *)
  if (current_bar = 0) then
    bar(x1,y1,x2,y2)
  else
    (* Alternate Bargraph Generator Call               *)
    (* Call 3D BAR Procedure with X1,Y1,X2,Y2 Coordinates *)
    bar3d(x1,y1,x2,y2,10,TRUE);
end;



{
  Output the COMMAND Text String at the Current Pointer
  Location.

  The location for the text is selected using the
  MOVE_CURSOR procedure. The font type and size are
  selected using the SET_FONT and SET_SIZE procedures.

  The default justification for is BOTTOM and LEFT.
  Additional procedures for establishing justification
  parameters could be written using the general model
  presented by these procedures.
}
procedure output_text(command : string);
begin
  (* Determine if Text is rotated and reset *)
  (* Justification Accordingly              *)
  if (current_style = 1) then settextjustify(2,0);

  outtext(command);

  (* Reestablsh Text Original Justification Parameters *)
  (* (X,Y) is the BOTTOM LEFT corner of the Text to be *)
  (* Displayed                                         *)
  if (current_style = 1) then settextjustify(0,0);
end;



{
  Draw a Pie Slice in the Current Color and fill it with the
  Current Shade.

  Draw a PIE around (X,Y) with radius R along a specific arc
  defined by a starting and ending angle. This procedure is
  used to produce a filled pie slice using the current color
  and shading pattern.
}
procedure draw_pie(command : string);
var
  x1,y1,code : integer;
  sd,ed,rad : word;
begin
  (* Convert TEXT Values into INTEGER Values *)
```

"Fig. 7-2
continued."

```
      VAL(copy(command,1,4),x1,code);
      VAL(copy(command,5,4),y1,code);
      VAL(copy(command,9,4),rad,code);
      VAL(copy(command,13,4),sd,code);
      VAL(copy(command,17,4),ed,code);

      (* Convert Y1 to Lower Left Origin *)
      Y1 := maxy - Y1;
      ed := sd + ed;

      (* Call The PIESLICE Procedure with X1,Y2,SD,ED,R Arguments *)
      pieslice(x1,y1,sd,ed,rad);
    end;

      {
        Draw Symbol Procedure. Identify Symbol and Execute
        Predefined Symbol Drawing Procedures.

        Unlike previous procedures that make use of predefined
        Turbo Pascal graphics objects, this procedure defines
        and draws symbols corresponding to the code passed in
        the command string.

        Symbols are positioned using the MOVE_CURSOR procedure.
      }
    procedure draw_symbol(command : string);
    var
      x, y, radius, dradius, symbol, code : integer;
    begin
      (* Convert TEXT Values into INTEGER Values *)
      VAL(command,symbol,code);
      x := getx;
      y := gety;
      radius := current_size + 1;
      dradius := 2*radius;
      setfillstyle(1,current_color);
      setlinestyle(0,0,1);

      (* Determine Symbol Type to Draw *)
      case symbol of
              (* POINT *)
          10 : putpixel(x,y,current_color);

              (* Empty Rectangle - SQUARE *)
          0 : rectangle(x-radius,y-radius,x+radius,y+radius);

              (* Empty Circle *)
          1 : arc(x,y,0,360,radius);

              (* Empty Triangle *)
          2 : begin
                line(x,y-radius,x-radius,y+radius);
                line(x-radius,y+radius,x+radius,y+radius);
                line(x+radius,y+radius,x,y-radius);
                moveto(x,y);
              end;

              (* Empty Inverted Triangle *)
          3 : begin
                line(x,y+radius,x-radius,y-radius);
                line(x-radius,y-radius,x+radius,y-radius);
                line(x+radius,y-radius,x,y+radius);
                moveto(x,y);
              end;

              (* Empty Diamond *)
```

"Fig. 7-2 continued."

```
        4 : begin
                line(x,y-radius,x+radius,y);
                line(x+radius,y,x,y+radius);
                line(x,y+radius,x-radius,y);
                line(x-radius,y,x,y-radius);
                moveto(x,y);
             end;

             (* Filled Square *)
        5 : bar(x-radius,y-radius,x+radius,y+radius);

             (* Filled Circle *)
        6 : circle(x,y,radius);

             (* Filled Triangle *)
        7 : begin
                line(x,y-radius,x-radius,y+radius);
                line(x-radius,y+radius,x+radius,y+radius);
                line(x+radius,y+radius,x,y-radius);
                moveto(x,y);
                moveto(x,y);
                floodfill(x,y,current_color);
             end;

             (* Filled Inverted Triangle *)
        8 : begin
                line(x,y+radius,x-radius,y-radius);
                line(x-radius,y-radius,x+radius,y-radius);
                line(x+radius,y-radius,x,y+radius);
                moveto(x,y);
                floodfill(x,y,current_color);
             end;

             (* Filled Diamond *)
        9 : begin
                line(x,y-radius,x+radius,y);
                line(x+radius,y,x,y+radius);
                line(x,y+radius,x-radius,y);
                line(x-radius,y,x,y-radius);
                moveto(x,y);
                floodfill(x,y,current_color);
             end;
      end;

  setfillstyle(current_shade,current_color);
  str(current_linetype,command);
  set_linetype(command);
end;



{
  Restore Graphics Mode, but don't Reload Graphics Driver.

  This procedure allows you to switch back and forth between
  graphics modes. If you add a text mode switching procedure
  this procedure could be used to switch back into graphics
  mode for additional graphics display.

  This program currently does not support Graphics/Text
  switching, however, you could add in these capabilities
  using the current procedures as model.
}
procedure restore_graph(command : string);
var
  code : integer;
```

"Fig. 7-2
continued."

```
begin
  (* Convert TEXT Values into INTEGER Values *)
  VAL(command,graphmode,code);

  (* Reset the graphics adapter to the selected mode *)
  setgraphmode(graphmode);
end;



{
  Set Text Direction, Either Horizontal or Vertical.

  This procedure enables you to select the orientation of the
  text to be displayed by the OUTPUT_TEXT command. The TEXT
  orientation capabilities of the fonts provided by Turbo
  Pascal enable this procedure to determine how text will
  be displayed at the current pointer.

  The position of the text is selected using the MOVE_CURSOR
  procedure. The orientation of the text is NOT affect and
  remains BOTTOM and LEFT, even for vertical text.

  There are some graphics programs which distinguish between
  the VERTICAL and DOWN orientations. VERTICAL corresponds to
  rotated text displayed in the VERTICAL orientation. DOWN is
  the use of not rotated text placed such that the word : DOWN
  appears as:


                                    D
                                    O
                                    W
                                    N

  No rotation has occurred, but the placement of the lettering is
  rotated.
}
procedure set_angle(command : string);
var
  code : integer;
begin
  (* Convert TEXT Values into INTEGER Values *)
  VAL(command,current_style,code);
  if (current_style = 90) then current_style := 1;

  (* Reset the orientation of text displayed *)
  settextstyle(current_font,current_style,current_size);
end;



{
  Set color of ALL Objects Drawn, including Text output using
  the OUTPUT_TEXT procedure.

  This procedure enables you to select a specific color for
  use in the drawing of objects and text.
}
procedure set_color(command : string);
var
  code : integer;
begin
  (* Convert TEXT Values into INTEGER Values *)
  VAL(command,current_color,code);

  (* Make sure the selected color is between 0 *)
```

"Fig. 7-2 continued."

```
        (* the maximum number of colors available in *)
        (* the current adapter and graphics mode      *)
        if (current_color > getmaxcolor) then current_color := 1;
        setcolor(current_color);
      end;


{
  Set Current Font for Display Text.

  This procedure takes the value passed to it in the
  COMMAND variable. The value is converted into a font
  code.

  This code is then passed to the SETTEXTSTYLE procedure
  as a font selection.
}
procedure set_font(command : string);
var
  code : integer;
begin
  (* Convert TEXT Values into INTEGER Values *)
  VAL(command,current_font,code);

  (* Set the current text font *)
  settextstyle(current_font,current_style,current_size);
end;


{
  Select BAR type when DRAW_BAR is selected.

  This procedure converts the code within the COMMAND variabl
  into a value for a global variable.

  The contents of this variable are then used by the DRAW_BAR
  procedure to determine whether to produce a 2D or 3D bar
  at the specified location.
}
procedure set_bar(command : string);
var
  code : integer;
begin
  (* Convert TEXT Values into INTEGER Values *)
  VAL(command,current_bar,code);
end;


{
  Set Current Shading for Solid Objects.

  This procedure uses the value contained in the COMMAND variable
  to determine which shade to use for filled or solid objects.

  Solid objects in this program include 2D and 3D BARS, and PIES.
  You can add additional object drawing capabilities using the
  current procedures as models.
}
procedure set_shade(command : string);
Const
    vlines    :    fillpatterntype = ($88,$88,$88,$88,$88,$88,$88,$88);
    checkered :    fillpatterntype = ($F0,$F0,$F0,$F0,$0F,$0F,$0F,$0F);
    grey50    :    fillpatterntype = ($AA,$55,$AA,$55,$AA,$55,$AA,$55);
```

"Fig. 7-2
continued."

```
Var
  code : integer;
begin
  (* Convert TEXT Values into INTEGER Values *)
  VAL(command,current_shade,code);

  (* Select a specific pattern based in the code     *)
  (* The codes used in this procedure are entirely   *)
  (* modifiable. They are the result of using a software *)
  (* package with predefined codes for specific patterns *)
  (* This procedure was modified to conform to the codes *)
  case current_shade of
    50 : setfillpattern(vlines,current_color);
    51 : setfillpattern(checkered,current_color);
    52 : setfillpattern(grey50,current_color);
   else
    begin
      current_shade := current_shade MOD 12;
      setfillstyle(current_shade,current_color);
    end;
  end;
end;


{
  Set size Multiplier for Display Text.

  This procedure is used to select the size of text displayed
  using the OUTPUT_TEXT command.
}
procedure set_size(command : string);
var
  code : integer;
begin
  (* Convert TEXT Values into INTEGER Values *)
  VAL(command,current_size,code);

  (* Set the size of text to be displayed by the *)
  (* OUTPUT_TEXT procedure                        *)
  settextstyle(current_font,current_style,current_size);
end;



{
  Set FONT and SIZE Simultaneously Based on a single Code.

  This procedure enables you to select both the FONT type
  and the SIZE of the character font using one command.
  The codes defined here provide for access to ALL of the
  fonts and many of the sizes available in Turbo Pascal.
}
procedure set_fontandstyle(command : string);
var
  tcommand : string;
  tempfont : integer;
  code : integer;
begin
  (* Convert TEXT Values into INTEGER Values *)
  VAL(command,tempfont,code);

  case tempfont of
      1,2,3,4,5 : begin
                    current_font := 0;
                    current_size := tempfont;
                  end;
```

"Fig. 7-2
continued."

```
      6,7,8,9,10 : begin
                     current_font := 1;
                     current_size := tempfont - 5;
                   end;
      11,12,13,14,15 : begin
                         current_font := 2;
                         current_size := tempfont - 10;
                       end;
      16,17,18,19,20 : begin
                         current_font := 3;
                         current_size := tempfont - 15;
                       end;
      21,22,23,24,25 : begin
                          current_font := 4;
                          current_size := tempfont - 20;
                        end
      else
        begin
          current_font := 0;
          current_size := 1;
        end;
    end;

  (* Set the SIZE and FONT using the current style  *)
  (* defined within the CURRENT_FONT, CURRENT_STYLE *)
  (* and CURRENT_SIZE global variables              *)
  settextstyle(current_font,current_style,current_size);
end;



{
  Erase the Specified Rectangular Area


}
procedure erase_window(command : string);
var
  dummy_bar : word;
begin
  (* Make sure to use the 2D bar when erasing a given area *)
  dummy_bar := current_bar;
  current_bar := 0;

  (* Call the DRAW_BAR procedure with the command string  *)
  (* intact. The bar is drawn and control returns to this *)
  (* procedure.                                           *)
  draw_bar(command);

  (* Restore the original value for the CURRENT_BAR global *)
  (* variable                                             *)
  current_bar := dummy_bar;
end;



{
  Clear Screen Procedure

  This procedure clears the screen using the CLEARDEVICE
  procedure.
}
procedure clear_screen;
begin
  cleardevice;
end;
```

"Fig. 7-2 continued."

```
{
    Process Command Text String Caught by SLIDESHOW Program
}
Procedure process_command(command : string);
var
  tstring : string;
begin
    (* Extract the leading two characters of the command *)
    (* string into the TSTRING variable to determine     *)
    (* which procedure to call                           *)
    tstring := copy(command,1,2);

    (* Copy the remainder of the string into the COMMAND  *)
    (* variable to be processed by the designated procedure *)
    command := copy(command,3,length(command) - 2);

    (* Determine which Screen Handling Procedure to Call *)
    (* and Execute it with the Text of the Command Line  *)
    if (tstring = 'A_') then draw_arc(command)
     else
    if (tstring = 'B_') then draw_bar(command)
     else
    if (tstring = 'CS') then clear_screen
     else
    if (tstring = 'FS') then set_fontandstyle(command)
     else
    if (tstring = 'I_') then initialize_driver(command)
     else
    if (tstring = 'L_') then draw_line(command)
     else
    if (tstring = 'LT') then set_linetype(command)
     else
    if (tstring = 'M_') then move_cursor(command)
     else
    if (tstring = 'O_') then output_text(command)
     else
    if (tstring = 'P_') then draw_pie(command)
     else
    if (tstring = 'PS') then draw_symbol(command)
     else
    if (tstring = 'RG') then restore_graph(command)
     else
    if (tstring = 'SA') then set_angle(command)
     else
    if (tstring = 'SB') then set_bar(command)
     else
    if (tstring = 'SC') then set_color(command)
     else
    if (tstring = 'SF') then set_font(command)
     else
    if (tstring = 'SH') then set_shade(command)
     else
    if (tstring = 'SS') then set_size(command)
     else
    if (tstring = 'T_') then program_pause
     else
    if (tstring = 'WE') then erase_window(command);
end;


{
    READ The Specified File One Line and ONE COMMAND at a Time
```

A file is specified to the program from DOS using the command line argument access capabilities of Turbo Pascal. The file is a simple ASCII text file in which each line represents a separate command.

"Fig. 7-2
continued."

The first two characters of each line of the file are used
to determine which procedure to call. The remaining characters
are used as arguments for the positioning of graphical objects,
parameters such as color, style, or pattern, or simply as text
to be output.

```pascal
}
procedure read_file(filenamestr : string);
var
  ch : char;
  f1 : TEXT;
  counter : integer;
  done : boolean;
begin
  (* Open file for input *)
  assign(f1, filenamestr);
  reset(f1);

  (* Initialize file access control variables *)
  done := false;
  i_found := FALSE;

  (* Read lines from the file and process them until the *)
  (* end of the file is reached                          *)
  (* In addition, processing of commands CANNOT be allowed *)
  (* until the graphics environment has been initialized   *)
  while NOT(EOF(f1)) AND (done = FALSE) do
    begin
      readln(f1, comline);
      if (copy(comline,1,2) = 'I_') AND (i_found) then done := TRUE;
      if (copy(comline,1,2) = 'I_') then i_found := TRUE;
      if (done = FALSE) then process_command(comline);
    end;

  (* After the file has been read completely then cause  *)
  (* the graphics adapter to reset to the original mode  *)
  (* prior to the initialization of the graphics adapter *)
  restorecrtmode;
  closegraph;
end;

{ Program Main Procedure }
Begin
  { Register all the drivers }
  code := RegisterBGIdriver(@CGADriverProc);
  code := RegisterBGIdriver(@EGAVGADriverProc);
  code := RegisterBGIdriver(@HercDriverProc);
  code := RegisterBGIdriver(@ATTDriverProc);
  code := RegisterBGIdriver(@PC3270DriverProc);
  code := RegisterBGIdriver(@IBM8514DriverProc);

  { Register all the fonts }
  code := RegisterBGIfont(@GothicFontProc);
  code := RegisterBGIfont(@SansSerifFontProc);
  code := RegisterBGIfont(@SmallFontProc);
  code := RegisterBGIfont(@TriplexFontProc);

  (* Retreive the name of the file to access from the command *)
  (* line argument procedures. If no filename or if an invalid *)
  (* filename is chosen then a default filename "PLOT.TMP" is  *)
  (* specified. After a filename is selected the READ_FILE     *)
  (* procedure is called                                       *)
  if (paramcount > 0) then
    begin
      comline := paramstr(1);
      if (comline = '') then comline := 'plot.tmp';
      read_file(comline);
```

"Fig. 7-2
continued."

```
        end
      else
        begin
          comline := 'plot.tmp';
          read_file(comline);
        end;
  end.
```

Vector graphics play a very important role in the basic operation of any graphics routine. Many graphics applications depend on the use of vector graphics to create images. If the graphics capabilities of Turbo Pascal were limited to placing lines on the screen, it would quickly get boring. Luckily, the graphics environment provides routines capable of producing not only lines but also squares, circles, pies, ellipses, and user-definable polygons. Each object type can be created as an empty shape, or as a filled object. The shading and color of an object are selected using separate set...procedures.

THE TURBO PASCAL GRAPHICS ENVIRONMENT

In order to understand how SlideShow functions, you must first look at the structure of the Turbo Pascal Graphics Environment. Starting with version 4.0, Turbo Pascal provided a device-independent graphics environment capable of operating on virtually every graphics adapter available on personal computers. When a graphics session is initialized, the environment can be instructed to load the driver for a specific adapter, or it can detect the most appropriate driver to load. There are no functions or procedures unique to any given driver. ALL graphics routines, except setrgbpalette, are available to any driver. The setrgbpalette is only available for the VGA and IBM8514 adapters.

The advantage of this environmental approach should be fairly obvious. Programmers can create applications capable of running on a variety of display devices without having to recode for each device. In addition, the get...commands such as getmaxcolor, getmaxx, getmaxy, etcetera, can be used to retrieve descriptive information about the current graphics device and mode. With this information, the advanced programmer can create applications that respond to different hardware while the program is running (run time). The advanced programmer tries to avoid hard-coding data such as the maximum and minimum resolution of a display adapter into their software. The reason for this is the constantly changing array of available hardware. A program can be instructed to detect the current display device and adapt to that device. This enables programmers to create generalized code capable of functioning with more than one display adapter using a minimum of effort and time.

Basic graphics programming is straightforward in Turbo Pascal. A graphics session is initialized by calling the initgraph procedure. This procedure loads the specified graphics driver and sets it to the indicated mode. This procedure can be instructed to detect the available display hardware, and then choose the most appropriate graphics mode. Once the graphics environment has been initialized, ALL procedures from the GRAPH unit are available for use. When you wish to terminate the graphics session, you call the closegraph procedure.

You might have noticed in the code for SlideShow that I call restorecrtmode and then closegraph. This is done to assure that the text mode in use prior to initializing graphics is properly restored. The restorecrtmode procedure restores the graphics display adapter to the original video mode. The closegraph procedure shuts down the graphics system. Memory used by the environment for variables or alternate display screens is freed up and given back to the operating system.

When the graphics environment is active, you have access to any function or procedure available in the GRAPH unit. A complete description of each procedure is presented in the Turbo Pascal reference guide. The routines can be grouped into five basic categories including: Environment Initialization and Termination, Parameter Setting, Parameter Retrieval, object Drawing and Image Management.

The Environment Initialization and Termination routines include procedures such as initgraph, resetcrtmode, and closegraph. These procedures control the active or inactive status of the environment. When initgraph is called, it not only selects the graphics driver and mode, but also the basic color palette, resolution variables, aspect ratio parameters and all basic information available through the get and set commands. The value of each of these parameters MUST be established before any image can be displayed.

The Environment Setting procedures enable the programmer, user or the program itself to establish basic parameters for the environment. Procedures such as setpalette, setmode, settextstyle, and setfillpattern establish the values for the environment parameters. The setpalette procedure enables the user or programmer to set the Color Palette for the current graphics session. The setmode procedure provides for the ability to reset the current graphics mode without reloading the graphics driver. The settextstyle procedure establishes Font, Orientation and Size of Text displayed by the outtext and outtextxy procedures. The setfillpattern procedure allows for the establishment of the filling pattern used for solid objects such as bars, filled ellipses, pie slices and filled polygons. Each of the set functions and procedures enables the programmer to tailor the current graphics environment to the requirements of the application.

The Environment Retrieval routines enable the programmer to retrieve information describing the current graphics session. Procedures such as getmaxcolor, getx and gety, getcolor and getfillsettings provide valuable information to a programmer or user. The getmaxcolor function enables the current application to determine the maximum number of colors available for the current driver and graphics mode. The `getx` and `gety` functions can be used to determine the position of the "Current Pointer" (CP) or graphics "cursor." The `getcolor` function returns the value of the current color. All graphics object drawing routines use the value of the current color for the objects they draw. The `getfillsettings` procedure is used to retrieve information about the fill pattern used for filled objects. The `get` routines can be used to help your application interact with the video display capabilities of the machine on which it runs. These routines enable your application to adapt to changing hardware platforms by providing basic information about the current graphics environment and the machine on which it is running.

The function of the Object Drawing procedures is clear. Procedures that draw objects require basic information about the location and size of the object to draw. The colors, line types, fill patterns, fonts and orientations are established using the `set` routines. The drawing routines take arguments such as position (X,Y), radius, width, height, starting angle, ending angle and so on. These routines provide the user with the ability to generate shapes of a basic type such as box, bar, circle and more complex shapes such as pie slices, ellipses and polygons. Basic and complex graphics images can be combined into a variety of shapes and images of even greater complexity.

The Image Management routines provide a service unlike any of the other procedures or functions. These routines enable the user or programmer to capture, save, display, erase or redisplay images on the graphics screen. Using these procedures, a programmer can produce amazing visual effects. Images can be overlaid. Basic as well as advanced forms of animation can be created by moving images around. The possibilities are as unlimited as your imagination. An example of some basic animation programming techniques for Turbo Pascal version 5.5 can be seen in chapter 8 of this book.

An excellent example of the basic and advanced graphics capabilities of your computer can be seen by loading, compiling and running the BGIDEMO.PAS program supplied with versions 5.0 and 5.5 of Turbo Pascal. The demo provides a sample of virtually every graphics routine available with the Turbo Pascal graphics environment. However, it is also a demonstration of the limitations of a hard-coded program. Each of the calls to a graphics routine is written directly into the program. To change the image, you must change the source code, recompile and then run. SlideShow provides for changing an image simply by editing the text file in which the command is located. No compilation is necessary to change the resulting display image.

USING SLIDESHOW

The SlideShow program closely emulates the workings of the Turbo Pascal Graphics Environment. Commands must be entered to initialize the environment. Arguments must be supplied for each procedure or function call. Some values used by the SlideShow application for the current color, shading filling, font type, font size and orientation are stored within the SlideShow program as global variables.

The SlideShow application takes the name of a file as its only argument. This file contains a series of commands for the SlideShow program to interpret and execute. Once the commands in the file have been processed, the SlideShow application automatically calls the restorecrtmode and closegraph procedures to restore the computer and its graphics adapter to their original states. During the processing of the file, any of the graphics commands supported by the SlideShow program can be called. There is no limit to the size of the file that can be read and interpreted—except the size of the disk on which it is stored.

Each line of the commands file contains a specific SlideShow command and the arguments needed by the procedure it calls. A typical SlideShow command is shown in FIG. 7-3. This command initializes the Turbo Pascal graphics environment. This command calls the initialize_driver procedure with three arguments. The first two characters of the command "I_" specify the procedure to call. All characters in the command after the first two are passed to the called procedure.

I_00090002C:\TURBO   Fig. 7-3. A typical SlideShow command.

For the initialize_driver procedure, thesc characters include three arguments. When more than one argument is used, and a numeric argument is one of them, then it must be formatted to occupy four characters in the command line. In the command, in FIG. 7-3, the characters "0009" are converted into the number 9. This value is used by initialize_driver to select the specific driver file to load during initialization. The characters "0002" are converted into the number 2. This value is used to select the specific graphics mode to activate. Finally, the last characters "C:\TURBO" are used to tell the initgraph procedure where to find the driver and font files. Because the SlideShow program links in all drivers and fonts (See the notes on compilation at the end of this chapter), this last argument is NOT necessary.

The reasons for the special formatting of numeric arguments are twofold. First, Turbo Pascal's val procedure that converts text strings into numbers CANNOT convert texts containing spaces or any other punctuation. The leading zeros "0" enable val to successfully convert "text representations" of numeric arguments into usable values. Second, a specific format length is necessary to be able to distinguish between multiple numeric arguments. Although "1" and "319" are both numeric, one has a character length of 1 and the other has a character length of 3. These two arguments both result in integer values but they are NOT the same length. If you saw the text "1319" you could make the numbers 1319, 1 and 319, 13 and 19, or 131 and "9." With so many different two-number combinations, there MUST be some form of standard numeric output to enable a program or a person to differentiate between them.

The SlideShow application does NOT support all graphics commands available in the Turbo Pascal Graphics Environment. However, the commands available enable programmers and users to create simple or complex displays. The available SlideShow commands and their corresponding SlideShow procedure calls are shown in FIG. 7-4.

```
I_                      Initialize_Driver(DRIVER CODE,
                                          MODE CODE,
                                          PATH TEXT)
T_                      Program_Pause
L_                      Draw_Line(X1,Y1,X2,Y2)
LT                      Set_LineType(SYMBOL CODE)
MC                      Move_Cursor(X1,Y1)
A_                      Draw_Arc(X1,Y1,RADIUS,START,ARCLENGTH)
B_                      Draw_Bar(X1,Y1,WIDTH,HEIGHT)
O_                      Output_Text(OUTPUT TEXT)
P_                      Draw_Pie(X1,Y1,RADIUS,START,ARCLENGTH)
PS                      Draw_Symbol(SYMBOL CODE)
RG                      Restore_Graph(MODE CODE)
SA                      Set_Angle(ANGLE CODE)
SB                      Set_Bar(BAR TYPE CODE)
SC                      Set_Color(COLOR CODE)
SF                      Set_Font(FONT CODE)
SH                      Set_Shade(SHADE CODE)
SS                      Set_Size(SIZE CODE)
FS                      Set_FontAndStyle(FS CODE)
WE                      Erase_Window(X1,Y1,WIDTH,HEIGHT)
CS                      Clear_Screen
```

Fig. 7-4. The SlideShow commands.

All CODE variables are integer values. The variables X1, X2, Y1, Y2, RADIUS, START, END, WIDTH and HEIGHT are also integer values. Integer values can range between 0 and 9999. These values are used for placement and sizing of objects. The CODE variables are used to select specific attributes and characteristics for objects and text. TEXT variables do not require conversion. The use of the PATH TEXT variable was discussed earlier. The OUTPUT TEXT variable is the actual text to display when the OUTPUT_TEXT procedure is called.

Although commands such as "L_" and "B_" require several arguments with specific numeric formats, commands like "SA" or "SF" use only a single argument. These commands with single numeric arguments do NOT require the numbers to be in a specified format because they have no leading spaces or numbers. With commands such as these, the format of the numeric arguments is irrelevant. The characters after the first two shouldn't have any leading or lagging characters that are NOT part of the argument.

The "I_" Command

The "I_" command calls the initialize_driver procedure. This procedure, as noted previously, initializes the graphics environment driver. If a driver and graphics mode are specified, an attempt is made to load that driver and initialize it accordingly. If no driver code is specified, then the procedure detects the video display equipment available, loads the appropriate driver, and initializes it to a default mode for the detected device. As you can see, this procedure is simply an interpretive layer built upon the Turbo Pascal initgraph procedure.

The "L" command tables three arguments: DRIVER CODE which is an integer, DRIVER MODE which is also an integer, and PATH which is a text in the form of a DOS directory indicating the location of the BGI and CHR files. An example of the use of the "L" command is shown in FIG. 7-5.

I_00090002C:\TURBO\   Fig. 7-5. A sample "L" command.

The driver codes and graphics mode codes for the SlideShow program are identical to those of Turbo Pascal version 5.5. The available graphics drivers and modes, and their corresponding codes, are shown in TABLE 7-1. They are described in more detail in chapter 12 of the Reference Guide for version 5.5 of Turbo Pascal.

The "T_" Command

The "T_" command calls the program_pause procedure. This procedure is used to control processing flow. Unlike a logical control statement, the "T_" command simply pauses for user input. When called, the "T_" command causes the text "press any key to continue" to appear in reverse video at the bottom of the display screen. This command takes no arguments. The program_pause procedure displays its message and then makes use of the standard Turbo Pascal readkey function to detect keyboard activity. After a key is pressed, control returns to the command processing procedure process_command. There is no limit to the number of times the "T_" command can be called within a single file. Your SlideShow script files can be written to include several "T_" commands to provide convenient stopping places for comment.

The "L" Command

The "L" command calls the draw_line procedure. This procedure is used to create a line on the display screen. The line style, thickness and color are chosen through other commands. This command accepts four integer arguments. These arguments combine to define the two end points of the line to be drawn. A typical line drawing command is shown in FIG. 7-6.

The individual integer values must be formatted to four character positions with the character "0" filling empty spaces in the command line. The locations for each point do NOT need to be in a specific sequence. However, the X and Y coordinates for each point must be placed adjacent to each other with the value for the X position placed before the value for Y.

Driver	Code	Mode	Code
Detect	0	CGAC0	0
CGA	1	CGAC1	1
		CGAC2	2
		CGAC3	3
		CGAHi	4
MCGA	2	MCGAC0	0
		MCGAC1	1
		MCGAC2	2
		MCGAC3	3
		MCGALo	4
		MCGAHi	5
EGA	3	EGALo	0
		EGAHi	1
EGA64	4	EGA64Lo	0
		EGA64Hi	1
EGAMono	5	EGAMonoHi	3
IBM8514	6	IBM8514Lo	0
		IBM8514Hi	1
HercMono	7	HercMonoHi	0
ATT400	8	ATT400C0	0
		ATT400C1	1
		ATT400C2	2
		ATT400C3	3
		ATT400Lo	4
		ATT400Hi	5
VGA	9	VGALo	0
		VGAMed	1
		VGAHi	2
PC3270	10	PC3270Hi	0

Table 7-1. The Graphics Drivers and Modes Available for Turbo Pascal Version 5.5

Fig. 7-6. A sample line drawing between the point (100,20) and (325,18).   L_0100002003250018

The "LT" Command

The "LT" command calls the set_linetype procedure. This procedure is used to select the specific line type in which a line may be drawn with the "L_" command. The available line types include single, double, dotted, dashed and combinations of dots and dashes. The available line types and their corresponding codes are listed in TABLE 7-2.

The SlideShow application through the "LT" command and the set_linetype procedure provide line types not available within the

Line Type	Code
Single	0
Double	1
Dotted	2
Dashed	3
Dot-Dash	4
Dot-Dot-Dash	5

Table 7-2. The SlideShow Line Styles

standard Turbo Pascal environment. You may define additional line types by making modifications to the set_linetype procedure.

Unlike the commands that take multiple integer arguments of a formatted type, the "LT" command requires only a single argument and it does NOT require special formatting. A typical "LT" command would be "LT3".

The reason for this apparent inconsistency resides in the fact that this command only takes a single argument. Formatting is required to differentiate between many arguments of differing lengths. Because only one argument is required to define a new line type, this command does not need to differentiate. The line type selection code can be extracted from the command text by converting ALL characters after the initial "LT" to a number. A determination is then made to see if that number matches any of the predefined line types. If it does, then the line type for the graphics environment is set to the appropriate value. If a match is not found, then no changes are made.

The "MC" Command

The "MC" command calls the move_cursor procedure. This procedure is used to move the Turbo Pascal "Current Pointer" (CP) to a specified location for text output or symbol placement. This command enables you to position a "graphics cursor" at any location on the graphics screen. When text is displayed on a standard text screen, it normally resides at specific predefined locations. Most standard screens can accommodate 25 lines and 80 characters per line. Regardless of the number of pixels used to construct a character, the placement is always within predefined locations.

The command in FIG. 7-7 demonstrates how the current pointer is positioned using the "MC" command. The "MC" command takes two arguments. These arguments correspond to the X and Y coordinates of the new location for the current pointer. Because more than one integer argument is used, formatting of the values is necessary to enable the "MC" command and its corresponding procedure to differentiate between the two coordinate values.

Fig. 7-7. A sample MC command.   MC03180183

This form of text placement is called cellular. When a Turbo Pascal graphics screen is initialized, there are no cellular contraints on the positioning of text characters. The "MC" command and move_cursor procedure are used to position the graphics cursor. The "O_" and "PS" commands are used to output text and symbols, respectively, at that selected location.

The "A_" Command

The "A_" command calls the draw_arc procedure. This procedure generates an arc around a specific center point (X1,Y1) and a radius (RADIUS). The extent of the arc is defined by two additional integer values, the starting angle (START) and the length of the arc (ARCLENGTH). All of these arguments are integer values. A sample call of the "A_" command is shown in FIG. 7-8.

Fig. 7-8. A sample "A_" command.   A_03190239004000000030

The command in FIG. 7-8 produces an arc centered around the point (319,239) with a radius of 40. The arc extends from 0 degrees to 30 degrees. An arc is the curved line produced by drawing a segment of the edge of a circle with the specified radius around the selected center point. The drawn portion of the edge is described by the starting angle (0 degrees) and the length of arc (30 degrees) which is expressed as an angle.

The "B_" Command

The "B_" command calls the DRAW_BAR procedure. This procedure draws a filled bar whose bottom left corner is described by a coordinate pair (X1, Y1) with a width (WIDTH) and a height (HEIGHT) specification. The bar is drawn in the current color and filled using the current shading. A sample call to the "B_" command is shown in FIG. 7-9.

Fig. 7-9. A sample "B_" command.   B_0300020000500100

The command in FIG. 7-9 creates a bar object whose lower left corner is located at coordinates (300,200). The width of the bar is specified to be 50. The height of the bar is specified to be 100. All values are integer, so formatting of the arguments is necessary to enable the "B_" command to differentiate.

The "O_" Command

The "O_" command calls the output_text procedure. This command is used to output a selected text to the screen. The placement of the

```
O_This is a sample text    Fig. 7-10. A sample "O_" command.
```

text is determined by a previous call to the "MC" command. After the current pointer is placed, the "O_" command is called with a text to output. A typical "O_" command is shown in FIG. 7-10.

The "P_" Command

The "P_" command calls the `draw_pie` procedure. This procedure generates a pie slice around a specified center point (X1,Y1) and a radius (RADIUS). The extent of the arc is defined by two additional integer values, the starting angle (START) and the length of the arch (ARCHLENGTH). All of these arguments are integer values. A sample call of the "P_" command is shown in FIG. 7-11.

```
P_03190239004000000030    Fig. 7-11. A sample "P_" command.
```

The command in FIG. 7-11 produces a pie centered around the point (319,239) with a radius of 40. The pie extends from 0 degrees to 30 degrees. An arc is the wedge of a circle line produced by drawing a segment of the edge of a circle with the specified radius around the selected center point and connecting each end of the line to the center point of the circle with straight lines. The drawn portion of the edge is described by the starting angle (0 degrees) and the length of arc (30 degrees) which is expressed as an angle.

The "PS" Command

The "PS" command calls the `draw_symbol` procedure. The `draw_symbol` procedure generates a single symbol at the location specified by the current pointer. The "PS" command takes only a single integer argument, the symbol code. Because only a single argument is required, no formatting of the code is necessary. Like the "LT" command, "PS" knows how to look for the code from the third to the last character in the command string. The available symbols and their corresponding codes are shown in TABLE 7-3.

The "RG" Command

The "RG" command calls the `restore_graph` procedure. This procedure restores the graphics mode and its original startup parameters. The "RG" command can also be used to select a different graphics mode from the current driver. This selection can be accomplished without reloading the driver for the current video display adapter. The advantage of this mode selection is the ability to modify the screen mode without a second call to the `initgraph` procedure. This command takes a single integer argument, so it does NOT require formatting.

Symbol	Code
Square	0
Circle	1
Triangle	2
Inverted Triangle	3
Diamond	4
Filled Square	5
Filled Circle	6
Filled Triangle	7
Filled Inverted Triangle	8
Filled Diamond	9
Point	10

Table 7-3. The SlideShow Symbols and Their Codes

The "SA" Command

The "SA" command calls the set_angle procedure. This procedure gives you the ability to change the orientation of the text displayed by the "O_" command. By selecting an angle of "O_," text appears on the screen as it would normally on a text screen. The orientation is called "horizontal." When an angle of "1" is selected, the text is rotated to a vertical orientation. This command takes a single integer argument, so it does NOT require formatting.

The "SB" Command

The "SB" command calls the set_bar procedure. This procedure establishes the type of bar generated by the "B_" command. The procedure sets an internal SlideShow global variable to either 0 or 1 to establish whether a 2-dimensional or 3-dimensional bar should be drawn. The default value for the SlideShow program is a 2-dimensional bar. The "SB" command takes a single integer argument, so it does not need to be formatted.

The "SC" Command

The "SC" command calls the SET_COLOR procedure. This procedure is used to establish the color used for any object drawn. This color will be used as the default color until another one is established by a subsequent call to the "SC" command. The "SC" command takes a single integer argument, so it does not need to be formatted. The colors available to the SlideShow application depend on the available video hardware and mode

Color	Code
Black	0
Blue	1
Green	2
Cyan	3
Red	4
Magenta	5
Brown	6
Light Gray	7
Dark Gray	8
Light Blue	9
Light Green	10
Light Cyan	11
Light Red	12
Light Magenta	13
Yellow	14
White	15

Table 7-4. The SlideShow and Turbo Pascal Colors and Their Codes

selection. However, the available colors and their codes correspond identically to the standard palette for Turbo Pascal. The standard Turbo Pascal colors and their corresponding codes are shown in TABLE 7-4.

The importance of this command is the ability to establish a drawing color for all procedures with a single command. This color is used for text as well as graphics, until a new color is selected using another call to the "SC" command.

The "SF" Command

The "SF" command calls the set_font procedure. This procedure is used to establish which font to use for subsequent text output. The "SF" command and the SlideShow application take advantage of the existing fonts and codes within Turbo Pascal. The available fonts and their codes are shown in TABLE 7-5.

Font Name	Code
DefaultFont	0
TriplexFont	1
SmallFont	2
SansSerifFont	3
GothicFont	4

Table 7-5. The Turbo Pascal Fonts and Their Codes

The "SF" command takes a single integer argument so it does not require formatting. The font selected by this command is used for all output generated by the "O_" command. The selected font is retained until the next call to the "SF" command.

The "SH" Command

The "SH" command calls the set_shade procedure. This procedure establishes the shading pattern for all calls to commands that created filled objects. Filled objects include bars, pie slices, filled ellipses and filled polygons. The "SH" command makes use of a combination of Turbo Pascal and SlideShow defined filling patterns. This was necessary to accommodate the requirements of the original driver table for which SlideShow was designed. The Turbo Pascal shade types and their corresponding codes are shown in TABLE 7-6. Descriptions of these fill types can be examined in chapter 12 of the Reference Guide for Turbo Pascal version 5.5.

Table 7-6. The SlideShow Shades and Codes

Shade Type	Code
EmptyFill	0
SolidFill	1
LineFill	2
LtSlashFill	3
SlashFill	4
BkSlashFill	5
LtBkSlashFill	6
HatchFill	7
XHatchFill	8
InterleaveFill	9
WideDotFill	10
CloseDotFill	11
Vertical Lines	50
Checker Board	51
50% Grey Scale	52

The SlideShow application defines three additional fill types called vertical lines, checker board, and 50% grey scale. The vertical lines and checker board shades are self-explanatory. The 50% grey scale shade is composed of closely spaced pixels in the shading area. The name for the 50% grey scale comes from the fact that half of the pixels are active, and the other half are not.

The "SS" Command

The "SS" command calls the set_size procedure. This procedure sets the size of text generated by the "O_" command. The "SS" command takes a single argument so it does not require formatting. The "SS" command was originally designed for Turbo Pascal 4.0, so it uses only a single argument to determine the height and width of characters. In addition, version 4.0 of Turbo Pascal's implementation of the settextstyle procedure allows for text size codes of 1 to 10. The addition of the setusercharsize procedure with Turbo Pascal 5.0 enables users to vary both the height and width of fonts 1 to 4. The procedure has no effect on character font 0. You might wish to modify this command and its corresponding procedure to accept user-defined height and width arguments.

The "FS" Command

The "FS" command calls the set_fontandstyle procedure. This procedure allows for the establishment of both the text font and size using only a single command and argument. The procedure defines a series of codes corresponding to specific combinations of size and font. The fonts, sizes and their codes are shown in TABLE 7-7.

If a value other than 1 to 25 is specified then the "FS" procedure will select the default font with a size of 1. Because this procedure takes only a single argument, is does not need to be formatted.

The "WE" Command

The "WE" command calls the erase_window procedure. This procedure takes four integer arguments to define a specific rectangular area of the display screen to fill with the background color and a solid filling. The erase window procedure takes four arguments similar to the "B_" procedure. In fact, the erase_window procedure calls the "B_" command without modification to the command line. The color is set to the background color, the fill pattern is set to solid fill. The "B_" command is then called by the "WE" command with the same command string passed to "WE." After the "B_" has executed, the color and fill pattern are reset to their original values. Because the "WE" and "B_" commands take more than one integer argument, formatting of the values is required.

The "CS" Command

The "CS" command calls the clear_screen procedure. This procedure clears the current display window. Unlike the "WE" command which provides the capability to define the extent of the erase window, the "CS" command simply erases the entire display screen. This command is normally used to prepare the screen for display of new images. It can also be used to clear the screen in between the display of several images. Like

Font and Size	Code
DefaultFont and 1	1
DefaultFont and 2	2
DefaultFont and 3	3
DefaultFont and 4	4
DefaultFont and 5	5
TriplexFont and 1	6
TriplexFont and 2	7
TriplexFont and 3	8
TriplexFont and 4	9
TriplexFont and 5	10
SmallFont and 1	11
SmallFont and 2	12
SmallFont and 3	13
SmallFont and 4	14
SmallFont and 5	15
SansSerifFont and 1	16
SansSerifFont and 2	17
SansSerifFont and 3	18
SansSerifFont and 4	19
SansSerifFont and 5	20
GothicFont and 1	21
GothicFont and 2	22
GothicFont and 3	23
GothicFont and 4	24
GothicFont and 5	25

Table 7-7. The SlideShow Combined Font and Size Codes

the "T_" command, the "CS" command can be used more than once within a single SlideShow script file.

GRAPHICS DEMONSTRATION FILES AND CORRESPONDING IMAGES

The SlideShow application was originally designed to work with a high-level statistical and graphical analysis package. This package has a programmable driver table that can accommodate a variety of commands. These commands can be written to a file to provide access to routines to initialize a graphics session, modify environmental parameters, draw graphical objects, and terminate a graphics session. SlideShow was designed as an on-screen "Plotter" emulator to display graphs using a VGA graphics adapter. Because Turbo Pascal 4.0, 5.0, and 5.5 provide drivers for VGA, EGA, CGA, ATT400, HERCULES and IBM 8514 video adapters, SlideShow can also accommodate these display devices.

The images presented in this section were created using an IBM PS/2 model 60 and an EPSON FX-286e printer. When the images were displayed, they were dumped to the printer using the PRTSC key. This technique of output generation will only work on machines with MS-DOS and PC-DOS 4.0 and higher.

The "Sample XY Graph" Image

The image in FIG. 7-12 is a simple "XY" graph. The graph demonstrates some of the basic uses of SlideShow. Variable size texts can be placed at specific positions on the screen. Orientation of text can be modified to provide vertically oriented text as can be seen on the Y axis label.

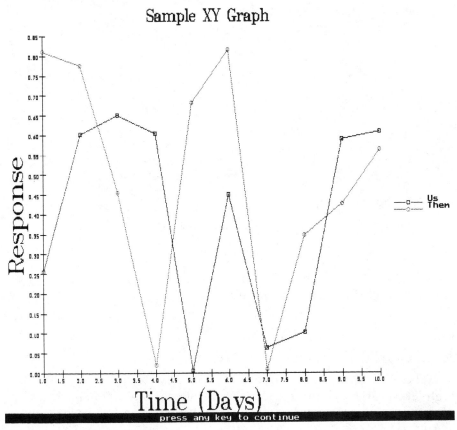

Fig. 7-12. An example of an XY graph.

The placement of graph symbols is also programmable. In both cases, the "Current Pointer" of the graphics environment is positioned using a call to the move_cursor procedure initiated with the "M_00010001" command. After the current position has been been set, a call with the "O_" command outputs text, or a call with the "PS" command places a symbol at the location. The SlideShow commands needed to create the image in FIG. 7-12 are shown in FIG. 7-13. The comments enclosed in brackets "[ ]" are not part of the file, and should not be incorporated into it. The comments are used to highlight interesting functions within the command file.

```
I_00090002         [ Initialize for VGA(9) 640x480x16Colors(2) ]
FS1                [ Select FONT and STYLE 1 ]
SA0                [ Set TEXT ANGLE to HORIZONTAL(0) ]
SC15               [ Set COLOR to WHITE(15) ]
SH0                [ Set SHADE to EMPTY Fill ]
CS                 [ Clear the Screen ]
L_0056004605350046 [ Draw a Line from (56,46) to (535,46) ]
L_0056005000560042 [ Draw a Line from (56,50) to (56,42) ]
FS12               [ Select FONT and STYLE 12 ]
M_00500036         [ Move the Current Pointer to (50,36) ]
O_1.0              [ Output the Text '1.0' ]
L_0083005000830042 [ Draw a Line from (83,50) to (83,42) ]
M_00760036         [ Move the Current Pointer to (76,36) ]
O_1.5              [ Output the Text '1.0' ]
L_0109005001090042 [ Draw a Line from (109,50) to (109,42) ]
M_01030036         [ Move the Current Pointer to (103,36) ]
O_2.0              [ Output the Text '2.0' ]
L_0136005001360042 [ Draw a Line from (136,50) to (136,42) ]
M_01290036         [ Move the Current Pointer to (129,36) ]
O_2.5              [ Output the Text '2.5' ]
L_0162005001620042 [ Draw a Line from (162,50) to (162,42) ]
M_01560036         [ Move the Current Pointer to (156,36) ]
O_3.0              [ Output the Text '3.0' ]
L_0189005001890042 [ Draw a Line from (189,50) to (189,42) ]
M_01830036         [ Move the Current Pointer to (183,36) ]
O_3.5              [ Output the Text '3.5' ]
L_0216005002160042 [ Draw a Line from (216,50) to (216,42) ]
M_02090036         [ Move the Current Pointer to (209,36) ]
O_4.0              [ Output the Text '4.0' ]
L_0242005002420042 [ Draw a Line from (242,50) to (242,50) ]
M_02360036         [ Move the Current Pointer to (236,36) ]
O_4.5              [ Output the Text '4.5' ]
L_0269005002690042 [ Draw a Line from (269,50) to (269,42) ]
M_02620036         [ Move the Current Pointer to (262,36) ]
O_5.0              [ Output the Text '5.0' ]
L_0296005002960042 [ Draw a Line from (296,50) to (296,42) ]
M_02890036         [ Move the Current Pointer to (289,36) ]
O_5.5              [ Output the Text '5.5' ]
L_0322005003220042 [ Draw a Line from (322,50) to (322,42) ]
M_03160036         [ Move the Current Pointer to (316,36) ]
O_6.0              [ Output the Text '6.0' ]
L_0349005003490042 [ Draw a Line from (349,50) to (349,42) ]
M_03420036         [ Move the Current Pointer to (342,36) ]
O_6.5              [ Output the Text '6.5' ]
L_0375005003750042 [ Draw a Line from (375,50) to (375,42) ]
M_03690036         [ Move the Current Pointer to (369,36) ]
O_7.0              [ Output the Text '7.0' ]
L_0402005004020042 [ Draw a Line from (402,50) to (402,42) ]
M_03950036         [ Move the Current Pointer to (395,36) ]
O_7.5              [ Output the Text '7.5' ]
L_0429005004290042 [ Draw a Line from (429,50) to (429,42) ]
M_04220036         [ Move the Current Pointer to (422,36) ]
O_8.0              [ Output the Text '8.0' ]
L_0455005004550042 [ Draw a Line from (455,36) to (455,42) ]
M_04490036         [ Move the Current Pointer to (449,36) ]
O_8.5              [ Output the Text '8.5' ]
L_0482005004820042 [ Draw a Line from (482,50) to (482,42) ]
M_04750036         [ Move the Current Pointer to (475,36) ]
O_9.0              [ Output the Text '9.0' ]
L_0508005005080042 [ Draw a Line from (508,50) to (508,42) ]
```

Fig. 7-13. The SlideShow code for the "Sample XY Graph" image.

"Fig. 7-13
continued."

```
M_05020036           [ Move the Current Pointer to (502,36) ]
O_9.5                [ Output the Text '9.5' ]
L_0535005005350042   [ Draw a Line from (535,50) to (535,42) ]
M_05270036           [ Move the Current Pointer to (527,36) ]
O_10.0               [ Output the Text '10.0' ]
L_0056004600560433   [ Draw a Line from (56,46) to (56,433) ]
L_0052004600600046   [ Draw a Line from (52,46) to (60,46) ]
M_00360043           [ Move the Current Pointer to (36,43) ]
O_0.00               [ Output the Text '0.00' ]
L_0052006900600069   [ Draw a Line from (52,69) to (60,69) ]
M_00360065           [ Move the Current Pointer to (36,65) ]
O_0.05               [ Output the Text '0.05' ]
L_0052009200600092   [ Draw a Line from (52,92) to (60,92) ]
M_00360088           [ Move the Current Pointer to (36,88) ]
O_0.10               [ Output the Text '0.10' ]
L_0052011400600114   [ Draw a Line from (52,114) to (60,114) ]
M_00360111           [ Move the Current Pointer to (36,111) ]
O_0.15               [ Output the Text '0.15' ]
L_0052013700600137   [ Draw a Line from (52,137) to (60,137) ]
M_00360134           [ Move the Current Pointer to (36,134) ]
O_0.20               [ Output the Text '0.20' ]
L_0052016000600160   [ Draw a Line from (52,160) to (60,160) ]
M_00360156           [ Move the Current Pointer to (36,156) ]
O_0.25               [ Output the Text '0.25' ]
L_0052018300600183   [ Draw a Line from (52,183) to (60,183) ]
M_00360179           [ Move the Current Pointer to (36,179) ]
O_0.30               [ Output the Text '0.30' ]
L_0052020500600205   [ Draw a Line from (52,205) to (60,205) ]
M_00360202           [ Move the Current Pointer to (36,202) ]
O_0.35               [ Output the Text '0.35' ]
L_0052022800600228   [ Draw a Line from (52,228) to (60,228) ]
M_00360225           [ Move the Current Pointer to (36,225) ]
O_0.40               [ Output the Text '0.40' ]
L_0052025100600251   [ Draw a Line from (52,251) to (60,251) ]
M_00360247           [ Move the Current Pointer to (36,247) ]
O_0.45               [ Output the Text '0.45' ]
L_0052027400600274   [ Draw a Line from (52,274) to (60,274) ]
M_00360270           [ Move the Current Pointer to (36,270) ]
O_0.50               [ Output the Text '0.50' ]
L_0052029600600296   [ Draw a Line from (52,296) to (60,296) ]
M_00360293           [ Move the Current Pointer to (36,293) ]
O_0.55               [ Output the Text '0.55' ]
L_0052031900600319   [ Draw a Line from (52,319) to (60,319) ]
M_00360316           [ Move the Current Pointer to (36,316) ]
O_0.60               [ Output the Text '0.60' ]
L_0052034200600342   [ Draw a Line from (52,342) to (60,342) ]
M_00360338           [ Move the Current Pointer to (36,338) ]
O_0.65               [ Output the Text '0.65' ]
L_0052036500600365   [ Draw a Line from (52,365) to (60,365) ]
M_00360361           [ Move the Current Pointer to (36,361) ]
O_0.70               [ Output the Text '0.70' ]
L_0052038700600387   [ Draw a Line from (52,387) to (60,387) ]
M_00360384           [ Move the Current Pointer to (36,384) ]
O_0.75               [ Output the Text '0.75' ]
L_0052041000600410   [ Draw a Line from (52,410) to (60,410) ]
M_00360407           [ Move the Current Pointer to (36,407) ]
O_0.80               [ Output the Text '0.80' ]
L_0052043300600433   [ Draw a Line from (52,433) to (60,433) ]
M_00360430           [ Move the Current Pointer to (36,430) ]
O_0.85               [ Output the Text '0.85' ]
SC4                  [ Select COLOR RED(4) ]
FS1                  [ Select FONT and STYLE 1 ]
M_00560162           [ Move the Current Pointer to (56,162) ]
PS0                  [ Put Symbol 'SQUARE'(0) at Current Pointer ]
L_0056016201090320   [ Draw Line between the CP (56,162) and
                       the next point on the graph (109,320) ]
M_01090320           [ Move the Current Pointer to (109,320) ]
PS0                  [ Put Symbol 'SQUARE'(0) at Current Pointer ]
L_0109032001620342   [ Draw a Line from (109,32) to (162,342) ]
M_01620342           [ Move the Current Pointer to (162,342)
PS0                  [ Put Symbol 'SQUARE'(0) at Current Pointer ]
L_0162034202160321   [ Draw a Line from (162,342) to (216,321) ]
```

"Fig. 7-13 continued."

```
M_02160321            [ Move the Current Pointer to (216,321) ]
PS0                   [ Put Symbol 'SQUARE'(0) at Current Pointer ]
L_0216032102690049    [ Draw a Line from (216,321) to (269,49) ]
M_02690049            [ Move the Current Pointer to (269,49) ]
PS0                   [ Put Symbol 'SQUARE'(0) at Current Pointer ]
L_0269004903220251    [ Draw a Line from (269,49) to (322,251) ]
M_03220251            [ Move the Current Pointer to (322,251) ]
PS0                   [ Put Symbol 'SQUARE'(0) at Current Pointer ]
L_0322025103750075    [ Draw a Line from (322,251) to (375,75) ]
M_03750075            [ Move the Current Pointer to (375,75) ]
PS0                   [ Put Symbol 'SQUARE'(0) at Current Pointer ]
L_0375007504290093    [ Draw a Line from (375,75) to (429,93) ]
M_04290093            [ Move the Current Pointer to (429,93) ]
PS0                   [ Put Symbol 'SQUARE'(0) at Current Pointer ]
L_0429009304820314    [ Draw a Line from (429,93) to (482,314) ]
M_04820314            [ Move the Current Pointer (482,314) ]
PS0                   [ Put Symbol 'SQUARE'(0) at Current Pointer ]
L_0482031405350323    [ Draw a Line from (482,314) to (535,323) ]
M_05350323            [ Move the Current Pointer to (535,323) ]
PS0                   [ Put Symbol 'SQUARE'(0) at Current Pointer ]
SC2                   [ Set COLOR to 'RED(2)' ]
M_00560415            [ Move the Current Pointer to (560,415) ]
PS1                   [ Put Symbol 'CIRCLE(1)' at Current Pointer ]
L_0056041501090399    [ Draw a Line from (560,415) to (109,399) ]
M_01090399            [ Move the Current Pointer to (109,399) ]
PS1                   [ Put Symbol 'CIRCLE(1)' at Current Pointer ]
L_0109039901620253    [ Draw a Line from (109,399) to (162,253) ]
M_01620253            [ Move the Current Pointer to (162,253) ]
PS1                   [ Put Symbol 'CIRCLE(1)' at Current Pointer ]
L_0162025302160055    [ Draw a Line from (162,253) to (216,55) ]
M_02160055            [ Move the Current Pointer to (216,55) ]
PS1                   [ Put Symbol 'CIRCLE(1)' at Current Pointer ]
L_0216005502690356    [ Draw a Line from (216,55) to (269,356) ]

M_02690356            [ Move the Current Pointer to (269,356) ]
PS1                   [ Put Symbol 'CIRCLE(1)' at Current Pointer ]
L_0269035603220417    [ Draw a Line from (269,356) to (322,417) ]
M_03220417            [ Move the Current Pointer to (322,417) ]
PS1                   [ Put Symbol 'CIRCLE(1)' at Current Pointer ]
L_0322041703750050    [ Draw a Line from (322,417) to (375,50) ]
M_03750050            [ Move the Current Pointer to (375,50) ]
PS1                   [ Put Symbol 'CIRCLE(1)' at Current Pointer ]
L_0375005004290204    [ Draw a Line from (375,50) to (429,204) ]
M_04290204            [ Move the Current Pointer to (429,204) ]
PS1                   [ Put Symbol 'CIRCLE(1)' at Current Pointer ]
L_0429020404820240    [ Draw a Line from (429,204) to (482,240) ]
M_04820240            [ Move the Current Pointer to (482,240) ]
PS1                   [ Put Symbol 'CIRCLE(1)' at Current Pointer ]
L_0482024005350302    [ Draw a Line from (482,240) to (535,302) ]
M_05350302            [ Move the Current Pointer to (535,302) ]
PS1                   [ Put Symbol 'CIRCLE(1)' at Current Pointer ]
SC15                  [ Set COLOR to WHITE (1) ]
FS7                   [ Select FONT and STYLE 7 ]
M_02060450            [ Move the Current Pointer to (206,450) ]
O_Sample XY Graph     [ Output the title text 'Sample XY Graph' ]
SA90                  [ Set TEXT ANGLE to Vertical ]
FS9                   [ Select FONT and STYLE 9 ]
M_00270160            [ Move the Current Pointer to (27,160) ]
O_Response            [ Output the Y Axis Label text 'Response' ]
SA0                   [ Set TEXT ANGLE to HORIZONTAL(0) ]
M_01860004            [ Move the Current Pointer to (186,4) ]
O_Time (Days)         [ Output the TEXT '0 Time (Days)' ]
SC4                   [ Set COLOR to 'GREEN(4)' ]
FS1                   [ Set FONT and STYLE ]
L_0556024005720240    [ Draw a Line from (556,240) to (572,240) ]
L_0580024005960240    [ Draw a Line from (580,240) to (596,240) ]
M_05760240            [ Move the Current Pointer to (576,240) ]
PS0                   [ Put Symbol 'SQUARE(0)' at Current Pointer ]
SC15                  [ Set COLOR to 'WHITE(15)' ]
M_06040240            [ Move the Current Pointer to (604,240) ]
O_Us                  [ Output the Text 'Us' ]
SC2                   [ Set COLOR to 'RED(2)' ]
L_0556023205720232    [ Draw a Line from (556,232) to (572,232) ]
L_0580023205960232    [ Draw a Line from (580,232) to (596,232) ]
```

```
M_05760232      [ Move the Current Pointer to (576,232) ]
PS1             [ Put Symbol 'CIRCLE(1)' at Current Pointer ]
SC15            [ Set COLOR to 'WHITE(15)' ]
M_06040232      [ Move the Current Pointer to (604,232) ]
O_Them          [ Output the Text 'Them' ]
T_              [ 'press any key to continue' ]
```

"Fig. 7-13 continued."

The code to produce the "XY" graph is stored in a file of 2566 bytes (without the comments in brackets "[ ]") when created by the original analysis application for display. Your file will take even less space to store. The same image of a VGA screen, if stored as an image in a file, would occupy approximately $640 \times 480 \times 16/8$ bytes of memory (over 600,000 bytes). The difference is in the fact that an image must store ALL screen information, while the SLIDESHOW command file only stores the information needed to create and place the lines, text and symbols.

COMPILATION NOTES

One of the first portions of code that you might have noticed about the SlideShow source code is the inclusion of two units called drivers and fonts. These units contain the object code for the Turbo Pascal device drivers and font files. When the files are linked into SlideShow, the separate ".BGI" and ".CHR" files are NOT required. Normally, when a graphics session is initiated, a call to the initgraph procedure is made with three arguments. These arguments are the codes for the desired device driver and the graphics mode and a text string containing a valid DOS path to the BGI and CHR files. Complete instructions on the use of the initgraph command can be found in the Turbo Pascal Reference Guide for versions 5.0 and 5.5.

The driver and font files are linked into a program as units with the uses command in the first part of the program, and subsequently registered into the executable file using the bgiregisterdriver and bgiregisterfont procedures in the main procedure section. You can create your own DRIVERS and FONTS units using the BGILINK.MAK application supplied with version 5.5 of Turbo Pascal. You might have noticed the use of a command to register the IBM 8514 driver into this application. The standard BGILINK.PAS application does NOT contain the code to create the IBM8514 driver file. If you examine the text of the BGILINK.MAK, BGILINK.PAS, and the DRIVERS.PAS program files on your distribution diskette, you will see that there is a generic method to converting and linking BGI files into the DRIVER.TPU unit. If you don't want to bother with the IBM8514 monitor for your SlideShow application, simply remove the register command for that driver from the code in the main procedure of the program.

ENHANCEMENTS

Some possible enhancements to the code might include additional object routine access. You might want the capability to specify and store certain portions of the screen image to a file. You might want to retrieve images from a file and redisplay them on the screen. The procedures imagesize, getimage, and putimage would be used to perform these actions. Another enhancement might be the capability for one SlideShow file to call another. This would involve taking the code for the read_file procedure in FIG. 7-2 and enabling it to be called from the process_command procedure in FIG. 7-2. Another addition might be to create a procedure that would automatically convert spaces of punctuation characters in the command string into zeros to ensure conversion by the val procedure. The expandability of this application is limited only by your imagination.

The real strength of the SlideShow program rests in what you decide to do with it. As a separate program, SlideShow can be called from other applications such as spreadsheets, database applications and statistical analysis packages. Assuming these programs have their own programming or macro languages, SlideShow files can be created automatically and then displayed. Many of these applications, like the Shell program from chapter 6, have the capability to call other programs and then resume their activities. In this case, a SlideShow file could be created and displayed, and then the "parent" application could continue running.

DISCUSSION

This chapter introduced the basic concept of vector graphics and its Turbo Pascal extension object graphics. The SlideShow application enables programmers and users to access these routines without the need to write, debug, and compile a Turbo Pascal program. A simple text file can be used to access and control a portion of Turbo Pascal's graphics capabilities. With your additions to the SlideShow code, more routines can be accessed.

SlideShow can be used as a standalone graphics display application. It can be used in conjunction with another application to provide enhanced graphics capabilities, and access to additional graphics drivers. Because the SlideShow application is written in Turbo Pascal, any enhancements made to the graphics environment for Turbo Pascal can be made available to the SlideShow program simply by recompiling.

To help fuel some graphics ideas of your own, I have included some additional images, and the SlideShow code for these images.

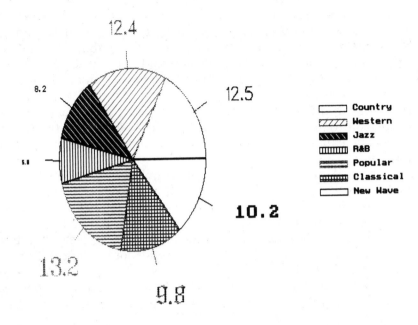

Fig. 7-14. An example of a pie chart.

```
I_00090002          [ Initialize for VGA(9) 640x480x16Colors(2) ]
FS1                 [ Set FONT and STYLE (1) ]
SA0                 [ Set TEXT Angle to HORIZONTAL (0) ]
SC15                [ Set COLOR to 15 ]
SY0                 [ Set STYLE to 0 ]
SH0                 [ Set SHADE to 0 ]
CS                  [ Clear the Display Screen ]
SC4                 [ Set COLOR to 4 ]
P_02510212010400000062  [ Draw a PieSlice at (251,212)
                          Radius=104, SAngle=0, ArcLength=62 ]
SC2                 [ Set COLOR to 2 ]
SH3                 [ Set SHADE to 3 ]
P_02500212010400620062  [ Draw a PieSlice at (250,212)
                          Radius=104, SAngle=62, ArcLength=62 ]
SC15                [ Set COLOR to 15 ]
SH6                 [ Set SHADE to 6 ]
P_02490212010401240041  [ Draw a PieSlice at (249,212)
                          Radius=104, SAngle=124, ArcLength=41 ]
SC1                 [ Set COLOR to 1 ]
SH50                [ Set SHADE to 50 ]
P_02490211010401650029  [ Draw a PieSlice at (249,211)
                          Radius=104, SAngle=165, ArcLength=29 ]
SC3                 [ Set COLOR to 3 ]
```

Fig. 7-15. The SlideShow code for the "Sample PieChart" image.

"Fig. 7-15 continued."

```
SH2                        [ Set SHADE to 2 ]
P_02490210010401940066     [ Draw a PieSlice at (249,210)
                             Radius=104, SAngle=149, ArcLength=66 ]
SC5                        [ Set COLOR to 5 ]
SH7                        [ Set SHADE to 7 ]
P_02500210010402600049     [ Draw a PieSlice at (250,210)
                             Radius=104, SAngle=260, ArcLength=49 ]
SC15                       [ Set COLOR to 15 ]
SH0                        [ Set SHADE to 0 ]
P_02510211010403090051     [ Draw a PieSlice at (250,211)
                             Radius=104, SAngle=309, ArcLength=51 ]
SC4                        [ Set COLOR to 4 ]
FS18                       [ Select Text FONT and STYLE to 18 ]
M_03740278                 [ Move Current Pointer to (374,278) ]
O_ 12.5                    [ Output the TEXT '12.5' ]
L_0357027603390265         [ Draw a Line from (357,276) to
                             (339,265) ]
SC2                        [ Set COLOR to 2 ]
M_02080356                 [ Move Current Pointer to (208,356) ]
O_ 12.4                    [ Output the TEXT '12.4' ]
L_0243033602440315         [ Draw a Line from (243,336) to
                             (244,315) ]
SC15                       [ Set COLOR to 15 ]
FS14                       [ Select Text FONT and STYLE to 14 ]
M_01000291                 [ Move Current Pointer to (100,291) ]
O_  8.2                    [ Output the TEXT '8.2' ]
L_0148028301650271         [ Draw a Line from (148,283) to
                             (165,271) ]
SC1                        [ Set COLOR to 1 ]
FS12                       [ Select Text FONT and STYLE to 12 ]
M_00840208                 [ Move Current Pointer to (84,208) ]
O_  5.8                    [ Output the TEXT '5.8' ]
L_0125021201460211         [ Draw a Line from (125,212) to
                             (146,211) ]
SC3                        [ Set COLOR to 3 ]
FS9                        [ Select Text FONT and STYLE to 9 ]
M_01000079                 [ Move the Current Pointer to (100,79) ]
O_ 13.2                    [ Output the TEXT '13.2' ]
L_0165011901790134         [ Draw a Line from (165,119) to
                             (179,134) ]
SC5                        [ Set COLOR to 5 ]
FS24                       [ Select Text FONT and  STYLE to 24 ]
M_02490045                 [ Move the Current Pointer to (249,45) ]
O_  9.8                    [ Output the TEXT '9.8' ]
L_0282009002760110         [ Draw a Line from (282,90) to
                             (286,110) ]
SC15                       [ Set COLOR to 15 ]
FS2                        [ Select Text FONT and STYLE to 2 ]
M_03810140                 [ Move the Current Pointer to (381,140) ]
O_ 10.2                    [ Output the TEXT '10.2' ]
L_0363015703440166         [ Draw a Line from (363,157) to
                             (344,166) ]
FS9                        [ Select Text FONT and STYLE to 9 ]
M_01000442                 [ Move the Current Pointer to (100,442) ]
O_Sample PieChart          [ Output the TEXT 'Sample PieChart' ]
FS1                        [ Select Text FONT and STYLE to 1 ]
M_02280426                 [ Move the Current Pointer to (228,426) ]
O_PIE 1                    [ Output the TEXT 'PIE 1' ]
SC4                        [ Set COLOR to 4 ]
B_0516026300400008         [ Draw a Bar from (516,263) using
                             Width=40 and Height=8 ]
L_0516026305550263         [ Draw a Line from (516,263) to
                             (555,263) ]
L_0555026305550270         [ Draw a Line from (555,263) to
                             (555,270) ]
L_0555027005160270         [ Draw a Line from (555,270) to
                             (516,270) ]
L_0516027005160263         [ Draw a Line from (516,270) to
                             (516,263) ]
SC15                       [ Set COLOR to 15 ]
M_05640263                 [ Move the Current Pointer to (564,263) ]
O_Country                  [ Output the TEXT 'Country' ]
SC2                        [ Set COLOR to 2 ]
```

"Fig. 7-15 continued."

```
SH3                      [ Set SHADE to 3 ]
B_0516024700400008       [ Draw a Bar from (516,247) using
                           Width=40 and Height=8 ]
L_0516024705550247       [ Draw a Line from (516,247) to
                           (555,247) ]
L_0555024705550254       [ Draw a Line from (555,247) to
                           (555,254) ]
L_0555025405160254       [ Draw a Line from (555,254) to
                           (516,254) ]
L_0516025405160247       [ Draw a Line from (516,254) to
                           (516,247) ]
SC15                     [ Set COLOR to 15 ]
M_05640247               [ Move the Current Pointer to (564,247) ]
O_Western                [ Output the TEXT 'Western' ]
SH6                      [ Set SHADE to 6 ]
FS1                      [ Select FONT and SIZE 1 ]
B_0044034300480007       [ Draw a Bar at (44,343) using
                           Width=48 and Height=7 ]
L_0044034300910343       [ Draw a Line from (44,343) to
                           (91,343) ]
L_0091034300910349       [ Draw a Line from (91,343) to
                           (91,349) ]
L_0091034900440349       [ Draw a Line from (91,394) to
                           (44,349) ]
L_0044034900440343       [ Draw a Line from (44,349) to
                           (44,343) ]
SC1                      [ Set COLOR to 1 ]
SH1                      [ Set SHADE to 1 ]
B_0044035000480112       [ Draw a Bar at (44,350) using
                           Width=48 and Height=112 ]
L_0044035000910350       [ Draw a Line from (44,350) to
                           (91,350) ]
L_0091035000910461       [ Draw a Line from (91,350) to
                           (91,461) ]
L_0091046100440461       [ Draw a Line from (91,461) to
                           (44,461) ]
L_0044046100440350       [ Draw a Line from (44,461) to
                           (44,350) ]
SC2                      [ Set COLOR to 2 ]
SH3                      [ Set SHADE to 3 ]
B_0044046300480002       [ Draw a Bar at (44,463) using
                           Width=48 and Height=2 ]
L_0044046300910463       [ Draw a Line from (44,463) to
                           (91,463) ]
L_0091046300910464       [ Draw a Line from (91,463) to
                           (91,464) ]
L_0091046400440464       [ Draw a Line from (91,464) to
                           (44,464) ]
L_0044046400440463       [ Draw a Line from (44,464) to
                           (44,463) ]
SH6                      [ Set SHADE to 6 ]
B_0100034300480006       [ Draw a Bar at (100,343) using
                           Width=48 and Height=6 ]
L_0100034301470343       [ Draw a Line from (100,343) to
                           (147,343) ]
L_0147034301470348       [ Draw a Line from (147,343) to
                           (147,348) ]
L_0147034801000348       [ Draw a Line from (147,348) to
                           (100,348) ]
L_0100034801000343       [ Draw a Line from (100,348) to
                           (100,343) ]
SC1                      [ Set COLOR to 1 ]
SH1                      [ Set SHADE to 1 ]
B_0100034900480110       [ Draw a Bar at (100,349) using
                           Width=48 and Height=110 ]
L_0100034901470349       [ Draw a Line from (100,349) to
                           (147,349) ]
L_0147034901470458       [ Draw a Line from (147,349) to
                           (147,458) ]
SC15                     [ Set COLOR to 15 ]
M_05640183               [ Move the Current Pointer to (564,183) ]
O_Classical              [ Output the TEXT 'Classical' ]
```

"Fig. 7-15 continued."

```
SH0                       [ Set SHADE to 0 ]
B_0516016700400008        [ Draw a Bar from (516,167) using
                            Width=40 and Height=8 ]
L_0516016705550167        [ Draw a Line from (516,167) to
                            (555,167) ]
L_0555016705550174        [ Draw a Line from (555,167) to
                            (555,174) ]
L_0555017405160174        [ Draw a Line from (555,174) to
                            (516,174) ]
L_0516017405160167        [ Draw a Line from (516,174) to
                            (516,167) ]
M_05640167                [ Move the Current Pointer to (564,167) ]
O_New Wave                [ Output the TEXT 'New Wave' ]
T_                        [ 'press any key to continue' ]
```

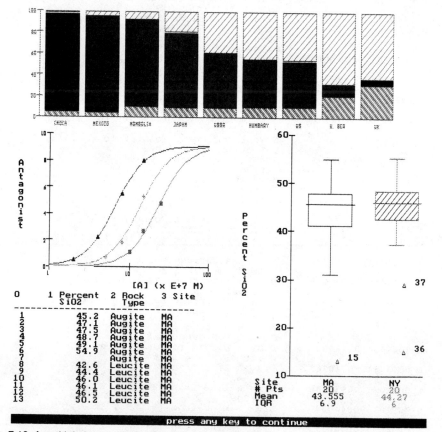

Fig. 7-16. A multiple image displayed using SlideShow.

```
I_00090002                [ Initialize for VGA(9) 640x480x16Colors(2)
FS1                       [ Select Text FONT and SHADE to 1 ]
SA0                       [ Set TEXT Angle to 0 ]
SC15                      [ Set COLOR to 15 ]
SY0                       [ Set Text STYLE to 0 ]
SH0                       [ Set SHADE to 0 ]
CS                        [ Clear the Display Screen ]
```

Fig. 7-17. The SlideShow code for the "Multiple On-Screen" image.

"Fig. 7-17 continued."

```
SC2                       [ Set COLOR to 2 ]
L_0036034305390343        [ Draw a Line from (36,343) to
                            (539,343) ]
FS12                      [ Select Text FONT and SHADE to 12 ]
M_00580333               [ Move the Current Pointer to (58,333) ]
O_INDIA                  [ Output the TEXT 'INDIA' ]
M_01120333               [ Move the Current Pointer to (112,333) ]
O_MEXICO                 [ Output the TEXT 'MEXICO' ]
M_01640333               [ Move the Current Pointer to (164,333) ]
O_MONGOLIA               [ Output the TEXT 'MONGOLIA' ]
M_02260333               [ Move the Current Pointer to (226,333) ]
O_JAPAN                  [ Output the TEXT 'JAPAN' ]
M_02840333               [ Move the Current Pointer to (284,333) ]
O_USSR                   [ Output the TEXT 'USSR' ]
M_03340333               [ Move the Current Pointer to (334,333) ]
O_HUNGARY                [ Output the TEXT 'HUNGARY' ]
M_04000333               [ Move the Current Pointer to (400,333) ]
O_US                     [ Output the TEXT 'US' ]
M_04480333               [ Move the Current Pointer to (448,333) ]
O_W. GER                 [ Output the TEXT 'W. GER' ]
M_05120333               [ Move the Current Pointer to (512,333) ]
O_UK                     [ Output the TEXT 'UK' ]
L_0036034300360465       [ Draw a Line from (36,343) to
                            (36,465) ]
L_0032034300400343       [ Draw a Line from (32,343) to
                            (40,343) ]
M_00280340               [ Move the Current Pointer to (28,340) ]
O_0                      [ Output the TEXT '0' ]
L_0032036700400367       [ Draw a Line from (32,367) to
                            (40,367) ]
M_00240364               [ Move the Current Pointer to (24,364) ]
O_20                     [ Output the TEXT '20' ]
L_0032039200400392       [ Draw a Line from (32,392) to
                            (40,392) ]
M_00240388               [ Move the Current Pointer to (24,388) ]
O_40                     [ Output the TEXT '40' ]
L_0032041600400416       [ Draw a Line from (32,416) to
                            (40,416) ]
M_00240413               [ Move the Current Pointer to (24,413) ]
O_60                     [ Output the TEXT '60' ]
L_0032044100400441       [ Draw a Line from (32,441) to
                            (40,441) ]
M_00240437               [ Move the Current Pointer to (24,437) ]
O_80                     [ Output the TEXT '80' ]
L_0032046500400465       [ Draw a Line from (32,465) to
                            (40,465) ]
M_00200462               [ Move the Current Pointer to (20,462) ]
O_100                    [ Output the TEXT '100' ]

SH6                       [ Set SHADE to 6 ]
FS1                       [ Select FONT and SIZE 1 ]
B_0044034300480007        [ Draw a Bar at (44,343) using
                            Width=48 and Height=7 ]
L_0044034300910343        [ Draw a Line from (44,343) to
                            (91,343) ]
L_0091034300910349        [ Draw a Line from (91,343) to
                            (91,349) ]
L_0091034900440349        [ Draw a Line from (91,394) to
                            (44,349) ]
L_0044034900440343        [ Draw a Line from (44,349) to
                            (44,343) ]
SC1                       [ Set COLOR to 1 ]
SH1                       [ Set SHADE to 1 ]
B_0044035000480112        [ Draw a Bar at (44,350) using
                            Width=48 and Height=112 ]
L_0044035000910350        [ Draw a Line from (44,350) to
                            (91,350) ]
L_0091035000910461        [ Draw a Line from (91,350) to
                            (91,461) ]
L_0091046100440461        [ Draw a Line from (91,461) to
                            (44,461) ]
L_0044046100440350        [ Draw a Line from (44,461) to
                            (44,350) ]
```

"Fig. 7-17
continued."

```
SC2                     [ Set COLOR to 2 ]
SH3                     [ Set SHADE to 3 ]
B_0044046300480002      [ Draw a Bar at (44,463) using
                          Width=48 and Height=2 ]
L_0044046300910463      [ Draw a Line from (44,463) to
                          (91,463) ]
L_0091046300910464      [ Draw a Line from (91,463) to
                          (91,464) ]
L_0091046400440464      [ Draw a Line from (91,464) to
                          (44,464) ]
L_0044046400440463      [ Draw a Line from (44,464) to
                          (44,463) ]
SH6                     [ Set SHADE to 6 ]
B_0100034300480006      [ Draw a Bar at (100,343) using
                          Width=48 and Height=6 ]
L_0100034301470343      [ Draw a Line from (100,343) to
                          (147,343) ]
L_0147034301470348      [ Draw a Line from (147,343) to
                          (147,348) ]
L_0147034801000348      [ Draw a Line from (147,348) to
                          (100,348) ]
L_0100034801000343      [ Draw a Line from (100,348) to
                          (100,343) ]
SC1                     [ Set COLOR to 1 ]
SH1                     [ Set SHADE to 1 ]
B_0100034900480110      [ Draw a Bar at (100,349) using
                          Width=48 and Height=110 ]
L_0100034901470349      [ Draw a Line from (100,349) to
                          (147,349) ]
L_0147034901470458      [ Draw a Line from (147,349) to
                          (147,458) ]
L_0147045801000458      [ Draw a Line from (147,458) to
                          (100,458) ]
L_0100045801000349      [ Draw a Line from (100,458) to
                          (100,349) ]
SC2                     [ Set COLOR to 2 ]
SH3                     [ Set SHADE to 3 ]
B_0100045900480006      [ Draw a Bar at (100,459) using
                          Width=48 and Height=6 ]
L_0100045901470459      [ Draw a Line from (100,459) to
                          (147,459) ]
L_0147045901470464      [ Draw a Line from (147,459) to
                          (147,464) ]
L_0147046401000464      [ Draw a Line from (147,464) to
                          (100,464) ]
L_0100046401000459      [ Draw a Line from (100,464) to
                          (100,459) ]
SH6                     [ Set SHADE to 6 ]
B_0156034300480013      [ Draw a Bar at (156,343) using
                          Width=48 and Height=13 ]
L_0156034302030343      [ Draw a Line from (156,343) to
                          (203,343) ]
L_0203034302030355      [ Draw a Line from (203,343) to
                          (203,355) ]
L_0203035501560355      [ Draw a Line from (203,355) to
                          (156,355) ]
L_0156035501560343      [ Draw a Line from (156,355) to
                          (156,343) ]
SC1                     [ Set COLOR to 1 ]
SH1                     [ Set SHADE to 1 ]
B_0156035600480099      [ Draw a Bar at (156,356) using
                          Width=48 and Height=99 ]
L_0156035602030356      [ Draw a Line from (156,356) to
                          (203,356) ]
L_0203035602030454      [ Draw a Line from (203,356) to
                          (203,454) ]
L_0203045401560454      [ Draw a Line from (203,454) to
                          (156,454) ]
L_0156045401560356      [ Draw a Line from (156,454) to
                          (156,356) ]
SC2                     [ Set COLOR to 2 ]
SH3                     [ Set SHADE to 3 ]
```

"Fig. 7-17 continued."

```
B_0156045500480010    [ Draw a Bar at (156,455) using
                        Width=48 and Height=10 ]
L_0156045502030455    [ Draw a Line from (156,455) to
                        (203,455) ]
L_0203045502030464    [ Draw a Line from (203,455) to
                        (203,464) ]
L_0203046401560464    [ Draw a Line from (203,464) to
                        (156,464) ]
L_0156046401560455    [ Draw a Line from (156,464) to
                        (156,455) ]
SH6                   [ Set SHADE to 6 ]
B_0212034300480012    [ Draw a Bar at (212,343) using
                        Width=48 and Height=12 ]
L_0212034302590343    [ Draw a Line from (212,343) to
                        (259,343) ]
L_0259034302590354    [ Draw a Line from (259,343) to
                        (259,354) ]
L_0259035402120354    [ Draw a Line from (259,354) to
                        (212,354) ]
L_0212035402120343    [ Draw a Line from (212,354) to
                        (212,343) ]
SC1                   [ Set COLOR to 1 ]
SH1                   [ Set SHADE to 1 ]
B_0212035500480085    [ Draw a Bar at (212,355) using
                        Width=48 and Height=85 ]
L_0212035502590355    [ Draw a Line from (212,355) to
                        (259,355) ]
L_0259035502590439    [ Draw a Line from (259,355) to
                        (259,439) ]
L_0259043902120439    [ Draw a Line from (259,439) to
                        (212,439) ]
L_0212043902120355    [ Draw a Line from (212,439) to
                        (212,355) ]
SC2                   [ Set COLOR to 2 ]
SH3                   [ Set SHADE to 3 ]
B_0212044100480024    [ Draw a Bar at (212,441) using
                        Width=48 and Height=24 ]
L_0212044102590441    [ Draw a Line from (212,441) to
                        (259,441) ]
L_0259044102590464    [ Draw a Line from (259,441) to
                        (259,464) ]
L_0259046402120464    [ Draw a Line from (259,464) to
                        (212,464) ]
L_0212046402120441    [ Draw a Line from (212,464) to
                        (212,441) ]
SH6                   [ Set SHADE to 6 ]
B_0268034300480012    [ Draw a Bar at (258,343) using
                        Width=48 and Height=12 ]
L_0268034303150343    [ Draw a Line from (268,343) to
                        (315,343) ]
L_0315034303150354    [ Draw a Line from (315,343) to
                        (315,354) ]
L_0315035402680354    [ Draw a Line from (315,354) to
                        (268,354) ]
L_0268035402680343    [ Draw a Line from (268,354) to
                        (268,343) ]
SC1                   [ Set COLOR to 1 ]
SH1                   [ Set SHADE to 1 ]
B_0268035500480062    [ Draw a Bar at (268,355) using
                        Width=48 and Height=62 ]
L_0268035503150355    [ Draw a Line from (268,355) to
                        (315,355) ]
L_0315035503150416    [ Draw a Line from (315,355) to
                        (315,416) ]
L_0315041602680416    [ Draw a Line from (315,416) to
                        (268,416) ]
L_0268041602680355    [ Draw a Line from (268,416) to
                        (268,355) ]
SC2                   [ Set COLOR to 2 ]
SH3                   [ Set SHADE to 3 ]
B_0268041700480048    [ Draw a Bar at (268,417) using
                        Width=48 and Height=48 ]
```

"Fig. 7-17
continued."

L_0268041703150417	[Draw a Line from (268,417) to (315,417)]
L_0315041703150464	[Draw a Line from (315,417) to (315,464)]
L_0315046402680464	[Draw a Line from (315,464) to (268,464)]
L_0268046402680417	[Draw a Line from (268,464) to (268,417)]
SH6	[Set SHADE to 6]
B_0324034300480013	[Draw a Bar at (324,343) using Width=48 and Height=13]
L_0324034303710343	[Draw a Line from (324,343) to (371,343)]
L_0371034303710355	[Draw a Line from (371,343) to (371,355)]
L_0371035503240355	[Draw a Line from (371,355) to (324,3550)]
L_0324035503240343	[Draw a Line from (324,355) to (324,34309)]
SC1	[Set COLOR to 1]
SH1	[Set SHADE to 1]
B_0324035600480054	[Draw a Bar at (324,356) using Width=48 and Height=54]
L_0324035603710356	[Draw a Line from (324,356) to (371,356)]
L_0371035603710409	[Draw a Line from (371,356) to (371,409)]
L_0371040903240409	[Draw a Line from (371,409) to (324,409)]
L_0324040903240356	[Draw a Line from (324,409) to (324,356)]
SC2	[Set COLOR to 2]
SH3	[Set SHADE to 3]
B_0324041000480055	[Draw a Bar at (324,410) using Width=48 and Height=55]
L_0324041003710410	[Draw a Line from (324,410) to (371,410)]
L_0371041003710464	[Draw a Line from (371,410) to (371,464)]
L_0371046403240464	[Draw a Line from (371,464) to (324,464)]
L_0324046403240410	[Draw a Line from (324,464) to (324,410)]
SH6	[Set SHADE to 6]
B_0380034300480013	[Draw a Bar at (380,343) using Width=48 and Height=13]
L_0380034304270343	[Draw a Line from (380,343) to (427,343)]
L_0427034304270355	[Draw a Line from (427,343) to (427,355)]
L_0427035503800355	[Draw a Line from (427,355) to (380,355)]
L_0380035503800343	[Draw a Line from (380,355) to (380,343)]
SC1	[Set COLOR to 1]
SH1	[Set SHADE to 1]
B_0380035600480052	[Draw a Bar at (380,356) using Width=48 and Height=52]
L_0380035604270356	[Draw a Line from (380,356) to (427,356)]
L_0427035604270407	[Draw a Line from (427,356) to (427,407)]
L_0427040703800407	[Draw a Line from (427,407) to (380,407)]
L_0380040703800356	[Draw a Line from (380,407) to (380,356)]
SC2	[Set COLOR to 2]
SH3	[Set SHADE to 3]
B_0380040900480056	[Draw a Bar at (380,409) using Width=48 and Height=56]
L_0380040904270409	[Draw a Line from (380,409) to (427,409)]

"Fig. 7-17 continued."

```
L_0427040904270464    [ Draw a Line from (427,409) to
                        (427,464) ]
L_0427046403800464    [ Draw a Line from (427,464) to
                        (380,464) ]
L_0380046403800409    [ Draw a Line from (380,464) to
                        (380,409) ]
SH6                   [ Set SHADE to 6 ]
B_0436034300480026    [ Draw a Bar at (436,343) using
                        Width=48 and Height=26 ]
L_0436034304830343    [ Draw a Line from (436,343) to
                        (483,343) ]
L_0483034304830368    [ Draw a Line from (483,343) to
                        (483,368) ]
L_0483036804360368    [ Draw a Line from (483,368) to
                        (436,368) ]
L_0436036804360343    [ Draw a Line from (436,368) to
                        (436,343) ]
SC1                   [ Set COLOR to 1 ]
SH1                   [ Set SHADE to 1 ]
B_0436036900480013    [ Draw a Bar at (436,369) using
                        Width=48 and Height=13 ]
L_0436036904830369    [ Draw a Line from (436,369) to
                        (483,369) ]
L_0483036904830381    [ Draw a Line from (483,369) to
                        (483,381) ]
L_0483038104360381    [ Draw a Line from (483,381) to
                        (436,381) ]
L_0436038104360369    [ Draw a Line from (436,381) to
                        (436,369) ]
SC2                   [ Set COLOR to 2 ]
SH3                   [ Set SHADE to 3 ]
B_0436038200480083    [ Draw a Bar at (436,382) using
                        Width=48 and Height=83 ]
L_0436038204830382    [ Draw a Line from (436,382) to
                        (483,382) ]
L_0483038204830464    [ Draw a Line from (483,382) to
                        (483,464) ]
L_0483046404360464    [ Draw a Line from (483,464) to
                        (436,464) ]
L_0436046404360382    [ Draw a Line from (436,464) to
                        (436,382) ]
SH6                   [ Set SHADE to 6 ]
B_0492034300480039    [ Draw a Bar at (492,343) using
                        Width=48 and Height=39 ]
L_0492034305390343    [ Draw a Line from (492,343) to
                        (539,343) ]
L_0539034305390381    [ Draw a Line from (539,343) to
                        (539,381) ]
L_0539038104920381    [ Draw a Line from (539,381) to
                        (492,381) ]
L_0492038104920343    [ Draw a Line from (492,381) to
                        (492,343) ]
SC1                   [ Set COLOR to 1 ]
SH1                   [ Set SHADE to 1 ]
B_0492038200480006    [ Draw a Bar at (492,382) using
                        Width=48 and Height=6 ]
L_0492038205390382    [ Draw a Line from (492,382) to
                        (539,382) ]
L_0539038205390387    [ Draw a Line from (539,382) to
                        (539,387) ]
L_0539038704920387    [ Draw a Line from (539,387) to
                        (492,387) ]
L_0492038704920382    [ Draw a Line from (492,387) to
                        (492,382) ]
SC2                   [ Set COLOR to 2 ]
SH3                   [ Set SHADE to 3 ]
B_0492038800480077    [ Draw a Bar at (492,388) using
                        Width=48 and Height=77 ]
L_0492038805390388    [ Draw a Line from (492,388) to
                        (539,388) ]
```

"Fig. 7-17
continued."

```
L_0539038805390464      [ Draw a Line from (539,388) to
                          (539,464) ]
L_0539046404920464      [ Draw a Line from (539,464) to
                          (492,464) ]
L_0492046404920388      [ Draw a Line from (492,464) to
                          (492,388) ]
SC15                    [ Set COLOR to 15 ]
L_0052017102770171      [ Draw a Line from (52,171) to
                          (277,171) ]
L_0052017500520167      [ Draw a Line from (52,175) to
                          (52,167) ]
FS12                    [ Select Text FONT and SIZE 12 ]
M_00500161              [ Move the Current Pointer to (50,161) ]
O_1                     [ Output the TEXT '1' ]
L_0165017501650167      [ Draw a Line from (165,175) to
                          (165,167) ]
M_01600161              [ Move the Current Pointer to (160,161) ]
O_10                    [ Output the TEXT '10' ]
L_0277017502770167      [ Draw a Line from (277,175) to
                          (277,167) ]
M_02710161              [ Move the Current Pointer to (271,161) ]
O_100                   [ Output the TEXT '100' ]
L_0052017100520324      [ Draw a Line from (52,171) to
                          (52,324) ]
L_0048017100560171      [ Draw a Line from (48,171) to
                          (56,171) ]
M_00440168              [ Move the Current Pointer to (44,168) ]
O_0                     [ Output the TEXT '0' ]
L_0048020200560202      [ Draw a Line from (48,202) to
                          (56,202) ]
M_00440198              [ Move the Current Pointer to (44,198) ]
O_2                     [ Output the TEXT '2' ]
L_0048023200560232      [ Draw a Line from (48,232) to
                          (56,232) ]
M_00440229              [ Move the Current Pointer to (44,229) ]
O_4                     [ Output the TEXT '4' ]
L_0048026300560263      [ Draw a Line from (48,263) to
                          (56,263) ]
M_00440259              [ Move the Currnet Pointer to (44,259) ]
O_6                     [ Output the TEXT '6' ]
L_0048029300560293      [ Draw a Line from (48,293) to
                          (56,293) ]
M_00440290              [ Move the Current Pointer to (44,290) ]
O_8                     [ Output the TEXT '8' ]
L_0048032400560324      [ Draw a Line from (48,324) to
                          (56,324) ]
M_00400321              [ Move the Current Pointer to (40,321) ]
O_10                    [ Output the TEXT '10' ]
SC4                     [ Set COLOR to 4 ]
FS1                     [ Select Text FONT and SIZE to 1 ]
M_00860179              [ Move the Current Pointer to (86,179) ]
PS7                     [ Draw SYMBOL 7 ]
M_01200205              [ Move the Current Pointer to (120,205) ]
PS7                     [ Draw SYMBOL 7 ]
M_01540255              [ Move the Current Pointer to (154,255) ]
PS7                     [ Draw SYMBOL 7 ]
M_01840293              [ Move the Current Pointer to (184,293) ]
PS7                     [ Draw SYMBOL 7 ]
SC3                     [ Set COLOR to 3 ]
M_01310182              [ Move the Current Pointer to (131,182) ]
PS9                     [ Draw SYMBOL 9 ]
M_01540199              [ Move the Current Pointer to (154,199) ]
PS9                     [ Draw SYMBOL 9 ]
M_01840252              [ Move the Current Pointer to (184,252) ]
PS9                     [ Draw SYMBOL 9 ]
SC2                     [ Set COLOR to 2 ]
M_01650188              [ Move the Current Pointer to (165,188) ]
PS5                     [ Draw SYMBOL 5 ]
M_01840212              [ Move the Current Pointer to (184,212) ]
PS5                     [ Draw SYMBOL 5 ]
```

"Fig. 7-17 continued."

```
M_02090244          [ Move the Current Pointer to (209,244) ]
PS5                 [ Draw SYMBOL 5 ]
SC14                [ Set COLOR to 14 ]
M_01840183          [ Move the Current Pointer to (184,183) ]
PS8                 [ Draw SYMBOL 8 ]
M_02090217          [ Move the Current Pointer to (209,217) ]
PS8                 [ Draw SYMBOL 8 ]
M_02320246          [ Move the Current Pointer to (232,246) ]
PS8                 [ Draw SYMBOL 8 ]
SC4                 [ Set COLOR to 4 ]
L_0052017300630174  [ Draw a Line from (52,173) to (63,174) ]
L_0063017400750176  [ Draw a Line from (63,174) to (75,176) ]
L_0075017600860179  [ Draw a line from (75,176) to (86,179) ]
L_0086017900970184  [ Draw a Line from (86,179) to (97,184) ]
L_0097018401080192  [ Draw a Line from (97,184) to (108,192) ]
L_0108019201200204  [ Draw a Line from (108,192) to (120,204) ]
L_0120020401310219  [ Draw a Line from (120,204) to (131,219) ]
L_0131021901420237  [ Draw a Line from (131,219) to (142,237) ]
L_0142023701530256  [ Draw a Line from (142,237) to (153,256) ]
L_0153025601650272  [ Draw a Line from (153,256) to (165,272) ]
L_0165027201760285  [ Draw a Line from (165,272) to (176,285) ]
L_0176028501870294  [ Draw a Line from (176,285) to (187,294) ]
L_0187029401980301  [ Draw a Line from (187,294) to (198,301) ]
L_0198030102100304  [ Draw a Line from (198,301) to (210,304) ]
L_0210030402210307  [ Draw a line from (210,304) to (221,307) ]
L_0221030702320308  [ Draw a Line from (221,307) to (232,308) ]
L_0232030802430309  [ Draw a Line from (232,308) to (243,309) ]
L_0243030902550309  [ Draw a Line from (243,309) to (255,309) ]
L_0255030902660310  [ Draw a Line from (255,309) to (266,310) ]
L_0266031002770310  [ Draw a Line from (266,310) to (277,310) ]
SC3                 [ Set COLOR to 3 ]
L_0052017100630172  [ Draw a Line from (52,171) to (63,172) ]
L_0063017200750172  [ Draw a Line from (63,172) to (75,172) ]
L_0075017200860173  [ Draw a Line from (75,172) to (86,173) ]
L_0086017300970174  [ Draw a Line from (86,173) to (97,174) ]
L_0097017401080175  [ Draw a Line from (97,174) to (108,175) ]
L_0108017501200178  [ Draw a Line from (108,175) to (120,178) ]
L_0120017801310183  [ Draw a Line from (120,178) to (131,183) ]
L_0131018301420191  [ Draw a Line from (131,183) to (142,191) ]
L_0142019101530202  [ Draw a Line from (142,191) to (153,202) ]
L_0153020201650217  [ Draw a Line from (153,202) to (165,217) ]
L_0165021701760235  [ Draw a Line from (165,217) to (176,235) ]
L_0176023501870253  [ Draw a Line from (176,235) to (187,253) ]
L_0187025301980270  [ Draw a Line from (187,253) to (198,270) ]
L_0198027002100284  [ Draw a Line from (198,270) to (210,284) ]
L_0210028402210294  [ Draw a Line from (210,284) to (221,294) ]
L_0221029402320300  [ Draw a Line from (221,294) to (232,300) ]
L_0232030002430304  [ Draw a Line from (232,300) to (243,304) ]
L_0243030402550307  [ Draw a Line from (243,304) to (255,307) ]
L_0255030702660308  [ Draw a Line from (255,307) to (266,308) ]
L_0266030802770309  [ Draw a Line from (266,308) to (277,309) ]
SC2                 [ Set COLOR to 2 ]
L_0052017100630171  [ Draw a Line from (52,171) to (63,171) ]
L_0063017100750171  [ Draw a Line from (63,171) to (75,171) ]
L_0075017100860171  [ Draw a Line from (75,171) to (86,171) ]
L_0086017100970172  [ Draw a Line from (86,171) to (97,172) ]
L_0097017201080172  [ Draw a Line from (97,172) to (108,172) ]
L_0108017201200173  [ Draw a Line from (108,172) to (120,173) ]
L_0120017301310175  [ Draw a Line from (120,173) to (131,175) ]
L_0131017501420177  [ Draw a Line from (131,175) to (142,177) ]
L_0142017701530182  [ Draw a Line from (142,177) to (153,182) ]
L_0153018201650188  [ Draw a Line from (153,182) to (165,188) ]
L_0165018801760198  [ Draw a Line from (165,188) to (176,198) ]
L_0176019801870212  [ Draw a Line from (176,198) to (187,212) ]
L_0187021201980229  [ Draw a Line from (187,212) to (198,229) ]
L_0198022902100248  [ Draw a Line from (198,229) to (210,248) ]
L_0210024802210266  [ Draw a Line from (210,248) to (221,266) ]
L_0221026602320280  [ Draw a Line from (221,266) to (232,280) ]
L_0232028002430291  [ Draw a Line from (232,280) to (243,291) ]
L_0243029102550298  [ Draw a Line from (243,291) to (255,298) ]
L_0255029802660303  [ Draw a Line from (255,298) to (266,303) ]
```

"Fig. 7-17
continued."

```
L_0266030302770306    [ Draw a Line from (266,303) to (277,306) ]
SC14                   [ Set COLOR to 14 ]
L_0052017100630171    [ Draw a Line from (52,171) to (63,171) ]
L_0063017100750171    [ Draw a Line from (63,171) to (75,171) ]
L_0075017100860171    [ Draw a Line from (75,171) to (86,171) ]
L_0086017100970171    [ Draw a Line from (86,171) to (97,171) ]
L_0097017101080171    [ Draw a Line from (97,171) to (108,171) ]
L_0108017101200172    [ Draw a Line from (108,171) to (120,172) ]
L_0120017201310172    [ Draw a Line from (120,172) to (131,172) ]
L_0131017201420173    [ Draw a Line from (131,172) to (142,173) ]
L_0142017301530175    [ Draw a Line from (142,173) to (153,175) ]
L_0153017501650177    [ Draw a Line from (153,175) to (165,177) ]
L_0165017701760182    [ Draw a Line from (165,177) to (176,182) ]
L_0176018201870188    [ Draw a Line from (176,182) to (187,188) ]
L_0187018801980199    [ Draw a Line from (187,188) to (198,199) ]
L_0198019902100212    [ Draw a Line from (198,199) to (210,212) ]
L_0210021202210230    [ Draw a Line from (210,212) to (221,230) ]
L_0221023002320248    [ Draw a Line from (221,230) to (232,248) ]
L_0232024802430266    [ Draw a Line from (232,248) to (243,266) ]
L_0243026602550281    [ Draw a Line from (243,266) to (255,281) ]
L_0255028102660291    [ Draw a Line from (255,281) to (266,291) ]
L_0266029102770298    [ Draw a Line from (266,291) to (277,298) ]
SC15                   [ Set COLOR to 15 ]
M_00080284            [ Move the Current Pointer to (8,284) ]
O_A                   [ Output the TEXT 'A' ]
M_00080276            [ Move the Current Pointer to (8,276) ]
O_n                   [ Output the TEXT 'n' ]
M_00080268            [ Move the Current Pointer to (8,268) ]
O_t                   [ Output the TEXT 't' ]
M_00080260            [ Move the Current Pointer to (8,260) ]
O_a                   [ Output the TEXT 'a' ]
M_00080252            [ Move the Current Pointer to (8,252) ]
O_g                   [ Output the TEXT 'g' ]
M_00080244            [ Move the Current Pointer to (8,244) ]
O_o                   [ Output the TEXT 'o' ]
M_00080236            [ Move the Current Pointer to (8,236) ]
O_n                   [ Output the TEXT 'n' ]
M_00080228            [ Move the Current Pointer to (8,228) ]
O_i                   [ Output the TEXT 'i' ]
M_00080220            [ Move the Current Pointer to (8,220) ]
O_s                   [ Output the TEXT 's' ]
M_00080212            [ Move the Current Pointer to (8,212) ]
O_t                   [ Output the TEXT 't' ]
M_00570145            [ Move the Current Pointer to (57,145) ]
O_            [A] (x E+7 M)
M_00040133            [ Move the Current Pointer to (4,133) ]
O_0      1 Percent   2 Rock    3 Site
M_00040125            [ Move the Current Pointer to (4,125) ]
O_          SiO2        Type
M_00040117            [ Move the Current Pointer to (4,117) ]
O_-------------------------------
M_00040109            [ Move the Current Pointer to (4,109) ]
O_ 1          45.2  Augite   MA
M_00040101            [ Move the Current Pointer to (4,101) ]
O_ 2          47.1  Augite   MA
M_00040093            [ Move the Current Pointer to (4,93) ]
O_ 3          47.5  Augite   MA
M_00040085            [ Move the Current Pointer to (4,85) ]
O_ 4          48.7  Augite   MA
M_00040077            [ Move the Current Pointer to (4,77) ]
O_ 5          49.1  Augite   MA
M_00040069            [ Move the Current Pointer to (4,69) ]
O_ 6          54.9  Augite   MA
M_00040061            [ Move the Current Pointer to (4,61) ]
O_ 7                Augite   MA
M_00040053            [ Move the Current Pointer to (4,53) ]
O_ 8          42.6  Leucite  MA
M_00040045            [ Move the Current Pointer to (4,45) ]
O_ 9          44.4  Leucite  MA
M_00040037            [ Move the Current Pointer to (4,37) ]
O_10          46.0  Leucite  MA
M_00040029            [ Move the Current Pointer to (4,29) ]
```

"Fig. 7-17 continued."

```
O_11              46.1   Leucite  MA
M_00040021               [ Move the Current Pointer to (4,21) ]
O_12              46.5   Leucite  MA
M_00040013               [ Move the Current Pointer to (4,13) ]
O_13              50.2   Leucite  MA
L_0394004805850048       [ Draw a Line from (398,48) to (585,48) ]
M_04420036               [ Move the Current Pointer to (442,36) ]
O_MA                     [ Output the TEXT 'MA' ]
M_05380036               [ Move the Current Pointer to (538,36) ]
O_NY                     [ Output the TEXT 'NY' ]
L_0394004803940324       [ Draw a Line from (394,48) to (394,324) ]
L_0390004803980048       [ Draw a Line from (390,48) to (398,48) ]
M_03740044               [ Move the Current Pointer to (374,44) ]
O_10                     [ Output the TEXT '10' ]
L_0390010303980103       [ Draw a Line from (390,103) to (398,103) ]
M_03740099               [ Move the Current Pointer to (374,99) ]
O_20                     [ Output the TEXT '20' ]
L_0390015803980158       [ Draw a Line from (390,158) to (398,158) ]
M_03740154               [ Move the Current Pointer to (374,154) ]
O_30                     [ Output the TEXT '30' ]
L_0390021403980214       [ Draw a Line from (390,214) to (398,214) ]
M_03740209               [ Move the Current Pointer to (374,209) ]
O_40                     [ Output the TEXT '40' ]
L_0390026903980269       [ Draw a Line from (390,269) to (398,269) ]
M_03740264               [ Move the Current Pointer to (374,264) ]
O_50                     [ Output the TEXT '50' ]
L_0390032403980324       [ Draw a Line from (390,324) to (398,324) ]
M_03740320               [ Move the Current Pointer to (374,320) ]
O_60                     [ Output the TEXT '60' ]
M_03460028               [ Move the Current Pointer to (346,28) ]
O_# Pts                  [ Output the TEXT '# Pts' ]
M_03460020               [ Move the Current Pointer to (346,20) ]
O_Mean                   [ Output the TEXT 'Mean' ]
M_03460012               [ Move the Current Pointer to (346,12) ]
O_IQR                    [ Output the TEXT 'IQP' ]
SC4                      [ Set COLOR to 4 ]
B_0418022000640038       [ Draw a Bar at (418,220) using
                           Width=64 and Height=38 ]
L_0418022004810220       [ Draw a Line from (418,220) to (481,220) ]
L_0481022004810257       [ Draw a Line from (481,220) to (481,257) ]
L_0481025704180257       [ Draw a Line from (481,257) to (418,257) ]
L_0418025704180220       [ Draw a Line from (418,257) to (418,220) ]
L_0415024504850245       [ Draw a Line from (415,245) to (485,245) ]
L_0450016404500220       [ Draw a Line from (450,164) to (450,220) ]
L_0439016404610164       [ Draw a Line from (439,164) to (461,164) ]
L_0450025804500296       [ Draw a Line from (450,258) to (450,296) ]
L_0439029604610296       [ Draw a Line from (439,296) to (461,296) ]
SC1                      [ Set COLOR to 1 ]
M_04620065               [ Move the Current Pointer to (462,65) ]
PS2                      [ Draw SYMBOL 2 ]
M_04780065               [ Move the Current Pointer to (478,65) ]
O_15                     [ Output the TEXT '15' ]
SC4                      [ Set COLOR to 4 ]
M_04420028               [ Move the Current Pointer to (442,28) ]
O_20                     [ Output the TEXT '20' ]
M_04260020               [ Move the Current Pointer to (426,20) ]
O_43.555                 [ Output the TEXT '43.555' ]
M_04380012               [ Move the Current Pointer to (438,12) ]
O_6.9                    [ Output the TEXT '6.9' ]
SC2                      [ Set COLOR to 2 ]
B_0514022800640033       [ Draw a Bar at (514,228) using
                           Width=64 and Height=33 ]
L_0514022805770228       [ Draw a Line from (514,228) to (577,228) ]
L_0577022805770260       [ Draw a Line from (577,228) to (577,260) ]
L_0577026005140260       [ Draw a Line from (577,260) to (514,260) ]
L_0514026005140228       [ Draw a Line from (514,260) to (514,228) ]
L_0511024705810247       [ Draw a Line from (511,247) to (581,247) ]
L_0546019905460228       [ Draw a Line from (546,199) to (546,228) ]
L_0535019905570199       [ Draw a Line from (535,199) to (557,199) ]
L_0546026105460298       [ Draw a Line from (546,261) to (546,298) ]
L_0535029805570298       [ Draw a Line from (535,298) to (557,298) ]
```

"Fig. 7-17
continued."

```
SC1                 [ Set COLOR to 1 ]
M_05580076          [ Move the Current Pointer to (558,76) ]
PS2                 [ Draw SYMBOL 2 ]
M_05740076          [ Move the Current Pointer to (574,76) ]
O_36                [ Output the TEXT '36' ]
M_05580153          [ Move the Current Pointer to (558,153) ]
PS2                 [ Draw SYMBOL 2 ]
M_05740152          [ Move the Current Pointer to (574,152) ]
O_37                [ Output the TEXT '37' ]
SC2                 [ Set COLOR to 2 ]
M_05380028          [ Move the Current Pointer to (538,28) ]
O_20                [ Output the TEXT '20' ]
M_05260020          [ Move the Current Pointer to (526,20) ]
O_44.27             [ Output the TEXT '44.27' ]
M_05420012          [ Move the Current Pointer to (542,12) ]
O_6                 [ Output the TEXT '6' ]
SC15                [ Set COLOR to 15 ]
M_03260226          [ Move the Current Pointer to (326,226) ]
O_P                 [ Output the TEXT 'P' ]
M_03260218          [ Move the Current Pointer to (326,218) ]
O_e                 [ Output the TEXT 'e' ]
M_03260210          [ Move the Current Pointer to (326,210) ]
O_r                 [ Output the TEXT 'r' ]
M_03260202          [ Move the Current Pointer to (326,202) ]
O_c                 [ Output the TEXT 'c' ]
M_03260194          [ Move the Current Pointer to (326,194) ]
O_e                 [ Output the TEXT 'e' ]
M_03260186          [ Move the Current Pointer to (326,186) ]
O_n                 [ Output the TEXT 'n' ]
M_03260178          [ Move the Current Pointer to (326,178) ]
O_t                 [ Output the TEXT 't' ]
M_03260170          [ Move the Current Pointer to (326,170) ]
O_                 [ Output the TEXT ' ' ]
M_03260162          [ Move the Current Pointer to (326,162) ]
O_S                 [ Output the TEXT 'S' ]
M_03260154          [ Move the Current Pointer to (326,154) ]
O_i                 [ Output the TEXT 'i' ]
M_03260146          [ Move the Current Pointer to (326,146) ]
O_O                 [ Output the TEXT 'O' ]
M_03260138          [ Move the Current Pointer to (326,138) ]
O_2                 [ Output the TEXT '2' ]
M_03460036          [ Move the Current Pointer to (346,36) ]
O_Site              [ Output the TEXT 'Site' ]
T_                  [ 'press any key to continue' ]
```

8

Object Oriented Programming and the "BALL" Applications

This chapter introduces the reader to the concepts of the Object Oriented Programming (OOP) extensions of Turbo Pascal version 5.5 and the Ball programs. This chapter includes two versions of the Ball application. The first version demonstrates the basic concepts of OOP. The second version of Ball extends the capabilities of the program to model a real-time environment using more advanced animated graphics. Object oriented programming is fundamentally different from typical procedural Turbo Pascal. Although the basic and advanced concepts of Turbo Pascal programming still apply, the control of the application changes dramatically.

It is NOT my intention to scare you away from OOP. However, you should be aware of the different thought process this type of programming requires.

As part of your preparation for this chapter, you might wish to review the graphics chapters in the Turbo Pascal Users Manual and the Reference Manual for versions 5.0 and 5.5.

PROCEDURAL LANGUAGES

Turbo Pascal 5.0 is a programming language based on the use of procedures and functions to accomplish a task. Any task that needs to be performed can be translated into one or more procedures to be executed.

Each procedure in a program corresponds to a portion of a task or a small task that is part of a larger application. Because of this structure for creating solutions to problems, the basic unit of Turbo Pascal prior to version 5.5 is the procedure.

Because of this basic unit of action, Pascal and other similar languages are referred to as *procedural.*

TURBO PASCAL 5.5

Turbo Pascal 5.5 as a language is identical to Turbo Pascal 5.0 in ALL respects. The distinction between Turbo Pascal 5.5 and 5.0 is made in the object oriented programming features available through the newer version of the compiler.

The functional enhancements to Turbo Pascal 5.5 include additional data type support as well as enhancements to overlay code and object-specific additions to the debugger. Each of these practical aspects of the OOP extension of Turbo Pascal are discussed in the OOP manual supplied with version 5.5.

If OOP were simply a matter of taking advantage of a new graphics procedure or a new data type, this chapter could easily describe it using a laundry list approach. Each new capability or function would have a single page description of its function, how it can be called, and some possible uses. In this manner each new element could be introduced individually, and then related to the language as a whole. As you might have guessed, OOP is NOT that simple, and a standard sequential approach to describing it is NOT applicable.

How then can the topic be explained? The OOP manual, included with version 5.5 of Turbo Pascal, begins by describing some basic components of OOP programming and then moving on to more complex elements. Some readers might find this useful, and they are encouraged to read the Turbo Pascal 5.5 OOP manual before, after or concurrently with this chapter. You will note some similarities and disparities between content and approach. It is my hope that you will find this diversity helpful in understanding the exciting new capabilities available within Turbo Pascal 5.5 and OOP.

WHAT AN OBJECT IS

Anything and everything is an object. This is not a joke. Anything within an OOP application that you write can be an object. This does not mean that everything MUST be an object, but everything has the potential.

In its simplest form, an *object* is an entity within your application that possesses one or more attributes. An attribute (or "method" as the OOP manual describes it) might be a characteristic or a capability within an object. Attributes can include graphical display characteristics such as color, fill pattern or a physical attribute such as size or velocity. An attribute might be something as simple as the radius of a circle, or as complex as a nonquantifiable characteristic such as mood or likability. The range or degree of an attribute is inconsequential. However, the fact that an object has one or more attributes makes it a viable entity within your Turbo Pascal application.

This chapter introduces the concept of graphical shapes as objects. Intuitively you know this to be true because you've worked with graphical objects such as circles, squares, rectangles, ectetera for your entire life. The world in which we live is made up of graphical objects with specific attributes. For a circle, the available attributes are listed in TABLE 8-1.

Table 8-1. Attributes of a Circle Object

Attribute
Center Position (X,Y)
Radius (R)
OutLine Thickness
Color
Filled (T or F)
Shading

The attributes describe in TABLE 8-1 reflect a combination of the Turbo Pascal `circle` and `filledellipse` procedures found in the GRAPH unit. These procedures each produce circular objects with the edge of the object drawn in the current color. The `filledellipse` generates additional graphical output by adding a filling to the object. The area inside the edge of the circle is filled with a specific color and pattern as selected by the `setfillpattern` procedure.

You might remember from chapter 7 that beginning with version 4.0 of Turbo Pascal, graphics procedures no longer contained complete lists of characteristics within their argument list definitions. Where version 3.0 contained arguments for `color` and `fillpattern` as well as X, Y, and `radius` within the call to the `circle` procedure, versions 4.0 to 5.5 contain only the X, Y and `radius` values. Specific colors, patterns and line types are set using other procedures. Because there is a disassociation of some attributes from specific procedural calls in later versions of Turbo Pascal, it is referred to as a "Graphics Environment."

The idea of an environment was a real breakthrough in graphics programming. Specific visual characteristics of objects could be established separately from calls to the procedures themselves. This made portions of the code needed to create a graphical shape reusable by other graphics procedures. It also reduced the amount of space needed to store the procedures. Graphical shapes could now be created with less code. That is more efficient.

Why explain the graphics environment? Because each graphics procedure within the GRAPH unit can be an object! Each object as it is drawn can assume an identity of its own. The data itself does NOT constitute the object, nor does the drawing procedure alone. An object is the merging of data and the actions performed on that data to generate and control the object. In addition, with Turbo Pascal 5.5 many of the graphics procedures in the GRAPH unit are referred to as though they were methods belonging to an object.

The Object Environment

In the simplest case, an *environment* is the place in which an object exists. The environment can exist apart from the object, but the object cannot exist without the environment. However, the really exciting part of OOP programming is generating and exploiting the relationship of an object to its environment.

An object is constituted by data and actions fused into a viable entity. An environment is the ocean upon which the object swims, dives or sails. Taking this analogy further, look at an aquarium as an environment.

Aquariums come in small, medium, large, extra large and public sizes. An aquarium has fish, some vegetation, bed covering, water filtration and an oxygenation system. Each of these elements (objects) performs a specific function to maintain the environment. The fish and other life forms cannot exist outside of their environment, as any fish out of water will tell you. More importantly, every component of the system can be described in object-like terms. Table 8-2 shows some characteristics of a fish.

Table 8-2. The Attributes of a "Fish" Object

Attribute
Movement - UP, DOWN, FORWARD, BACKWARD, RIGHT and LEFT
Extracts Oxygen from Water
Extracts Nourishment from Water, or Plants
Swims in Schools
Reproduces

Besides the obvious physical attributes of a fish, two of the more interesting capabilities of the object are "Swims in Schools" and "Reproduces." These two capabilities demonstrate that a fish can not only interact with its environment, but it can also interact with other fish objects.

Why is it important that objects interact? One of the uses of object oriented programming is to describe real life systems such as the interior structure of a solid and the interactions of molecules. Of course, that type of scientific application might not appeal to everyone. Another application might actually be to create an electronic aquarium in which the fish-type objects can not only move, but also interact.

The previous discussion has been primarily theoretical to introduce a new concept and not clutter your mind with the practical aspects of OOP just yet. It is important to be certain in your own mind of what constitutes an object, an attribute (referred to by the OOP manual as a "method"), and an environment. The theoretical implications of OOP should make more sense as you work through the examples in this chapter, and those described in the OOP manual. If a concept does not make sense here, do not hesitate to look through the OOP manual for clarification.

Initiating the Environment

The creation of an object oriented program begins on paper, and in the simpler cases it is already done for you. In many graphics OOP programs, the boundaries of the environment are obviously the screen or the current window in which your object will be drawn. For this chapter, the graphics environment is optimal because its boundaries are intuitively obvious.

What can be accomplished in this environment? In the Turbo Pascal graphics environment, objects can be placed anywhere within the boundaries of the screen. Colors and fill patterns can be assigned to these objects prior to display. Palettes may be modified to affect object color before and after image display. Objects can appear in part, or in their entirety, depending on the clipping nature of the current display window. If an image is placed on the screen using the put image procedure, the image can be drawn using the and, or, or xor operator for a variety of display effects.

What objects exist within this environment? Any objects that you wish to define. The program FIGURES.PAS, which comes with the Turbo Pascal 5.5 product, contains OOP definitions for a "location," a "point" and a "circle" object. The definitions for these objects were made easily extendable. Other programs supplied with the Turbo Pascal distribution disks include a version of the popular "Breakout" game and an information tracking programming that uses lists to store data. So as not to reinvent the wheel, and to make this chapter compatible with what you might have previously read in the FIGURES.PAS program, I'll define an extension of the "point" and "circle" objects called a "ball."

Defining an Object

When you look at the source code for the FIGURES.PAS program, you will note the use of the type section to define the procedure headers (methods) and the variables (data) for the object. The "ball" object contains such a definition in its type section. That definition is shown in FIG. 8-1.

```
type
  Ball = object
            Direction : Boolean;
            X, Y, Radius : Integer;
            Speed, Color, Pattern : Integer;
            Constructor Init(InitX, InitY, InitRadius,
                             InitSpeed, InitColor,
                             InitPattern : Integer);
            procedure Show;
            procedure Hide;
            procedure Bounce;
          end;
```

Fig. 8-1. The Ball object declaration.

As FIG. 8-1 shows, a Ball has data and actions that combine to create an object. The type definition is NOT a complete one, and you are encouraged to experiment and add additional methods and data to the definition.

The X, Y and Radius variables hold values to define the physical dimensions and position of the BALL. The Color and Pattern variables hold values that define the color and fill pattern of the BALL. Finally, the Speed variable defines the number of pixels (picture elements) to move the BALL when it bounces. By themselves, these pieces of data can do nothing except describe a theoretical object. However, when the data is combined with the procedures listed in the type definition, a true object results.

The procedures defined in the BALL object are Init, Show, Hide and Bounce. Each of these procedures has a specific function for the object. When a method is defined for the object, the procedure header is defined in the type section, although the actual procedure definition is located later in the program or unit. A method can be a procedure or function. It can take arguments, return values, or call other procedures. For the definition portion of the object, a method is a procedure.

In addition to the standard capabilities of Turbo Pascal procedures, OOP methods can also be defined as "virtual." A *virtual* method is simply a method that can be used by other objects. You might have noticed in the FIGURES.PAS unit the definition for the POINT object contains several declarations which include the phrase virtual; just after them. This definition allows the methods defined in one object to be passed down to other objects. When this type of relationship is established, the original object is called the *ancestor* and the later object which calls the original is called the *descendant*. Although the BALL object is based on POINT, it is not a descendant of it. To be a descendant of POINT, BALL would need to be defined as shown in FIG. 8-2.

The BALL object is made a descendant of POINT by including (point) next to the word object in the type definition. You may also notice that the X and Y variables are no longer defined. This is because they are defined in the POINT object and do not need to be redefined here.

```
type
   Ball = object (point)
              Direction : Boolean;
              Radius : Integer;
              Speed, Color, Pattern : Integer;
              Constructor Init(InitX, InitY, InitRadius,
                               InitSpeed, InitColor,
                               InitPattern : Integer);
           procedure Show;
           procedure Hide;
           procedure Bounce;
           end;
```

Fig. 8-2. BALL as a Descendant of POINT.

A program that uses the definition of BALL in FIG. 8-2 would also need to use the FIGURES.TPU unit created by "making" the FIGURES.PAS program. As the definitions for each of the methods of the BALL object are explained, I will point out the differences in code for BALL as a standalone object, and as a descendant of the POINT object.

The first method to define for an object is its initialization procedure. You might notice that this procedure has a special declaration identifier Constructor. This is an object-specific extension of the Turbo Pascal language. Other than that, the initialization method is typical of any procedure. It can have an argument list. It can have its own type and var sections, and it can call other procedures or functions. However, unlike other procedures and methods used by the object, this procedure MUST be the first one called when the object is initialized. This is necessary to ensure that ALL data and variables are initialized properly. Figure 8-3 shows the definition of the BALL object initialization constructor Ball. Init. You should note the way the procedure is referenced using the period (.) record delimiter as the delimiter between the object name Ball and the Init method.

```
          Constructor Ball.Init(InitX, InitY, InitRadius,
                                InitSpeed, InitColor,
                                InitPattern : Integer);
       begin
          X           := InitX;
          Y           := InitY;
          Radius      := InitRadius;
          Speed       := InitSpeed;
          Color       := InitColor;
          Pattern     := InitPattern;
          Direction := True;
       end;
```

Fig. 8-3. The BALL initialization procedure.

This definition shows the Init procedure for a nondescendant object. Figure 8-4 shows the Ball.Init procedure as it would be defined for a descendant of the POINT object. Note the lack of an assignment of Initx

```
Constructor Ball.Init(InitX, InitY, InitRadius,
                      MaxHeight, MinHeight, InitSpeed,
                      InitColor, InitPattern : Integer);
begin
  (* Initialize Ancestor POINT Object *)
  POINT(InitX,InitY);

  Radius    := InitRadius;
  Speed     := InitSpeed;
  Color     := InitColor;
  Pattern   := InitPattern;
  Direction := True;
end;
```

Fig. 8-4. The BALL initialization as a POINT descendant.

to X and Inity to Y. This assignment has already been performed by Point.Init which in turn called Location.Init. If you haven't done so already, look at the FIGURES.PAS unit definition program and verify this for yourself.

Every variable that is specific to the BALL object that has not been defined by descendance to an ancestor object is assigned a value in Ball.Init. These values can be passed to the Init procedure using arguments, or they may be prompted for, using other methods for the object. In fact, they can be assigned initial values in other method procedures. However, they should be assigned in the Init procedure.

Just as the Constructor method is used to initialize the object, there is another method, called Destructor, which is used to terminate the object. While an object MUST have a Constructor method to be created, it does not need a Destructor to be destroyed. The Destructor method can be used to deallocate memory or variables used by the method. It can also be used to remove graphical objects from the screen. In general, the Destructor method performs the opposite function of the Constructor for its object.

As I mentioned before, the POINT object is itself a descendant of the LOCATION object as defined in the FIGURES.TPU unit. What makes the POINT and BALL objects different is to have a modifiable location. POINT allows movement interactively using the MoveTo method. Each BALL object initializes with a movement speed, and proceeds noninteractively from there taking into account the speed, location, and maximum and minimum vertical height of the graphics environment. For the BALL object, the Bounce method allows for movement of the object on the screen. The definition for Bounce, or Ball.Bounce as it would be referred to in the program, is shown in FIG. 8-5.

The Ball.Bounce procedure enables the BALL object to "move" and "react" to its environment. The environment is the current Turbo Pascal graphics window, and its constraints are defined by the graphics adapter on board your computer. The constraints for this object are the maximum and minimum addressable vertical positions on the screen. In addition,

```
procedure Ball.Bounce;
begin
  hide;
  if (Direction) then
    Y := Y + Speed
  else
    Y := Y - Speed;

  if (Y < 0) then
    begin
      Direction := NOT(Direction);
      Y := Y + (2 * Speed);
    end;
  if (Y > GRAPH.GetMaxY) then
    begin
      Direction := NOT(Direction);
      Y := Y - (2 * Speed);
    end;
  show;
end;
```

Fig. 8-5. The Bounce procedure for the BALL object.

any variables declared within the object definition in the type section of the program, are global to the object, but NOT the program.

The Ball.Bounce procedure, based on the value of the Direction variable, adds or subtracts the value of the Speed variable to or from the current Y location of the BALL. If the result of the addition or subtraction is beyond the range of the minimum or maximum possible vertical coordinate of the environment, then the Direction variable assumes its opposite value. When the Direction variable reverses, the direction of movement of the ball is also reversed.

Although the Ball.Bounce method controls changes in position, the hide and show methods allow you to see the change. These methods control the visibility of the image on the screen, and as such are called by Bounce before and after the value of the Y variable changes. These procedures are shown in FIG. 8-6.

These methods allow the object to "move" visually by drawing the BALL in the selected color and pattern defined in the call to Ball.Init. The Ball.Show procedure displays the BALL or ELLIPSE in the current color and pattern as defined by the Color and Pattern variables. You should note the fact that any procedure from the GRAPH unit is called as though the procedure were a method, and GRAPH were an object. This is done to eliminate confusion on the part of the compiler, and it's good programming technique for Turbo Pascal 5.5. If you examine the definition of the CIRCLE object in the FIGURES.PAS program, you will see that the CIRCLE object uses this same syntax. This is necessary because there is a CIRCLE object and there is a Graph procedure (method?) called Circle.

The Hide method provides the BALL object with the capability to remove itself from view while its position changes. This procedure redraws the BALL object with the same dimensions as defined by the X, Y, and Radius variables. However, the drawing is done in the background color for the current graphics driver and mode. The apparent result is the

```
procedure Ball.Show;
var
   xasp, yasp : word;
begin
   Graph.SetColor(Color);
   Graph.SetFillStyle(Pattern,Graph.GetColor);
   Graph.GetAspectRatio(xasp,yasp);
   Graph.FillEllipse(X,Y,Radius,ROUND((xasp/yasp) * Radius));
end;

procedure Ball.Hide;
var
   xasp, yasp : Word;
begin
   Graph.SetColor(GetBkColor);
   Graph.SetFillStyle(1,Graph.GetColor);

   (* Draw the Ellipse in the background color to hide it *)
   Graph.GetAspectRatio(xasp,yasp);
   Graph.FillEllipse(X,Y,Radius,ROUND((xasp/yasp) * Radius));
   Graph.SetColor(Color);
   Graph.SetFillStyle(Pattern, Color);
end;
```

Fig. 8-6. The Hide and Show methods for the BALL Object.

removal of the BALL from the display screen. Although the POINT and CIRCLE objects both have these two methods defined, the Ball.Hide method MUST be defined specifically for the BALL object.

The currently defined Ball.Bounce method allows for a bouncing movement in the vertical direction. This method could also be expanded to include movement in the horizontal direction.This would require the addition of an initial angle of movement as well as variables to track horizontal direction and the horizontal component of the movement of the ball. Later in this chapter the advanced version of the BALL application will demonstrate how these methods may be added to the BALL object's characteristics.

Together, these methods and data constitute the BALL object. The BALL has position, dimension, color, texture and speed. Next, the environment must be created in which the BALL will move and interact. For the demonstration of the BALL object, the constraints are the physical dimensions of the display screen for your computer. For a CGA screen, the maximum value of the Y variable can be 199, and the minimum value 0. For a program that uses a single or a known number of balls, the program in FIG. 8-7 demonstrates the functionality of the BALL object.

The Basic_Ball program creates a specific environment for a variable number of ball objects to interact with the graphics environment. The data and methods for the BALL object clearly define its range of capabilities and display attributes. In the environment of the program, you must activate the objects so that their behavior can be observed. You should closely examine the method by which objects are created and set in motion.

```
program Basic_Ball;

uses Crt, DOS, Graph, Drivers, Fonts;

type
  Ball = object
           Direction : Boolean;
           X, Y, Radius : Integer;
           Speed, Color, Pattern : Integer;
           Constructor Init(InitX, InitY, InitRadius,
                            InitSpeed, InitColor,
                            InitPattern : Integer);
           procedure Show;
           procedure Hide;
           procedure Bounce;
           end;

  BPointer     = ^Ball;
  Ball_Pointer = ^Ball_Record;
  Ball_Record  = record
                   NextBall : Ball_Pointer;
                   TheBall  : BPointer;
                 end;

var
  GraphDriver : Integer;
  GraphMode : Integer;
  ErrorCode : Integer;
  HalfInt, Interval : Integer;
  Front, Back, Current, ABall : Ball_Pointer;
  Num_Balls, Counter : Integer;

{-----------------------------------------------------------}
{ Ball's method declarations:                               }
{-----------------------------------------------------------}

{
  This CONSTRUCTOR is used to initialize the BALL object and
  provide the ball with the basic data required to show color
  shade, and movement. Othe arguments include physical position
  and size, as well as upper and lower bounds for movement.
}
Constructor Ball.Init(InitX, InitY, InitRadius,
                      InitSpeed, InitColor,
                      InitPattern : Integer);
begin
  X          := InitX;
  Y          := InitY;
  Radius     := InitRadius;
  Speed      := InitSpeed;
  Color      := InitColor;
  Pattern    := InitPattern;
  Direction  := True;
end;

{
  This procedure SHOWs the BALL at the Current (X,Y) position
  with radius RADIUS, color COLOR, and Fill Pattern PATTERN.
}
procedure Ball.Show;
var
  xasp, yasp : word;
```

Fig. 8-7. The Basic_Ball program.

"Fig. 8-7
continued."

```
begin
  Graph.SetColor(Color);
  Graph.SetFillStyle(Pattern,Graph.GetColor);
  Graph.GetAspectRatio(xasp,yasp);
  Graph.FillEllipse(X,Y,Radius,ROUND((xasp/yasp) * Radius));
end;


{
  This procedure HIDEs the BALL at the Current (X,Y) position
  with Radius RADIUS, by drawing the BALL in the Background
  color of the current graphics mode.
}
procedure Ball.Hide;
var
  TempColor, xasp, yasp : Word;
begin
  TempColor := Graph.GetColor;
  Graph.SetColor(GetBkColor);
  Graph.SetFillStyle(1,Graph.GetColor);

  (* Draw the Ellipse in the background color to hide it *)
  Graph.GetAspectRatio(xasp,yasp);
  Graph.FillEllipse(X,Y,Radius,ROUND((xasp/yasp) * Radius));
  Graph.SetColor(Color);
  Graph.SetFillStyle(Pattern, Color);
end;


{
  This function controls the MOVEMENT of the Ball Object
  by using HIDE and SHOW.

  MOVEMENT is determined by the SPEED and DIRECTION of movement
  Wheÿ thí positioÿ oì thí balš extendµ beyond GRAPH.GETMAXÄ o·
  0, the DIRECTION changes
}
procedure Ball.Bounce;
begin
  hide;
  if (Direction) then
    Y := Y + Speed
   else
    Y := Y - Speed;

  if (Y < 0) then
    begin
      Direction := NOT(Direction);
      Y := Y + (2 * Speed);
    end;
  if (Y > GRAPH.GetMaxY) then
    begin
      Direction := NOT(Direction);
      Y := Y - (2 * Speed);
    end;
  show;
end;


{-----------------------------------------------------------}
{ Linked List Procedures                                    }
{-----------------------------------------------------------}
{
  This procedure initializes and extends a linked list
  of BPOINTER records.
}
procedure Create_Ball_List;
```

"Fig. 8-7
continued."

```
begin
  (* Determine the Number of Balls to Create *)
  (* and their spacing on the display screen *)
  randomize;
  Num_Balls := random(7) + 2;
  HalfInt := ROUND(GetMaxX / (Num_Balls * 2));
  Interval := 2 * HalfInt;

  (* Initialize the Linked List of Ball Objects *)
  new(ABall);
  ABall^.TheBall :=
    new(BPointer, Init(HalfInt, 100, random(95) + 5,
        random(GetMaxY DIV 4) + 1, random(Graph.GetMaxColor)+1,
        random(10) + 2));

  ABall^.NextBall := nil;
  front := ABall;
  back := ABall;

  (* Complete the Chain *)
  for counter := 2 to Num_Balls do
    begin
      new(ABall);
      ABall^.TheBall :=

        new(BPointer, Init(Halfint + (counter - 1) * Interval,
            100, random(95) + 5, random(GetMaxY DIV 4) + 1 ,
            random(Graph.GetMaxColor)+1, random(10) + 2));

      ABall^.NextBall := nil;
      back^.NextBall := ABall;
      back := ABall;
    end;
end;

{
  This procedure cycles through the LIST of objects causing
  movement by calling the BOUNCE method using pointer
  indirection.
}
procedure Cycle;
begin
  (* Cycle through the List Until a Key is Pressed *)
  while NOT(keypressed) do
    begin
      Current := Front;
      while(Current <> nil) do
        begin
          (* Bounce the Ball *)
          Current^.TheBall^.Bounce;
          (* Move to the Next Link *)
          Current := Current^.NextBall;
        end;
    end;
end;


{-----------------------------------------------------------}
{ Main program:                                             }
{-----------------------------------------------------------}

begin
  (* Register the CGA Graphics Driver *)
  (* and link it to the resulting EXE *)
  (* program                         *)
  errorcode := RegisterBGIdriver(@CGADriverProc);
```

"Fig. 8-7
continued."

```
(* We've linked the CGA driver to the *)
(* program, but let the BGI determine *)
(* what board is onboard the computer *)
GraphDriver := Detect;

DetectGraph(GraphDriver, GraphMode);
InitGraph(GraphDriver, GraphMode,'');
if GraphResult <> GrOK then
  begin
    WriteLn('>>Halted on graphics error:',
            GraphErrorMsg(GraphDriver));
    Halt(1)
  end;

(* Create the Ball List with Random Arguments *)
Create_Ball_List;
(* Make the Balls Move until a Key is Pressed *)
Cycle;

CloseGraph;
RestoreCRTMode;
end.
```

The most important facet of the Basic_Ball program is the use of the "dynamic" creation of BALL objects. The number of bouncing balls is determined using the standard Turbo Pascal random( ) function. The structure that tracks the balls is a linked list of record objects. The definition of the record is shown in FIG. 8-8.

```
type
  Ball = object
            Direction : Boolean;
            X, Y, Radius : Integer;
            Speed, Color, Pattern : Integer;
            Constructor Init(InitX, InitY, InitRadius,
                             InitSpeed, InitColor,
                             InitPattern : Integer);
          procedure Show;
          procedure Hide;
          procedure Bounce;
          end;

  BPointer      = ^Ball;
  Ball_Pointer = ^Ball_Record;
  Ball_Record  = record
                   NextBall : Ball_Pointer;
                   TheBall  : BPointer;
                 end;
```

Fig. 8-8. The Ball_Record definition.

Remember, pointers are simply variables that contain memory locations of other variables, procedures, functions or in this case objects. The Ball_Record record is composed of a pointer to a BALL object and a pointer to another Ball_Record. The first pointer enables the programmer to create objects dynamically, and to set the pointers in Ball_Record to them. The second pointer allows for the creation of a list of ball objects.

Because the number of items in the list is determined at run time, and not defined at compile time, they are referred to as *dynamic*.

The ability to create dynamic lists of objects within a program provides for some real advantages in programming. As you can see from the "Linked List" procedures in the Basic_Ball program, the amount of code necessary to initialize and extend the list is minimal. The maintenance of the objects is accomplished by the objects themselves. Remember, the aim of OOP is to create objects capable of viable existence within their environment. The ultimate object is one that can be set in motion with initial values and simply left alone.

The BALL object is designed to be able to Show, Hide, and Bounce within its environment. The values needed by the object from the environment are initial parameters to run. After initial data has been supplied, the object can perform on its own. When the BALL object has been defined as dynamic, then you never need to address the object directly, only by its pointer. You should consider it imperative to refrain from manipulating an object's data from outside of the object. All this means is that only an object's own methods should be used to manipulate or modify an object's data.

One of the major OOP extensions to Turbo Pascal available within version 5.5 is the ability to dynamically create objects. When properly defined, as in FIG. 8-8, the pointer and the object can be allocated using the new procedure. The OOP extension to this function allows you to initialize the object during the call to new. However, the procedure called by new during the allocation MUST be the Constructor. The method used to dynamically create a BALL object is shown in FIG. 8-9.

```
        (* Initialize the Linked List of Ball Objects *)
        new(ABall);
        ABall^.TheBall :=

          new(BPointer,
              Init(HalfInt, 100, random(95) + 5, random(50) + 1,
              random(Graph.GetMaxColor)+1, random(10) + 2));


        ABall^.NextBall := nil;
        front := ABall;
        back := ABall;
```

Fig. 8-9. Creating a dynamic object.

As you can see, the randon function plays a vital role in the initialization of the dynamic object. When a new pointer ABall is created, a new Ball_Record is created. Memory is allocated for the record, but the ball object it points to is not allocated. This is the conventional call to new. The OOP call to the new procedure creates a new BPointer variable, and a dynamic BALL object to which it points. In the process, the Ball.Init procedure is called with arguments for X, Y, Radius, Speed, Color, and Pattern. The general OOP call to new is shown in FIG. 8-10.

```
NEW(Pointer, Init(argument list));
```
Fig. 8-10. A generic OOP call to the new( ) procedure.

It was previously mentioned that along with a Constructor method, an object may also have a Destructor method. Destructors are normally used to clean up an object for termination. The destructor method for a dynamic object performs the same function. For dynamic objects the destructor method additionally performs the function of returning ALL memory used for the object back to the operating system. The definition of the destructor does not need to be complicated to perform this task. The definition of the Finish method for the BALL object is shown in FIG. 8-11.

```
Destructor BALL.FINISH;
begin
end;
```
Fig. 8-11. The Ball.Finish method.

The Finish method does NOT need to contain any code in order to perform this function. Because the Init function is called using the new procedure, one might guess the Finish function could be called with Dispose. In fact Dispose is used and with the same syntax as new. Although Basic_Ball does not require the use of the Finish method, it would be called as shown in FIG. 8-12.

```
Dispose(BPointer, Finish);
```
Fig. 8-12. Disposing of a dynamic object.

After the dynamic object and its parent record have been created and initialized, the pointers to the beginning and ending of the list are initialized. After this, the remainder of the list is allocated and initialized. In the Basic_Ball program, the number of balls to generate is selected using the random function. Based on this number, an interval X distance separation is selected and passed as an argument to the Init procedure for each link in the list of BALL objects. The code to complete the list of BPOINTER records is shown in FIG. 8-13.

After this portion of code has executed, all of the BALL objects are initialized and waiting for their Ball.Bounce methods to be executed. This only describes how to create complex data structures. However, it does not explain how methods within objects can be instructed to perform their functions.

With static objects that are simply defined as variables in the var section of the program, methods are called using the period record delimiter. When a static object variable Ball1 is defined for a program, the Init method can be called as shown in FIG. 8-14.

Remember that the Ball.Hide and Ball.Show methods reference procedures from the GRAPH unit using the "GRAPH.FILLELLIPSE" syntax. Similarly, the methods of an object are referenced using this syntax.

```
procedure Create_Ball_List;
begin
  (* Determine the Number of Balls to Create *)
  (* and their spacing on the display screen *)
  randomize;
  Num_Balls := random(7) + 2;
  HalfInt := ROUND(GetMaxX / (Num_Balls * 2));
  Interval := 2 * HalfInt;

  ...

  (* Complete the Chain *)
  for counter := 2 to Num_Balls do
    begin
      new(ABall);
      ABall^.TheBall :=

        new(BPointer,
            Init(Halfint +  (counter - 1) * Interval,
            100, random(95) + 5, random(GetMaxY DIV 4) + 1 ,
            random(Graph.GetMaxColor)+1, random(10) + 2));

      ABall^.NextBall := nil;
      back^.NextBall := ABall;
      back := ABall;
    end;
end;
```

Fig. 8-13. Creating the remaining BPointer links.

```
Type
  Ball = object ...
Var
  Ball1 : Ball;
begin
  (* Initialize the BALL1 Object Variable *)
  BALL1.INIT(XStart, YStart, RStart,
             SpeedStart,ColorStart,PatternStart);

  (* Make BALL1 Bounce until a key is pressed *)
  while NOT(keypressed) do
    begin
      BALL1.BOUNCE;
    end;
end.
```

Fig. 8-14. Causing the BALL to BOUNCE.

An OOP extension of the Turbo Pascal with command allows the program code to access methods within a specific object. A sample of an object call using with is shown in FIG. 8-15.

For a dynamic object, methods must be accessed using the indirection available through pointers. With a single pointer to the object, the call is fairly straightforward. The only difference between a simple dynamic object method call and a static call is the use of the pointer (^) indicator character. Figure 8-16 shows the code used to call a method using single level indirection.

```
         with (BALL1) do
           begin
             INIT(XStart, YStart, RStart,
                  SpeedStart,ColorStart,PatternStart);

             (* Make BALL1 Bounce until a key is pressed *)
             while NOT(keypressed) do
               begin
                 BOUNCE;
               end;
             end;
         end;
```

Fig. 8-15. Accessing an object's methods using WITH.

```
        Type
          Ball = object ...
          Ball_Pointer = ^Ball;
        Var
          Ball1 : Ball_Pointer;
        begin
          (* Create a New Dynamic Ball Object *)
          (* Initialize the BALL1 Object Variable *)
          NEW(Ball1, INIT(XStart, YStart, RStart,
                          SpeedStart,ColorStart,PatternStart);

          (* Make BALL1 Bounce until a key is pressed *)
          while NOT(keypressed) do
            begin
              BALL1^.BOUNCE;
            end;
        end.
```

Fig. 8-16. Causing the dynamic BALL to BOUNCE.

The Basic_Ball program uses two levels of indirection because of the variable length linked list of BALL objects. Each link in a list is accessed through a pointer variable. In turn, each link is a record composed of two pointers, the first pointing to the next link in the chain and the second pointing to the BALL object for that record. In order to access the method within the BALL object, two levels of pointer indirection must be established. A call to the Bounce method used in the Basic_Ball program is shown in FIG. 8-17.

```
        procedure Cycle;
        begin
          (* Cycle through the List Until a Key is Pressed *)
          while NOT(keypressed) do
            begin
              Current := Front;
              while(Current <> nil) do
                begin
                  (* Bounce the Ball *)
                  Current^.TheBall^.Bounce;
                  (* Move to the Next Link *)
                  Current := Current^.NextBall;
                end;
            end;
        end;
```

Fig. 8-17. Calling an object's method from a linked list.

The code in FIG. 8-17 demonstrates the typical method of using records and pointers to create and move through a linked list. The OOP extension is the ability to execute a method defined within an object. The construct "Current^.TheBall^.Bounce" calls the Bounce method through the TheBall record structure pointer, which has been pointed to by the Current pointer. If Bounce were a function, a value could be returned to the calling procedure or routine using the code in FIG. 8-18.

Fig. 8-18. Returning a value from an object method.

```
(* Bounce the Ball *)
Value := Current^.TheBall^.Bounce;
```

When you have decided how the environment for your objects will function, you can better decide whether indirection is necessary at all. You might then decide what level of indirection is appropriate. The Basic_Ball program requires two levels of indirection because it uses dynamic objects and a variable length linked list.

The Basic_Ball program provides a general introduction into the workings of the object oriented programming extensions available in Turbo Pascal version 5.5. If you have entered the code for the program into Turbo Pascal and attempted to run it, you have seen how the program generates images and moves them in a vertical direction. This is all well and good as a demonstration of beginning concepts—however, it lacks the reality needed to fully appreciate even the most basic capabilities of OOP. The next section will provide you with a more complete understanding of OOP, as well as a more advanced demonstration of its capabilities.

THE "BALL_ADVANCED" APPLICATION

The Ball_Advanced application is a more advanced implementation of the concepts introduced previously in the Basic_Ball program. The BALL object has now been expanded to allow for passing of data from internal variables to external procedure calls. The Ball.Bounce method has been expanded to include movement in the horizontal as well as the vertical direction. The argument list and methods declaration sections of the BALL object have been expanded to accommodate more information. Finally, the Ball.Init, Ball.Show and Ball.Hide methods have been modified and superceded to allow for the use of the PutImage procedure.

These enhancements enable the BALL object to move in two dimensions simultaneously. The BALL can reacts not only to the upper and lower edges of the screen, but also the right and left. Changes in direction can also be made in two dimensions simultaneously. The BALL object can now sense the presence of not only the environment, but also other objects. Collisions can also occur with other BALL objects. Collisions can cause changes in direction and speed. An enhancement to the Ball.Bounce method provides for transfer of momentum between balls traveling in the same direction at different speeds. Finally, a tone now is sounded when a collision occurs. Different tones indicate collisions with the environment or other ball objects. The source code for the Ball_Advanced application is shown in FIG. 8-19.

Several new and improved procedures and functions have been added to the original Basic_Ball application. These features enable the BALL object to more fully "sense" its position and status in the environment. Other features enable the ball object to act and react in an entirely new dimension. Finally, the BALL cannot only display its position and interactions, it can express and differentiate collisions using sound.

```
Program BALL_ADVANCED;

{
  This program demonstrates some of the more advanced
  capabilities of objects. In this demonstration
  Objects can react to each other as well as to the
  boundaries of the environment.
}


uses Crt, DOS, Graph, Drivers, Fonts;


{
  The definition of the BALL object is similar to the
  BALL_BASIC program. The main differences are the
  'Ball.Get' functions which enable an external program
  to retrieve data directly from an object without
  referencing the data directly.
}
type
  BPointer      = ^Ball;
  Ball_Pointer = ^Ball_Record;
  Ball_Record  = record
                          NextBall : Ball_Pointer;
                          TheBall  : BPointer;
                        end;

  Ball = object
              XDirection, YDirection, Visable : Boolean;
              X, Y, XRadius, YRadius, Id : Integer;
              Xasp, Yasp : Word;
              XSpeed, Yspeed, Color, Pattern : Integer;
              Image : Pointer;
              Constructor Init(InitX, InitY, InitRadius,
                             InitSpeed, InitAngle,
                             InitColor, InitPattern,
                             InitId : Integer);
              Destructor Done;
              procedure PutImage;
              procedure ChangeXDir;
              procedure ChangeYDir;
              procedure ChangeXSpeed(NewSpeed : Integer);
              procedure ChangeYSpeed(NewSpeed : Integer);
              function  GetXDirection : Boolean;
              function  GetYDirection : Boolean;
              function  GetXPosition : Integer;
              function  GetYPosition : Integer;
```

Fig. 8-19. The source code for the Ball_Advanced program.

"Fig. 8-19
continued."

```
               function  GetXSpeed : Integer;
               function  GetYSpeed : Integer;
               function  GetXRadius : Integer;
               function  GetYRadius : Integer;
               function  GetIDNum   : Integer;
               procedure Collisions(List_Pointer : Ball_Pointer);
               procedure Bounce(List_Pointer : Ball_Pointer);
            end;

  var
    GraphDriver : Integer;
    GraphMode : Integer;
    ErrorCode : Integer;
    HalfInt, Interval : Integer;
    Front, Back, Current, ABall : Ball_Pointer;
    Num_Balls, Counter : Integer;

  {------------------------------------------------------------}
  { Ball's method declarations:                                }
  {------------------------------------------------------------}

  {
    This CONSTRUCTOR is used to initialize the BALL object and
    provide the ball with the basic data required to show color
    shade, and movement. Other arguments include physical position
    and size, as well as upper and lower bounds for movement.

    Unlike the BALL object in the BasicBallDemo program, this
    constructor creates the object image, dynamically allocates
    memory to store the image, stores it and then removes it
    from the screen.

    Because of this action, the need for the procedures SHOW and
    HIDE from the original object have been eliminated. The
    GRAPH.PUTIMAGE procedure can be used for both functions and
    provides for cleaner, faster graphics.
  }
  Constructor Ball.Init(InitX, InitY, InitRadius,
                        InitSpeed, InitAngle,
                        InitColor, InitPattern,
                        InitId : Integer);
  Var
    dreal : real;
    image_size : word;
  begin
    (* Determine the Aspect Ratio of the Current Screen and Mode *)
    GRAPH.GetAspectRatio(Xasp,Yasp);

    (* Initialize Working Variables *)
    Id         := InitId;
    X          := InitX;
    Y          := InitY;
    XRadius    := InitRadius;
    YRadius    := ROUND(InitRadius * Xasp / Yasp);
    dreal      := InitSpeed;
    XSpeed     := ROUND(cos(InitAngle) * dreal);
    YSpeed     := ROUND((sin(InitAngle) * dreal) * Yasp/Xasp);
    Color      := InitColor;
    Pattern    := InitPattern;
    XDirection := (XSpeed > 0);
    XSpeed := ABS(Xspeed);
    YDirection := (YSpeed > 0);
    YSpeed := ABS(Yspeed);

    (* Determine the Amount of memory to Store the Ball's Image *)
```

"Fig. 8-19
continued."

```
    Image_Size := GRAPH.ImageSize(X - XRadius,
                                  Y - YRadius,
                                  X + XRadius,
                                  Y + YRadius);

  (* Allocate the Memory to the Untyped Image Pointer *)
  GetMem(Image, Image_Size);

  (* Place the Image on the Screen *)
  Graph.SetColor(Color);
  Graph.SetFillStyle(Pattern,Graph.GetColor);
  Graph.GetAspectRatio(xasp,yasp);
  Graph.FillEllipse(X,Y,XRadius,YRadius);
  Visable := True;

  (* Capture the Image in the Allocated Image Variable *)
  GRAPH.GetImage(X - XRadius, Y - YRadius,
                 X + XRadius, Y + YRadius,
                 Image);

  (* Remove the Image from the Screen *)
  Graph.SetFillStyle(0,Graph.GetBkColor);
  Graph.Bar(X - XRadius, Y - YRadius,
            X + XRadius, Y + YRadius);
  Visable := False;
end;


{
  The procedure releases memory used to store the BALL's
  image. An inherent feature of ANY Destructor which does
  NOT need to be defined is the DISPOSAL of the Dynamic
  BALL itself.
}
Destructor Ball.Done;
begin
  Dispose(Image);
end;


{
  This procedure SHOWs or HIDEs the BALL Image Depending
  on the current contents of the Image area on the screen

  If the Ball's Image IS NOT on screen, then this procedure
  will place it there. If the Image IS on screen, then this
  procedure will remove it. For more information of PUTIMAGE
  and the XOR method of screen painting, consult the Turbo
  Pascal 5.0 User's Guide and Reference Manual.
}
procedure Ball.PutImage;
begin
  (* Determine the Aspect Ratio of the Current Screen and Mode *)
  GRAPH.GetAspectRatio(Xasp,Yasp);

  (* XOR the Image onto the Screen *)
  GRAPH.PutImage(X - XRadius,
                 Y - YRadius,
                 Image, XorPut);
end;


{
  This procedure allows an external routine to change
  the XDIRECTION value without accessing the value
  directly.
}
procedure Ball.ChangeXDir;
begin
  XDirection := NOT(XDirection);
```

"Fig. 8-19
continued."

```
end;


{
  This procedure allows an external routine to change
  the YDIRECTION value without accessing the value
  directly
}
procedure Ball.ChangeYDir;
begin
  YDirection := NOT(YDirection);
end;


{
  This procedure allows an external routine to change
  the XSPEED value without accessing the target value
  directly
}
procedure Ball.ChangeXSpeed(NewSpeed : Integer);
begin
  YSpeed := NewSpeed;
end;


{
  This procedure allows an external routine to change
  the YSPEED value without accessing the target value
  directly
}
procedure Ball.ChangeYSpeed(NewSpeed : Integer);
begin
  XSpeed := NewSpeed;
end;


{
  These functions return the values of the object's position,
  physical dimension, movement parameters and identification
  parameters.

  We do NOT want an external procedure or function to access
  the data in this object directly.
}
function Ball.GetXDirection : Boolean;
begin
  GetXDirection := XDirection;
end;
function Ball.GetYDirection : Boolean;
begin
  GetYDirection := YDirection;
end;
function Ball.GetXPosition : Integer;
begin
  GetXposition := X;
end;
function Ball.GetYPosition : Integer;
begin
  GetYPosition := Y;
end;
function Ball.GetXSpeed : Integer;
begin
  GetXSpeed := XSpeed;
end;
function Ball.GetYSpeed : Integer;
begin
  GetYSpeed := YSpeed;
end;
function Ball.GetXRadius : Integer;
```

"Fig. 8-19 continued."

```
begin
  GetXRadius := XRadius
end;
function Ball.GetYRadius : Integer;
begin
  GetYRadius := YRadius;
end;
function Ball.GetIDNum : Integer;
begin
  GetIDNum := ID;
end;

{
  This procedure checks the positions of all other BALL
  objects to determine if a collision has occurred. If a
  collision does occur then it determines which DIRECTION
  and SPEED variables to alter to graphically demonstrate
  the collision.
}
procedure Ball.Collisions(List_Pointer : Ball_Pointer);
var
  XPos, YPos   : Integer;
  XMine, YMine : Integer;
  XSpd, YSpd   : Integer;
  OXRad, OYRad : integer;
  OXDir, OYdir : boolean;
begin
  XMine := X;
  YMine := Y;
(* Move down the linked list pointed to by the   *)
(* LIST_POINTER variable. Determine if another   *)
(* object is within the collision range defined  *)
(* by the radii of this object and the other.    *)
while(List_Pointer^.NextBall <> nil) do
  begin
    if (List_Pointer^.TheBall^.GetIDNum <> Id) then
      begin
        (* Retrieve the current position *)
        (* and speed parameters for the  *)
        (* other object                  *)
        OXDir := List_Pointer^.TheBall^.GetXDirection;
        OYDir := List_Pointer^.TheBall^.GetYDirection;
        XSpd  := List_Pointer^.TheBall^.GetXSpeed;
        YSpd  := List_Pointer^.TheBall^.GetYSpeed;
        OXRad := List_Pointer^.TheBall^.GetXRadius;
        OYRad := List_Pointer^.TheBall^.GetYRadius;
        XPos  := List_Pointer^.TheBall^.GetXPosition;
        YPos  := List_Pointer^.TheBall^.GetYPosition;

        (* Determine if a collision has occurred by *)
        (* checking distance between the centers of *)
        (* the objects and the sum of the radii.    *)
        (* Compare the two distances *)
        if (ABS(Ypos - Ymine) <= (YRadius + OYRad)) AND
           (ABS(Xpos - Xmine) <= (XRadius + OXRad)) then
          begin
            (* A collision has occurred : Determine *)
            (* which direction to change            *)

            (* Make a sound 2000hz to indicate *)
            (* collisions with other balls objects *)
            sound(2000);
            delay(10);
            nosound;
```

"Fig. 8-19
continued."

```
                              (* If the Other Ball ABOVE *)
                              (* ot BELOW this ball      *)
                              if ((YPos - YMine) <= 0) then
                                begin
                                  (* Is the Other Ball is ABOVE this Ball *)
                                  if ((OYDir) AND NOT(YDirection)) then
                                    begin
                                      (* Yes, Collision causes a reversal of *)
                                      (* Y Directions of Both Ball Objects   *)
                                      ChangeYDir;
                                      List_Pointer^.TheBall^.ChangeYDir;
                                    end
                                  else
                                    begin
                                      (* No, But a collision DID OCCUR   *)
                                      (* so transfer YSPEEDs between the *)
                                      (* objects to conserve MOMENTUM.   *)
                                      List_Pointer^.TheBall^.ChangeYSpeed(XSpeed);
                                      YSpeed := XSpd;
                                    end;
                                end
                              else
                                begin
                                  (* Is the Other Ball BELOW this Ball *)
                                  if (NOT(OYDir) AND (YDirection)) then
                                    begin
                                      (* Yes, Collision causes a reversal of *)
                                      (* Y Directions of Both Ball Objects   *)
                                      ChangeYDir;
                                      List_Pointer^.TheBall^.ChangeYDir;
                                    end
                                  else
                                    begin
                                      (* No, But a collision DID OCCUR   *)
                                      (* so transfer YSPEEDs between the *)
                                      (* objects to conserve MOMENTUM.   *)
                                      List_Pointer^.TheBall^.ChangeYSpeed(XSpeed);
                                      YSpeed := XSpd;
                                    end;
                                end;

                              (* Is the Other Ball to the LEFT of this Ball *)
                              if ((XPos - XMine) <= 0) then
                                begin
                                  if ((OXDir) AND NOT(XDirection)) then
                                    begin
                                      (* Yes, Collision causes a reversal of *)
                                      (* X Directions of Both Ball Objects   *)
                                      ChangeXDir;
                                      List_Pointer^.TheBall^.ChangeXDir;
                                    end
                                  else
                                    begin
                                      (* No, But a collision DID OCCUR   *)
                                      (* so transfer XSPEEDs between the *)
                                      (* objects to conserve MOMENTUM.   *)
                                      List_Pointer^.TheBall^.ChangeXSpeed(YSpeed);
                                      XSpeed := YSpd;
                                    end;
                                end
                              else
                                begin
                                  (* Is the Other Ball to the RIGHT of this Ball *)
                                  if (NOT(OXDir) AND (XDirection)) then
                                    begin
```

"Fig. 8-19 continued."

```
                            (* Yes, Collision causes a reversal of *)
                            (* X Directions of Both Ball Objects   *)
                            ChangeXDir;
                            List_Pointer^.TheBall^.ChangeXDir;
                        end
                      else
                        begin
                            (* No, But a collision DID OCCUR   *)
                            (* so transfer XSPEEDs between the *)
                            (* objects to conserve MOMENTUM.   *)
                            List_Pointer^.TheBall^.ChangeXSpeed(YSpeed);
                            XSpeed := YSpd;
                        end;
                end;
            end;
        end;
      List_Pointer := List_Pointer^.NextBall;
    end;
end;

{
  This function controls the MOVEMENT of the Ball Object
  by using HIDE and SHOW.

  MOVEMENT is determined by the SPEED, DIRECTION of movement,
  MAXH and MINH parameters supplied to INIT. When the position
  of the ball extends beyond, MAXH or MINH, the DIRECTION changes
}
procedure Ball.Bounce(List_Pointer: Ball_Pointer);
begin
  (* Remove the image from the display screen *)
  if (Visable) then
    begin
      Ball.PutImage;
      Visable := False;
    end;

  (* Based on DIRECTION of movement ADD or SUBTRACT *)
  (* the SPEED to or from the current Y Position    *)
  if (YDirection) then
    Y := Y + YSpeed
   else
    Y := Y - YSpeed;

  (* If the NEW Position is less than the Environment *)
  (* minimum then modify the direction and the NEW    *)
  (* position                                         *)
  if (Y < (YRadius + 1)) then
    begin
      YDirection := NOT(YDirection);
      Y := Y + (2 * YSpeed);

      (* Make a sound 3500hz to indicate *)
      (* collisions with the environment *)
      sound(3500);
      delay(10);
      nosound;
    end;

  (* If the NEW Position is greater than the Environment *)
  (* maximum then modify the direction and the NEW       *)
  (* position                                            *)
  if (Y > (GRAPH.GetMaxY - Yradius - 1)) then
    begin
      YDirection := NOT(YDirection);
      Y := Y - (2 * YSpeed);
```

"Fig. 8-19
continued."

```
            (* Make a sound 3500hz to indicate *)
            (* collisions with the environment *)
            sound(3500);
            delay(10);
            nosound;
          end;

        (* Based on DIRECTION of movement ADD or SUBTRACT *)
        (* the SPEED to or from the current X Position    *)
        if (XDirection) then
          X := X + XSpeed
        else
          X := X - XSpeed;

        (* If the NEW Position is less than the Environment *)
        (* minimum then modify the direction and the NEW    *)
        (* position                                         *)
        if (X < (Xradius + 1)) then
          begin
            XDirection := NOT(XDirection);
            X := X + (2 * XSpeed);

            (* Make a sound 3500hz to indicate *)
            (* collisions with the environment *)
            sound(3500);
            delay(10);
            nosound;
          end;

        (* If the NEW Position is greater than the Environment *)
        (* maximum then modify the direction and the NEW       *)
        (* position                                            *)
        if (X > (GRAPH.GetMaxX - Xradius - 1)) then
          begin
            XDirection := NOT(XDirection);
            X := X - (2 * XSpeed);

            (* Make a sound 3500hz to indicate *)
            (* collisions with the environment *)
            sound(3500);
            delay(10);
            nosound;
          end;

        (* Test for Collisions *)
        Collisions(List_Pointer);

        (* Replace image on the display screen *)
        Ball.PutImage;
        Visable := True;
end;
{-------------------------------------------------------------}
{ Linked List Procedures                                      }
{-------------------------------------------------------------}
{
  This procedure initializes and extends a linked list
  of BALL records.
}
procedure Create_Ball_List;
begin
  (* Determine the Number of Balls to Create *)
  (* and their spacing on the display screen *)
  randomize;
  Num_Balls := random(12) + 1;
  HalfInt := ROUND(GetMaxX / (Num_Balls * 2));
  Interval := 2 * HalfInt;
```

"Fig. 8-19
continued."

```
(* Initialize the Linked List of Ball Objects *)
new(ABall);
ABall^.TheBall := new(BPointer,
                      Init(random(GRAPH.GetMaxX - 50) + 25,
                           random(GRAPH.GetMaxY - 50) + 25,
                           GRAPH.GetMaxX DIV 30,
                           GRAPH.GetMaxY DIV HalfInt,
                           (* (GRAPH.GetMaxX DIV Num_Balls) DIV 10,*)
                           random(359) + 1,
                           Random(GetMaxColor) + 1,
                           random(10) + 2,
                           1));
ABall^.NextBall := nil;
front := ABall;
back := ABall;

(* Complete the Chain *)
for counter := 2 to Num_Balls do
  begin
    new(ABall);
    ABall^.TheBall := new(BPointer,
                          Init(random(GRAPH.GetMaxX - 50) + 25,
                               random(GRAPH.GetMaxY - 50) + 25,
                               GRAPH.GetMaxX DIV 30,
                               GRAPH.GetMaxY DIV HalfInt,
                               (* (GRAPH.GetMaxX DIV Num_Balls) DIV 10, *)
                               random(359) + 1,
                               Random(GetMaxColor) + 1,
                               random(10) + 2,
                               counter));

    ABall^.NextBall := nil;
    back^.NextBall := ABall;
    back := ABall;
  end;
end;
  {
    This procedure cycles through the LIST of objects
    causing movement by calling the BOUNCE method.

    An argument FRONT is supplied to the current
    object to allow it to determine where it is
    located with respect to other objects in the
    linked list of bouncing balls.

    This argument is used to determine if a collision
    has occurred with another object and then acts
    upon that information.
  }
procedure Cycle;
begin
  (* Cycle through the List Until a Key is Pressed *)
  while NOT(keypressed) do
    begin
      Current := Front;
      while(Current <> nil) do
        begin
          (* Bounce the Ball *)
          Current^.TheBall^.Bounce(front);
          (* Move to the Next Link *)
          Current := Current^.NextBall;
        end;
    end;
end;
```

"Fig. 8-19
continued."

```
{ ------------------------------------------------------------ }
{ Main program:                                                }
{ ------------------------------------------------------------ }

begin
  (* Register and Link the following : *)
  (* CGA, EGA and VGA Graphics Drivers *)
  (* to the final EXE file             *)
  errorcode := RegisterBGIdriver(@CGADriverProc);
  errorcode := RegisterBGIdriver(@EGAVGADriverProc);

  GraphDriver := Detect;      (* Let the BGI determine what *)
                              (* board you're using         *)
  DetectGraph(GraphDriver, GraphMode);
  InitGraph(GraphDriver, GraphMode,'');
  if GraphResult <> GrOK then
    begin
      WriteLn('>>Halted on graphics error:',
               GraphErrorMsg(GraphDriver));
      Halt(1)
    end;

  (* Create the Ball List with Random Arguments *)
  Create_Ball_List;
  (* Make the Balls Move until a Key is Pressed *)
  Cycle;

  CloseGraph;
  RestoreCRTMode;
end.
```

Detecting Other Objects

The most important enhancements of the Ball_Advanced application are the Get functions. These functions enable an object to obtain information about other objects in the environment. Why is this important? When an object is moving in an environment with other objects, some form of interaction will occur. For the Ball_Advanced application the interaction is "collision." The Get functions enable the "current" ball to determine if its position and the position of another ball overlap. If an overlap is detected, then a collision has occurred and appropriate action must be taken.

Interactions need not be limited to collisions. Ball objects might stick to each other, Ball objects of the same color or shade might "fuse" to form a larger ball object. Ball objects of specific combinations might create "new" balls. You might remember from earlier in this chapter, the description of a "fish" object. One of the characteristics noted for fish was the capability to reproduce. If a fish object can reproduce, there is no reason a ball object couldn't be defined to do the same. In short, an interaction can be any characteristic you might wish to define. The initiation of an action, based on an interaction need not be limited to the overlapping of two objects. However, for our demonstration, this interaction suits the ball object well. The Ball.Get...functions are shown in FIG. 8-20.

```
{
  These functions return the values of the object's position,
  physical dimension, movement parameters and identification
  parameters.

  We do NOT want an external procedure or function to access
  the data in this object directly.
}
function Ball.GetXDirection : Boolean;
begin
  GetXDirection := XDirection;
end;
function Ball.GetYDirection : Boolean;
begin
  GetYDirection := YDirection;
end;
function Ball.GetXPosition : Integer;
begin
  GetXposition := X;
end;
function Ball.GetYPosition : Integer;
begin
  GetYPosition := Y;
end;
function Ball.GetXSpeed : Integer;
begin
  GetXSpeed := XSpeed;
end;
function Ball.GetYSpeed : Integer;
begin
  GetYSpeed := YSpeed;
end;
function Ball.GetXRadius : Integer;
begin
  GetXRadius := XRadius
end;
function Ball.GetYRadius : Integer;
begin
  GetYRadius := YRadius;
end;
function Ball.GetIDNum : Integer;
begin
  GetIDNum := ID;
end;
```

Fig. 8-20. The Ball.Get functions.

When the Ball.Bounce procedure for the current ball in the linked list is called, it is passed the pointer value of the start of the linked list, as an argument. This value is used to call the get functions of other objects to detect their position and, if necessary, to change them. Like the linked-list controlling procedure Cycle, the Ball.Collisions procedure moves down the linked list from start to finish. As it moves to a link, it determines the position, speed and direction of the ball pointed to by that link.

The Ball.GetXDirection function enables the current ball to detect the direction of horizontal movement of another ball. The Ball.GetY-Direction function enables the current ball to detect the direction of vertical movement of another ball. These values are used to determine if a collision is head-on or going in the same direction.

The Ball.GetXPosition enables the current ball to detect the current horizontal location of the other ball. the Ball.GetYPosition function enables the current ball to detect the current vertical position of the other ball. The Ball.GetXRadius and Ball.GetYRadius functions provide information on the size of the other ball. The Ball_Advanced application uses a constant size ball for demonstration purposes. However, you could modify the size of the Create_Ball_List procedure to create balls of variable sizes. These values are used to determine if the current ball and another ball are overlapping. If an overlap is detected, then a collision has occurred.

The Ball.GetXSpeed and Ball.GetYSpeed functions, along with the Ball.Collisions procedure, are used to detect the speed of the other ball. If the conditions are right, the speed of the current ball is changed to the speed of the other ball. In addition, the speed of the other ball is changed to the original speed of the current ball. The Ball. ChangeXSpeed and Ball.ChangeYSpeed procedures enable the current ball to tell the other ball what horizontal and vertical speeds to assume. If the collision is "head-on" then changes in direction can be made by calling the Ball.ChangeXDir and Ball.ChangeYDir procedures for both the current ball and the other ball.

One of the most important of the Ball.Get...functions is Ball.GetIDNum. When a ball is initialized by Create_Ball_List, it is assigned a unique identification number. This number can be obtained through the Ball.GetIDNum function. The value returned by this function can then be compared to the value in the ID variable of the current ball. If the values match, then the current and the other ball are the same, and NO detection of collisions should be performed. If collisions were detected as normal with the current and other ball being the same, then a collision would ALWAYS be detected. This condition would cause the machine to freeze by putting it into the equivalent of an infinite loop.

One of the most important procedures in the Ball_Advanced application is the Ball.Collisions procedure. The Ball.Collisions procedure uses the Ball.Get... functions to determine when a collision has occurred between ball objects. When a collision does occur, a determination is made of what kind of collision it was. This information is then used to change the direction, speed or position of the ball in response to the collision. The BALL.COLLISIONS procedure is shown in FIG. 8-21.

The detection of a collision is made by determining whether the image of one ball has overlapped the image of another. The detection is made using the center positions of both balls and the radii of both balls. The images are created using the Graph.FilledEllipse procedure. This procedure requires the use of a radius argument for both the X and Y direction. The values for the X and Y radii can be used to detect an overlap as well.

```
procedure Ball.Collisions(List_Pointer : Ball_Pointer);
var
  XPos, YPos    : Integer;
  XMine, YMine  : Integer;
  XSpd, YSpd    : Integer;
  OXRad, OYRad  : integer;
  OXDir, OYdir  : boolean;
begin
  XMine := X;
  YMine := Y;

  (* Move down the linked list pointed to by the  *)
  (* LIST_POINTER variable. Determine if another  *)
  (* object is within the collision range defined *)
  (* by the radii of this object and the other.   *)
  while(List_Pointer^.NextBall <> nil) do
    begin
      if (List_Pointer^.TheBall^.GetIDNum <> Id) then
        begin
          (* Retrieve the current position *)
          (* and speed parameters for the  *)
          (* other object                  *)
          OXDir := List_Pointer^.TheBall^.GetXDirection;
          OYDir := List_Pointer^.TheBall^.GetYDirection;
          XSpd  := List_Pointer^.TheBall^.GetXSpeed;
          YSpd  := List_Pointer^.TheBall^.GetYSpeed;
          OXRad := List_Pointer^.TheBall^.GetXRadius;
          OYRad := List_Pointer^.TheBall^.GetYRadius;
          XPos  := List_Pointer^.TheBall^.GetXPosition;
          YPos  := List_Pointer^.TheBall^.GetYPosition;

          (* Determine if a collision has occurred by  *)
          (* checking distance between the centers of  *)
          (* the objects and the sum of the radii.     *)
          (* Compare the two distances *)
          if (ABS(Ypos - Ymine) <= (YRadius + OYRad)) AND
             (ABS(Xpos - Xmine) <= (XRadius + OXRad)) then
            begin
              (* A collision has occurred : Determine *)
              (* which direction to change            *)

              (* Make a sound 2000hz to indicate *)
              (* collisions with other balls objects *)
              sound(2000);
              delay(10);
              nosound;

              (* If the Other Ball ABOVE *)
              (* or BELOW this ball       *)
              if ((YPos - YMine) <= 0) then
                begin
                  (* Is the Other Ball is ABOVE this Ball *)
                  if ((OYDir) AND NOT(YDirection)) then
                    begin
                      (* Yes, Collision causes a reversal of *)
                      (* Y Directions of Both Ball Objects   *)
                      ChangeYDir;
                      List_Pointer^.TheBall^.ChangeYDir;
                    end
                  else
                    begin
                      (* No, But a collision DID OCCUR  *)
```

Fig. 8-21. The Ball.Collisions procedure.

```
                                  (* so transfer YSPEEDs between the *)
                                  (* objects to conserve MOMENTUM.   *)
                                  List_Pointer^.TheBall^.ChangeYSpeed(XSpeed);
                                  YSpeed := XSpd;
                                end;
                         end
                       else
                        begin
                           (* Is the Other Ball BELOW this Ball *)
                           if (NOT(OYDir) AND (YDirection)) then
                             begin
                               (* Yes, Collision causes a reversal of *)
                               (* Y Directions of Both Ball Objects   *)
                               ChangeYDir;
                               List_Pointer^.TheBall^.ChangeYDir;
                             end
                           else
                             begin
                               (* No, But a collision DID OCCUR   *)
                               (* so transfer YSPEEDs between the *)
                               (* objects to conserve MOMENTUM.   *)
                               List_Pointer^.TheBall^.ChangeYSpeed(XSpeed);
                               YSpeed := XSpd;
                             end;
                        end;

                    (* Is the Other Ball to the LEFT of this Ball *)
                    if ((XPos - XMine) <= 0) then
                      begin
                         if ((OXDir) AND NOT(XDirection)) then
                           begin
                             (* Yes, Collision causes a reversal of *)
                             (* X Directions of Both Ball Objects   *)
                             ChangeXDir;
                             List_Pointer^.TheBall^.ChangeXDir;
                           end
                         else
                           begin
                             (* No, But a collision DID OCCUR   *)
                             (* so transfer XSPEEDs between the *)
                             (* objects to conserve MOMENTUM.   *)
                             List_Pointer^.TheBall^.ChangeXSpeed(YSpeed);
                             XSpeed := YSpd;
                           end;
                      end
                    else
                      begin
                         (* Is the Other Ball to the RIGHT of this Ball *)
                             if (NOT(OXDir) AND (XDirection)) then
                               begin
                                 (* Yes, Collision causes a reversal of *)
                                 (* X Directions of Both Ball Objects   *)
                                 ChangeXDir;
                                 List_Pointer^.TheBall^.ChangeXDir;
                               end
                             else
                               begin
                                 (* No, But a collision DID OCCUR   *)
                                 (* so transfer XSPEEDs between the *)
                                 (* objects to conserve MOMENTUM.   *)
                                 List_Pointer^.TheBall^.ChangeXSpeed(YSpeed);
                                 XSpeed := YSpd;
                               end;
                           end
                      end;
```

"Fig. 8-21
continued."

```
        end;
    List_Pointer := List_Pointer^.NextBall;
  end;
end;
```

A collision of BALL objects occurs when the image of one ball overlaps the image of another ball. In numeric terms this means that the distance between the centers of the balls is less than the sum of the radii. The mathematical expression for a collision determination is shown in FIG. 8-22.

```
        Center Distance = SQRT(SQR(Y1 - Y2) + SQR(X1 - X2))

          Collision Distance = SQRT(SQR(R1 + R2))


  X1 = X position of Ball 1
  Y1 = Y position of Ball 1
  R1 = Radius of Ball 1

  X2 = X position of Ball 2
  Y2 = Y position of Ball 2
  R2 = Radius of Ball 2
```

Fig. 8-22. A mathematical expression of a collision.

A collision occurs when the "Center Distance" is less than the "Collision Distance." As you might have noticed, the equation used to determine collisions within the Ball_Advanced application is somewhat different. The difference originates in the fact that the radius values used for the X and Y direction are not the same. because the ratio of X and Y picture elements is NOT the same for any of the video display adapters, a circle is NOT really a circle. For a CGA screen, the vertical resolution is 200 pixels, and the horizontal resolution is 640 pixels. In order for a circle or ball to appear round, a correction for the ratio of vertical to horizontal pixels must be incorporated into the drawing of the ball. This generates complications for the calculation of the collision distance because of the variability of the radius from the Y radius to the X radius and back. The equation used by the Ball.Collisions procedure is the best compromise to accommodate the variability of the ball's radius. Once a collision has occurred, the Ball.Collisions procedure determines what kind of collision it is.

DISCUSSION

The concepts involved in object oriented programming are built upon the basic ideas of Turbo Pascal. The reorganization of these basic ideas provides the programmer with the ability to design and implement objects. The OOP extensions in Turbo Pascal version 5.5 give programmers considerable flexibility and power in implementing the objects either as static or dynamic structures.

The BALL object represents only a fraction of the true potential of object oriented programming. It moves, it makes sounds, it senses, it acts and it reacts. The importance of these capabilities is the demonstration of the ability of an object to interact with other objects as well as the environment. These interactions must be well detailed and broken down into he necessary mathematical relationships, but they can all be expressed. And any methods defined for one object can be applied to any other object of the same type. The logical extension of the ball application is to enhance it to include other object types.

9

Advanced Applications and Beyond

This chapter summarizes the concepts presented in the previous eight chapters. Emphasis is placed on the concepts of advanced programming rather than detailed line-by-line explanations of code. Specific emphasis is placed on the origins of each application, why it was needed, how requirements were determined and how the applications were developed. This chapter also provides some information concerning where new ideas for applications may be obtained. Lastly, I want to try and give you some ideas for other applications that you might have been thinking about, but were a little hesitant to pursue.

THE ORIGINS OF THE APPLICATIONS
IN CHAPTERS 5, 6, 7, AND 8

This text presents information and instructions for the creation and enhancement of some of the advanced applications that can be created using Turbo Pascal. These applications represent only a fraction of the potential of the Turbo Pascal language for enhancing the capabilities of the Personal Computer's functionality and operating environment. This information and the examples in this book may be used to create even more advanced applications. The use of this information is ultimately up to you.

I believe the most important aspects of the book are really the presentation of concepts rather than finished applications. The applications represent my vision of some of the uses of these concepts. If you have read the previous eight chapters of the book you should have an understanding of some of the uses of these concepts. Remember, my applications and uses are certainly NOT the last word in programming. Think of them as merely a starting point for your own programs. I'm confident that you will find additional uses for these concepts that I haven't even considered.

"KeyClick"

The KeyClick application originated with a friend who traveled a lot on business. He is a touch-typist with a laptop computer and a need to be able to "hear" the keys as characters are entered.

We talked about the requirements of an application to provide the functionally he wanted. He took several business trips a month on a variety of aircraft. The background noise for each flight varied considerably because of different aircraft and seating assignments on each flight. He needed to hear a "key click" when he was using his word processor, notepad application and several other desk accessories. He wanted control over the "click" generator to control whether sound was generated or not. He did NOT want to reload the sound generator every time he used an application. Finally, he did NOT want to be required to modify the sound generator each time he reloaded it.

The requirements for this application were not extensive. However, their implementation was a little tricky. The sound generator needed to be able to operate while another application was executing. The function of the other application is variable. The user must be able to modify the pitch of the key click while within an application. This allows the user to modify the "click" to accommodate changing noise levels.

The purpose of the other application that runs while KeyClick executes should be irrelevent. However, because so many applications exist for the PC, and because so much functionality is available, I couldn't totally disregard the functioning of the other program. The KeyClick program had to be designed to be able to operate successfully without infringing on the functionality of another application.

The complete solution for this project included the use of Terminate but-Stay-Resident (TSR) programming techniques. This solution was inevitable to allow for generation of sound within several applications. The purpose and capabilities of the other application would probably NOT be known to the KeyClick application. Otherwise, I might have needed to create a word processor, and several desktop utilities. The use of a TSR application means I do not need to recreate all the functionality of each of the applications to get a tone when a key was pressed.

The ability to modify the pitch of the sound required the definition of specific key command sequence. These key combinations needed to be easy to enter and execute, and yet be unique enough not to be used by other applications. The use of control-key sequences is easy enough. The use of the CTRL key and the arrow keys in combination provides a reasonably unique series of commands. Although I have seen applications that make use of these key combinations, they are not very numerous. In addition, none of the applications currently used by my associate incorporated these command combinations.

"Shell"

The Shell application is a fairly advanced program based on a very simple idea. The DOS operating system provides an extremely limited ability to recall and edit previous commands. The most recent command can be recalled in its entirety using the "F3" key. The "F1" key can be used to recall the previous command, character-by-character. New characters can be entered at a specific section. The "F1" command can then be used to add the remaining characters from the previous command, until all the characters have been used up.

The current "command recall" system is limited to retrieving only a single command. No new characters can be inserted into the command using the F1 key. These restrictions cause users to be restricted in their ability to reuse commands other than the most recently executed. The Shell program provides for these capabilities. The current implementation enables users to recall up to 20 previous commands. The simplicity and beauty of the Shell program lie in its character entry functionality.

The Shell application started out as an attempt to create a programmable data entry procedure. Many applications allow for input of data at specific locations on the display screen. The procedures that provide this capability can use either text or graphics screens, and sometimes both. The advantage of these procedures is that they can be programmed to accept data of a specific type (e.g., text, numeric), or format (10 digits and 3 decimal, 10 alphanumeric characters). The current state of the procedure is that of a limited text editor allowing for entry on a single line.

As an exercise, you might consider how the basic functionality of this procedure might be modified to allow for predefined input. I mentioned previously that you might construct a general data entry function. Actually you might consider creating several. One function could get text input. Another could be used to prompt for and validate an integer number. A third could be used to prompt and validate a real number. You could do the same thing for Boolean or YES and NO responses.

Finally, you might consider a function that takes an array of strings values as one of the arguments. The procedure would prompt for a text value and compare it to the text strings in the string array. If the entered value and matched one of the values in the array, then that value would be accepted. If there was no match then you would reprompt for an acceptable response. The value of functions such as this is that they present generic methods for obtaining data. They also provide basic type checking to make sure that a prompt that requires integer data will get integer data.

One of the weakest links in the code of any application is a prompt for user input. The IBM compatible personal computers are some of the easiest computers to use. People with little or no computer experience can be taught to use these machines in very little time. Unfortunately, teaching a person to input data and then having that person input the correct data are two entirely different tasks. When you validate the data entered at a specific prompt, you are creating a more bulletproof application and reducing the potential for frustration of the user.

One final note about data entry functions. When you make use of the same functions each time you require data, you standardize the method by which data comes into your programs. When you standardize, you create a consistent interface to which the user can become accustomed. You reduce the amount of code needed to create a prompt for user input. You reduce the potential for user frustration. Finally, your efforts will likely result in a series of entry procedures that can be incorporated into a source code library or a Turbo Pascal Unit library (TPU file) and used with other applications.

The EXEC Procedure   The EXEC procedure enables an application to take entered command text and pass it to the operating system. If a command is of the proper format it will be accepted by the COMMAND.COM program and executed as though it was entered at the DOS command prompt. If its format is inappropriate or incompatable with DOS syntax, or it is a call to a nonexistent program, then an error will result. In any case, you can use the functionality of Turbo Pascal to detect and process "success" or "failure" of an EXEC statement. For more information you should consult the EXECDEMO.PAS program supplied with your distribution media, the Turbo Pascal User's Guide or the Turbo Pascal Reference Manual.

The need for command recall and command text editing capabilities first came to my attention because of the need to have a read or readln type procedure for graphics screens. I perceived the lack of a command-line recall and editing utility as a deficiency in DOS. I believed then, and continue to believe now, that command line recall and editing could be combined within the structure of the Shell application to provide the desired capabilities. This new functionality enhances the DOS environment without losing the versatility and convenience of a command driven operating system.

The reason I have mentioned the origins of separate portions of the Shell application is twofold. First, the text entry and editing procedures were created for an entirely different application. However, it was created using a generic-enough structure to allow its code to be inserted into this application. With minor modifications, the code was made compatible with the Shell program. Secondly, source code for the command line storage, recall and execute portions of the application originated in an entirely different language. However, by using structured programming techniques in the other language, and for the other application, the intent and functionality of these procedures were easily translated into Turbo Pascal.

Nearly every beginning programming text available in your local book store contains the phrase "Structured Programming." This method of program development has little to do with the specific language in which you write your applications. The extent of the application of structured programming techniques is up to you. One of the main advantages of these techniques is the ease with which you can convert routines from one language to another. One of the major benefits is the ability to translate procedures and functions with very little modification. This is a benefit of structured programming, and it helps you to generate a source code library of routines in any language. This library, although it is written in one language, might be perfectly applicable in another.

It is important to understand the inherent value of a source code library of routines. The Shell program represents some of the advantages of possessing such a software library. One of the most important procedures for the Shell application had already been written and debugged. Conversion to another language required additional debugging, but not as much as if the procedure had been written from scratch. Your routines, if well-written and documented, regardless of their origins, can be generally applied in any application and language. Of course, there are certain functions provided in some languages that are not available in others. However, the basic capabilities of virtually all high level languages are fairly common.

"SlideShow"

The slide application originated as an enhancement to the display capabilities of an existing software program. The introduction of Turbo Pascal version 4.0 and subsequent updates allowed for access to a variety of graphics adapters Drivers for advanced graphics display adapters such as the VGA and 8514 were provided. Files containing fonts for Triplex, Small, SansSerif and Gothic text styles were also provided. Graphics object routines were added to provide even greater flexibility in graphics presentation.

Because SlideShow is a standalone application, it can be used by itself or in combinations with other applications. The application for which SlideShow was originally designed uses a programmable driver table system. New drivers can be added simply by programming a specific row in the driver table with the commands used by SlideShow to generate graphics. This table has specific columns designed to hold commands to select shade, color, font, line style and other graphics parameters. Other columns hold commands to generate graphics objects such as lines, boxes, circles and pie slices, to name a few.

Many programmable driver systems make use of assembly level programming to provide additional device support. For certain spreadsheet applications, this has proved to be an excellent method for accommodating new devices. The drawback is that drivers written for a spreadsheet application usually cannot be used by a graphics or drawing program. Although many programs have methods of transferring images between themselves using graphics formats, images will look different when you switch applications because of the different drivers. The SlideShow application is different because it provides the same graphics procedures regardless of the application. This means that images can be stored separately from the original application from which they were generated, in SlideShow script files. It also means that images can be displayed separately from their parent applications.

The generic graphics language used by the SlideShow application can be generated manually or automatically. Any application such as a spreadsheet or database manager with an internal macro language can be enhanced to produce SlideShow code. Whether this much effort is needed to provide enhanced output is up to you. There are a variety of text-based applications that might benefit from some form of graphical representation of data.

The standalone nature of Slideshow enables it to be accessed from any application you desire. Of course the application must have the capability to call SlideShow from within its macro language. Many of the more advanced applications have this capability. In addition, they possess memory management capabilities capable of providing SlideShow with the appropriate amount of memory needed to execute properly.

Basic_Ball and Ball_Advanced

The Basic_Ball and Ball_Advanced applications are not enhancements to the functionality of an existing program. These programs help to demonstrate some of the capabilities of the object oriented programming extensions available with Turbo Pascal version 5.5. These extensions provide the basis for the creation of environments in which custom objects can move, act, react or interact.

Objects are entities existing within an object oriented environment that you define. For the Ball programs, the environment is the display screen. BALL objects move and react within the environment by sensing their position. They are designed to determine their location relative to the boundaries or "walls" of the display screen. For the advanced version, the BALL objects cannot only sense their own location, but also the location of every other BALL object in the environment.

These applications make use of different versions of the BALL object. The basic object is common to both applications, but the methods vary to accommodate different methods of movement and reactions. The ball object can also be used as the basis for other objects that you might wish to create. Your objects might vary in function, but the basic concepts introduced and expanded upon in this text should provide you the working understanding of OOP.

THE PHILOSOPHY OF PROGRAMMING

Most programming texts provide instruction on the general use of a programming language. Many of these texts also provide details on the advantages of structured programming. One of the problems with these texts is that they don't detail the process by which the requirements are turned into a blueprint for the source code. Anyone can sit back and tell you how you should do something. They might try to tell you how a method works for them, and how it can work for you. The problem with learning another programmer's method is that it might not work for you.

Although I am an avid fan of the basic principles of structured programming, I know there are some aspects of the method that I don't always perform. One step that I always perform is to understand the use of the application. This might sound pretty basic, but it is very important. Knowing how a program will be used is considerably different from knowing how a program works.

Knowing how a program will be used enables you to create applications geared to the user. Knowing how an application works limits you to an understanding of the mechanics of the application you write. The difference is like night and day. A user's perspective enables you to create applications that are logically structured, easy-to-learn and easy-to-use. Knowing how a program works tells you what actions the individual functions and procedures perform. Knowing how a program works doesn't tell you how the actions will be applied.

Structured programming techniques emphasize the creation of a functional specification. This document contains lists of routines, their function, arguments and other routines and procedures that might be called. The specification contains a technical description of the interelationship of data, routines and command sequences, but it doesn't give the programmer a clear idea of what the user is actually doing. The original idea for the application and its functionality is the basis for the specification. However, somewhere in the development of many of the documents I have seen, the user gets forgotten.

I try to approach programming using a more humanistic approach. My experiences as a project leader, programmer/analyst, network administrator and customer technical representative have impressed upon me the basic difference between expectations and requirements. An *expectation* is a user-oriented term used to describe what an end-user wants for functionality. A *requirement* is what the programmer uses as a definition for that functionality. The real art of programming is to bring the user's expectations and the programmer's understandings of the requirements as close to each other as possible.

All too often the programmer/analyst will have preconceived notions about the task they are undertaking. The user will also have their own idea about the final application. Just like a store, the customer (user) is always right. Remember, the user is the one who has to work with this application. As a programmer you create the application and you might have some knowledge abouts its use. However, the user's vision of the application MUST be the final gauge by which the success or failure of the programming effort is measured.

Some might argue that the end-user might not have a valid perspective concerning the realities of computer programming. It can also be argued that the programmer might not have a valid perspective concerning the requirements of the application. It is the responsibility of the programmer to inform the user of the limitations of the system on which the application will perform. It is the responsibility of the user to describe the needs of the finished application to the programmer. If the originator of the idea for the application and the programmer are the same person, then there is no problem. However, if the user and programmer are two different people, then communications MUST be established to reconcile the two understandings of the project.

Right now, many of the applications you write are destined to remain with you. For each application, you are both the programmer and the user. As your involvement with computers increases, the tasks you will be asked to perform might increase in complexity and scope. These projects could include requirements that you did not create. These projects could also be used by people other than yourself.

When you create applications for yourself, you already know what to expect. You know the prompts, the type of data input expected, and you most likely know the output that will be generated. However, you know these things because YOU wrote the program. A user does not possess the same knowledge as you do. Are there any applications which you have not written that you know as intimately as your own? I am not saying that users should be pampered and lead through every facet of your application, but you should strive to make your applications as intuitively obvious as possible.

Because most problems with applications arise due to incorrect user input, your applications should attempt to make input as straightforward as possible. Input should be validated. Validation might require making sure that entered text is of a specific length. Numeric data entry might require differentiation of integer and real data. Entry of data for YES or NO responses might require the acceptance of not only these values, but also TRUE and FALSE. Prompts for input must be fully explained and concise. Although they must be informative, prompts must NOT be verbose. This type of programming produces user-friendly applications.

As important as are user-friendliness, and ease of use, your application must also possess a certain degree of intuitive instruction. You can make use of arrows, icons, and other images to convey direction. You can convey information using visual or audio signals. A tone from the computer can indicate acceptance of data. Specific signals can be used to tell the user the current state of the application or the computer. There are a variety of signalling capabilities available. As usual, the choice is up to you.

As the originator of an application to be used by others, it is your responsibility to make your application usable. This usability can be provided with complete documentation. It can be made available through on-line help. Users need help at specific locations within the application so you might want to add "context sensitive" help to your program. This type of help simply means that there is specific help available at each data input prompt of the current function, procedure or complete application.

NEW INFORMATION

How do I get information on new programming techniques? One obvious answer is to read about it. One of the reasons you purchased this text was to find out more about TSR, Shell, Graphics and OOP programming. Other sources of information include the trade magazines. These magazines usually have articles about advanced programming concepts. The first TSR application I ever wrote was based on an article I saw in one of these magazines. Other sources of information include computer users groups, on-line services such as bulletin boards, or interactive call-in services. The on-line services require a modem, but they provide access to other on-line services. The last, certainly not least, and most important source of information and new techniques is other programmers. The user groups provide access to these people, as do some on-line electronic mail systems.

CONCLUSION

This book trys to introduce the reader to some of the more popular programming concepts available through Turbo Pascal. Instruction and working applications have been included as demonstrations of these concepts. I have also attempted to provide short term direction to build on these applications by suggesting enhancements. The long term direction you take with this information is up to you. It is my hope that the presentation of these concepts and applications has increased your appreciation of Turbo Pascal's capabilities, and expanded your awareness of your own programming potential.

Index

Index

Other Bestsellers of Related Interest

UPGRADE YOUR IBM® COMPATIBLE AND SAVE A BUNDLE—Aubrey Pilgrim

Here is the book millions of PC owners have been waiting for! In this new addition to his highly praised *"...Save a Bundle"* series, Pilgrim explores dozens of cost-effective ways to breathe new life into aging hardware. It shows how you can use commercialy available hardware upgrade products, and provides guidelines and helpful advice in choosing the upgrade options best-suited to your needs and your budget. 224 pages, 60 illustration. Book No. 3468, $16.95 paperback, $26.95 hardcover.

COMPUTER SYSTEMS TECHNIQUES: Development, Implementation and Software Maintenance—Jag Sodhi

Systems engineer Jag Sodhi provides a comprehensive view of computer systems techniques that covers the entire process: initiaion, project management, the software engineering lifecycle, development, system implementation, and software maintenance in accordance with Department of Defense standards (DOD-STD-2167). 180 pages, Illustrated. Book No. 3376, 21.95 hardcover only.

LOGISTIC SUPPORT ANALYSIS HANDBOOK—James V. Jones

James V. Jones provides in-depth information on support principles and analytical strategies. He details specific tasks required for successful logistic support analysis, program planning and control, organized dynamics, and more. By focusing on the development of practical applications of LSA principles in both military and commercial environments, Jones has provided a complete set of resources for establishing LSA programs that comply with government requirements. 400 pagegs, 173 illustrations. Book No. 3351, $39.95 hardcover only.

THE FAX HANDBOOK—Gerald V. Quinn

This comprehensive guide explores what a fax machine can do for yor business's bottom line, and explains all of the elements of owning and operation a fax machine. you will understand how fax machines work, and why the have become as crucial to today's workstation as the photocopier. This book also gives you set up and operation guidelines for your fax. You'll find tipson power supplies, connecting to the telephone, adn the best locations for the machine within the workstation. 160 pages, 42 illustrations. Book No. 3341, $8.95 paperback, $16.95 hardcover.

PROGRAMMING WITH IBM® PC BASIC® AND THE PICK® DATABASE SYSTEM—David L. Clark

This is the only comparative gide available in the integration of IBM PC BASIC and the PICk database system Organized alphabetically by topic, it allows programmers who are already familiar with one system to perform similar operations in the other quickly and easily. David Clark thoroughly explains compatible system operations, gives parallel examples in other languages, and provides sample programs and testing routines for duplicating applications between systems. 448 pages, 77 illustrations. Book No. 3322, $34.95 hardcover only.

EXCEL MACROS FOR THE IBM® PC—Shelley Satonin

All the information you need to set up and use macros to change worksheets, print out, create graphs and charts, and manipulatte databases in fraction of the usual time. Santonin uses many simple examples and illustrations to explain the basics of macro writing and includes a complete directory of macro writing and includes a complete directory of Excel macro functions for easy reference. You'll find recipes for building dozens of advanced macros that you can use or customize for your own applications. 272 pages, 151 illustrations. Book No. 3293, $19.95 paperback only.

COMPUTER TECHNICIAN'S HANDBOOK—3rd Edition—Art Margolis

"This is a clear book, with concise and sensible language and lots of large diagrams...use (it) to cure or prevent problems in (your) own system...the (section on troubleshooting and repair) is worth the price of the book."—**Science Software Quarterly**

MORE than just a how-to manual of do-it-yourself fix-it techniques, this book offers complete instructions on interacing and modification that will help yo get the most out of your PC. 580 pages, 97 illustrations. Book No. 3279, $24.95 paperback, $36.95 hardcover.

HANDBOOK OF MANAGEMENT FOR SCIENTIFIC AND TECHNICAL PERSONNEL
—Dimitris N. Chorafas

Chorafas explains essential techniques in forecasting, planning, marketing, product development, finance, and office automation. Key areas covered include mathematical forecasting, long-term planning, developing new products, administering finances, budgets, and product pricing, controlling a marketing and sales network, and preparing for the challenges of the network communications system. 304 pages, 81 illustrations. Book No. 3263, $39.95 hardcover only.

HANDBOOK OF DATABASE MANAGEMENT AND DISTRIBUTED RELATIONAL DATABASES
—Dimitris N. Chorafas

This book provides database users and designers with the tools necessary to make informed decisions and to keep pace with the advancement of database technology. Now you can identify your needs, define the requirements, evalate your priorities, choose supports, and determine solutions that are effective both in terms of cost and performance. 720 pages. Book No. 3253, $49.95 hardcover

WORDPERFECT 5.0®: Power Word Processing Made Easy—Jennifer de Lasala

Three essential resources in one easy-to-use volume—a complete tutorial, an advanced user's manual, and a toolbox librar of commands, function keys, and more! Bases on WordPerfect 5.0, this practical reference is perfect for any level of user. It will guide you from the initial steps of setting up your system to a fuller, more complete understanding of the advanced features. 544 pages, 92 illustrations. Book No. 3249, $24.95 paperback.

WORKING WITH ORACLE® VERSION 6.0
—Jack L. Hursch, Ph.D. and Carolyn J. Hursch, Ph.D.

It's fast. It's SQL based. It's available on vitrually every operating system on microcomputers and mainframes—including MS-DOS based IBM PCs and compatibles! Now, Jack and Carolyn Hursch show how you can tap the remarkable capabilities of this top-ranked database management system with this practical programmer's reference. 416 pages, 50 illustrations. Book No. 3246, $21.95 paperback.

HANDBOOK OF DECISION SUPPORT SYSTEMS
—Stephen J. Andriole

This practical, working text outlines design strategies that will help your organization perform real-world tasks such as forecasting budgets and planning sales promotions more quickly and efficiently. Andriole deals directly with evaluation questions in helping you set up a realistic, requirements-driven system that will be adaptable to, but not dependant on, future technologies. With this book, you'll be able to select software and hardware that suit your needs. 256 pages. Book No. 3240, $29.95 hardcover.

MS-DOS® BEYOND 640K: Working with Extended and Expanded Memory—James Forney

Find out how some relatively inexpensive hardware and software enhancements can give you 8088, 80286, or 80386-based computer the ability to run larger applications, create multiple simultaneous work environments, maintain larger files, and provide all the memory you need. This book provides a clear picture of all the alternatives and options available, even up-to-the-minute tips and techniques for using Lotus 1-2-3®, Release 3.0, in extended memory! 248 pages, Illustrations. Book No. 3239, $19.95 paperback, $29.95 hardcover.

ARTIFICIAL INTELLIGENCE AND NATIONAL DEFENSE: Opportunity and Challenge
—Paul E. Lehner

This book examines artifical intelligence technology from the persepective of its potential contribution to national defense—from military intelligence analysis and data fusion to SDI. Lehner explores a variety of A1 systems and techniques, and then enumerates the difficulties, successes and failures that have been part of bringing A1 to military applications. 204 pages, Illustrations. Book No. 3235, $34.95 hardcover.

dBASE IV™: A Comprehensive User's Manual for Nonprogrammers—Kerman D. Bharucha

Bring the power of dBASE IV into your business world. Kerman Bharucha's clear learn-by-example approach makes this the perfect guide if you want to start producing with dBASE IV immediately. Bharucha guides you on a logical path through the three methods of using dBASE IV: interactive dot prompt, programming, and the Control Center. 656 pages, 321 illustrations. Book No. 3224, $21.95 paperback, $31.95 hardcover.

MICROSOFT® WORKS: IBM® Applications Made Easy—Paul Dlug

Now, you can take full advantage of the powerful features of the Microsoft Works Version 1.0 integrated software system. Through a series of application problems, Paul Dlug provides a practical, hands-on course in the many features of Works, including: creating macros, integration, mail merge, graphics, use of modems, and more. It's the perfect guide for novices and experienced programmers alike! 256 pages, 229 illustrations. Book No. 3213, $17.95 paperback.

ENCYCLOPEDIA OF LOTUS® 1-2-3® , RELEASE 3: The Master Reference—Robin Stark

"A comprehensive and highly useful guide to 1-2-3...a worthwhile addition to your library..."

Incorporating the same painstaking detail, three-part indexing system, and cross-referencing of the earlier edition, this book provides a comprehensive and easy-to-use guide to all commands, functions, and macro commands offered by 3, with example applications for each. 560 pages, 183 illustrations. Book No. 3211, $24.95 paperback, $34.95 hardcover.

CLIPPER™: A Programmer's Guide—Gary Beam

Here are never-before-published techniques for getting the most from Clipper Version Summer '87! This book is designed to be an applications guide for Clipper Summer '87, the enhanced version of the dBASE language compiler from Nantucket Corporation. Many new commands and functions have been provided. Beam covers: utilization, user-defined functions, arrays, telecommunications, graphics, and functions libraries. 240 pages, Illustrations. Book No. 3207, $19.95 paperback.

DACEASY™ ACCOUNTING AND PAYROLL MADE EASY, Version 3.0—Gary West and william Mills

For the small business owners and operators who need to set up and operate a computer-based accounting and payroll system, this bestselling book is now more valuable than ever. the authors examine every aspect of computerizing your books, and give a thorough course in the DacEasy system, including the enhancements incorporated in Version 3.0. Through a series of tutorials, you'll see how DacEasy can handle all of your record-keeping tasks. 400 pages, 269 illustrations. Book No. 3204, $21.95 paperback, $31.95 hardcover.

COMPUTER TOOLS, MODELS AND TECHNIQUES FOR PROJECT MANAGEMENT—Dr. Adedeji B. Badiru and Dr. Gary E. Whitehouse

Badiru and Whitehouse provide you with practical, down-to-earth guidance on the use of project management tools, models, and techniques. You'll find this book filled with helpful tips and advice. You'll also discover ways to use your current computer hardware and softwware resources to more effectively enhance jproject management functions. 320 pages, 112 illustrations. Book No. 3200, $32.95 hardcover.

ENCYCLOPEDIA OF EXCEL—The Master Reference—Robin Stark and Shelly Satonin

Here is the definitive handbook to Excel for the IBM versions. A comprehensive guide to Excel commands and functions, it includes over 250 alphabetically arranged entries! To ensure quick access to needed facts, *Encyclopedia of Excel* is thoroughly cross-referenced and indexed three ways. In addition to the comprehensive main indes, an index of applications directs you to specific examples. 420 pages, 150 illustrations. Book No. 3191, $22.95 paperback, $31.95 hardcover.

BUILD YOUR OWN 80383 IBM® COMPATIBLE AND SAVE A BUNDLE—Aubrey Pilgrim

Now you really can have the power of a PS/2-compatible microcomputer at just a fraction of the normal retail cost. Or, you can upgrade your present IBM compatible to include all of the up-to-date features of new 80386-based machiens for even less! The secret? Assembling it yourself! All you need is a pair of pliers, a couple of screwdrivers, and the parts you can buy for considerably less than a complete, assembled machines. 224 pages, 83 illustrations. Book No. 3131, $16.95 paperback, $24.95 hardcover.

Prices Subject to Change Without Notice.

Look for These and Other TAB Books at Your Local Bookstore

To Order Call Toll Free 1-800-822-8158
(in PA, AK, and Canada call 717-794-2191)

or write to TAB BOOKS, Blue Ridge Summit, PA 17294-0840.

Title	Product No.	Quantity	Price

☐ Check or money order made payable to TAB BOOKS

Charge my ☐ VISA ☐ MasterCard ☐ American Express

Acct. No. _____ Exp. _____

Signature: _____

Name: _____

Address: _____

City: _____

State: _____ Zip: _____

Subtotal $ _____

Postage and Handling
($3.00 in U.S., $5.00 outside U.S.) $ _____

Add applicable state
and local sales tax $ _____

TOTAL $ _____

TAB BOOKS catalog free with purchase; otherwise send $1.00 in check or money order and receive $1.00 credit on your next purchase.

Orders outside U.S. must pay with international money order in U.S. dollars.

TAB Guarantee: If for any reason you are not satisfied with the book(s) you order, simply return it (them) within 15 days and receive a full refund. **BC**